STEVENSON • WATTERS • LEYH • ALLEN • NOWAK • LAIHO

LUMBERJANES™

BAND TOGETHER

BOOM!
BOX™

Ross Richie..CEO & Founder
Matt Gagnon...Editor-in-Chief
Filip Sablik...............President of Publishing & Marketing
Stephen Christy....................President of Development
Lance Kreiter.................VP of Licensing & Merchandising
Phil Barbaro...VP of Finance
Bryce Carlson.....................................Managing Editor
Mel Caylo...Marketing Manager
Scott Newman.....................Production Design Manager
Irene Bradish.................................Operations Manager
Sierra Hahn...Senior Editor
Dafna Pleban.........................Editor, Talent Development
Shannon Watters..Editor
Eric Harbun...Editor
Whitney Leopard....................................Associate Editor
Jasmine Amiri.......................................Associate Editor
Chris Rosa...Associate Editor

Alex Galer...Associate Editor
Cameron Chittock.................................Associate Editor
Mary Gumport..Assistant Editor
Matthew Levine......................................Assistant Editor
Kelsey Dieterich................................Production Designer
Jillian Crab..Production Designer
Michelle Ankley.................................Production Designer
Grace Park.....................................Production Design Assistant
Aaron Ferrara...............................Operations Coordinator
Elizabeth Loughridge..................Accounting Coordinator
Stephanie Hocutt.....................Social Media Coordinator
José Meza...Sales Assistant
James Arriola..Mailroom Assistant
Holly Aitchison....................................Operations Assistant
Sam Kusek......................Direct Market Representative
Amber Parker.................................Administrative Assistant

BOOM! BOX™

LUMBERJANES Volume Five, December 2016. Published by BOOM! Box, a division of Boom Entertainment, Inc. Lumberjanes is ™ & © 2016 Shannon Watters, Grace Ellis, Noelle Stevenson & Brooke Allen. Originally published in single magazine form as LUMBERJANES No. 13, 18-20. ™ & © 2015 Shannon Watters, Grace Ellis, Noelle Stevenson & Brooke Allen. All rights reserved. BOOM! Box™ and the BOOM! Box logo are trademarks of Boom Entertainment, Inc., registered in various countries and categories. All characters, events, and institutions depicted herein are fictional. Any similarity between any of the names, characters, persons, events, and/or institutions in this publication to actual names, characters, and persons, whether living or dead, events, and/or institutions is unintended and purely coincidental. BOOM! Box does not read or accept unsolicited submissions of ideas, stories, or artwork.

A catalog record of this book is available from OCLC and from the BOOM! Studios website, www.boom-studios.com, on the Librarians Page.

BOOM! Studios, 5670 Wilshire Boulevard, Suite 450, Los Angeles, CA 90036-5679. Printed in China. First Printing.

ISBN: 978-1-60886-919-0, eISBN: 978-1-61398-590-8

THIS LUMBERJANES FIELD MANUAL BELONGS TO:

NAME:_____

TROOP:_____

DATE INVESTED:_____

FIELD MANUAL TABLE OF CONTENTS

LUMBERJANES
FIELD MANUAL

For the Intermediate Program

Tenth Edition • May 1984

Prepared for the

Miss Qiunzella Thiskwin
Penniquiqul Thistle Crumpet's
CAMP FOR ~~GIRLS~~ HARDCORE LADY-TYPES

"Friendship to the Max!"

A MESSAGE FROM THE LUMBERJANES HIGH COUNCIL

miss
Quinzella Thiskwin
Penniquiqul Thistle Crumpet's
Camp for
HARDCORE LADY TYPES
FRIENDSHIP to the MAX!

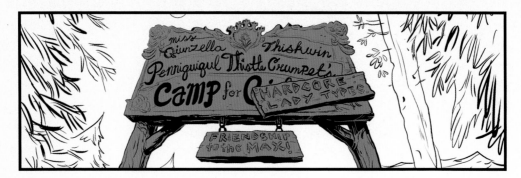

Friendship is amazing. There are many valuable things in life, but friendship may be one of the most important. To live life without the experience of friendship, would be a life that we would not wish upon anyone. Human interaction is a necessity to survival, and when it comes to survival at camp, that could be literal. Developed friendships, friendships that will truly last the ages, are essential to the successful well being of anyone.

The definition of a friend is, "A person whom one knows, likes, and trusts." But to us here with the Lumberjane Scouts, friendship is so much more than that. Our entire camp curriculum is built around the long lasting relationships that we hope every Lumberjane Scout has a chance to build in their time here. We don't need to define friendship based off of actions or words, but by emotional connection that will form naturally as we all learn to work and live together. During your time at camp, we hope that you experience many great things. We want you to know what it feels like to fall from great heights with the wind surrounding you, and know that you will be caught. You will also have someone waiting for you at the bottom to catch you so that you may be able to make the climb again together. One of our greatest goals for you is to experience freedom, the ability to be yourself and let go of any pressures of the world outside of this camp.

We want you to feel free to be who you truly are, to be the hardcore lady-type, the amazing Lumberjanes that you are on the inside and outside. We look forward to watching you, and your friends, take on the world one day at a time.

THE LUMBERJANES PLEDGE

I solemnly swear to do my best
Every day, and in all that I do,
To be brave and strong,
To be truthful and compassionate,
To be interesting and interested,
To pay attention and question
The world around me,
To think of others first,
To always help and protect my friends,
[redacted]
And to make the world a better place
For Lumberjane scouts
And for everyone else.

THEN THERE'S A LINE ABOUT GOD, OR WHATEVER

LUMBERJANES™

BAND TOGETHER

Chapter 17 Written by
Noelle Stevenson & Shannon Watters

Chapters 18-20 Written by
Shannon Watters & Kat Leyh

Chapter 17 Illustrated by
Brooke Allen

Chapters 18-20 Illustrated by
Carolyn Nowak

Colors by
Maarta Laiho

Letters by
Aubrey Aiese

Cover by
Brooke Allen
with colors by **Maarta Laiho**

Badge Design by
Scott Newman
Designer
Kelsey Dieterich
Associate Editor
Whitney Leopard
Editor
Dafna Pleban
Special thanks to **Kelsey Pate** for giving the Lumberjanes their name.

Created by **Shannon Watters, Grace Ellis, Noelle Stevenson & Brooke Allen**

LUMBERJANES FIELD MANUAL
CHAPTER SEVENTEEN

Lumberjanes "Out-of-Doors" Program Field

BEGINNER'S LUCK BADGE

"Everyone Starts Somewhere"

Every story has a beginning, and every race has a start line. You don't finish things halfway, you begin and complete them from start to finish. Nature is a great place to gain experience in the light of the sun but a true Lumberjane knows the importance of learning things from square one. It is at Lumberjanes Camp that our Lumberjanes will be able to learn new skills and lessons throughout their time there. We don't expect every camper to come in with the knowledge already in their heads because one of the joys of this camp is being able to pass on knowledge to your fellow campers.

The *Beginner's Luck* badge is the for Lumberjane who jumps feet first into the unknown. The Lumberjane who is willing to learn as they go through camp, who will take the experiences and lessons of others and apply them in their day-to-day life at camp. The *Beginner's Luck* badge is earned by multiple methods, by either jumping into a course or curriculum without any prior knowledge and using their already acquired skills to come out with top marks. Or, a Lumberjane is able to earn the *Beginner's Luck* badge through a series of tests that are set up by their counselor. This is not only the most popular way to earn the badge, but often accepted as the most enjoyable since often time the tests will include working together with your cabin, with your friends.

The history of the *Beginner's Luck* badge starts at the beginning of the Lumberjane camp history. It is in fact one of the original badges from that time, just with a better name. Back then, the *Beginner's Luck* badge was often referred to as the *Guppy* badge, but after much deliberation, we find that while we teach a lot of the same lessons in both the badges, the *Beginner's Luck* badge is just a better name. The biggest and most important lesson to keep in mind with this badge is that while everyone has to start at the beginning, you might be able to skip a step or two but you won't be able to know which steps until you start.

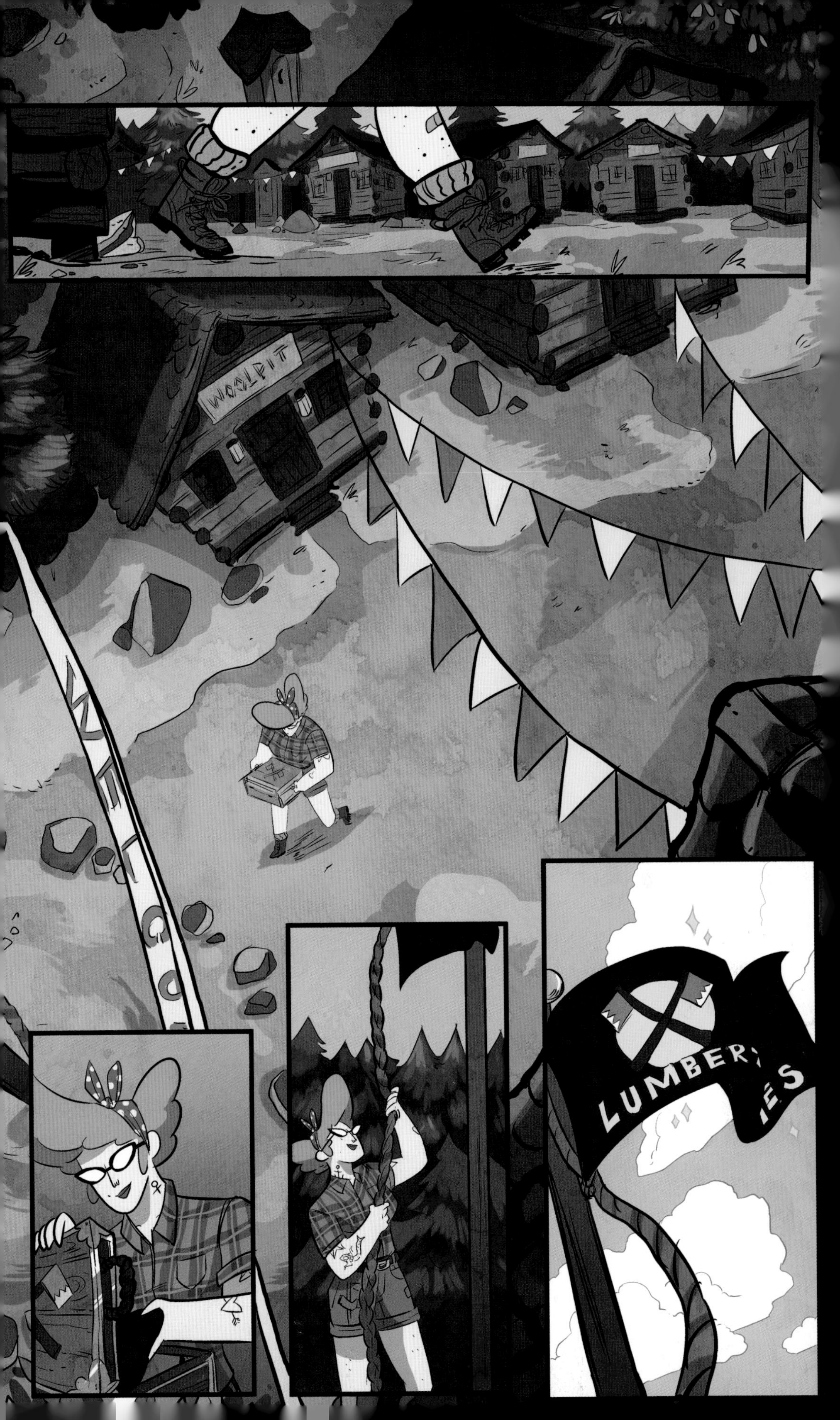
WOOLPIT
LUMBER

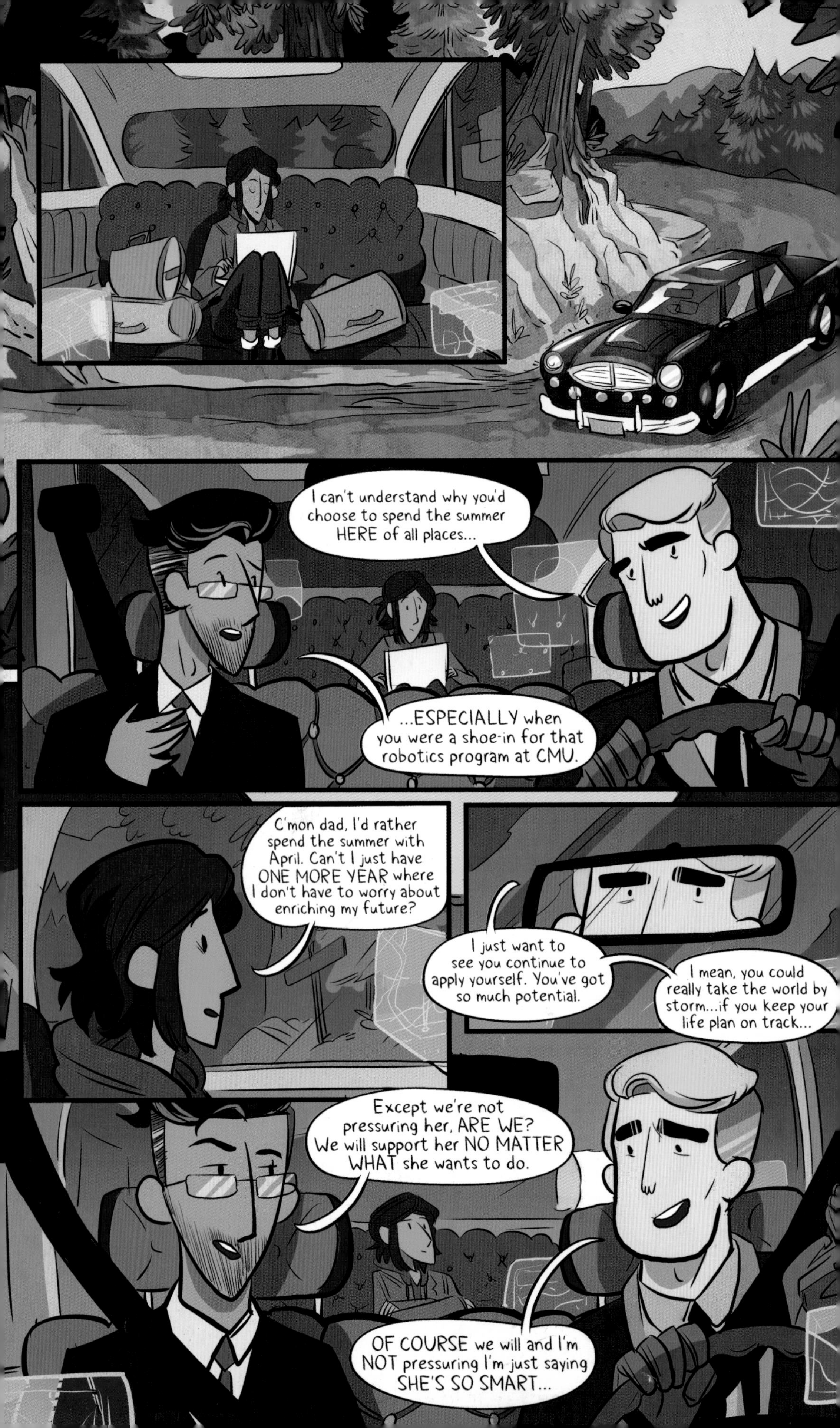
I can't understand why you'd choose to spend the summer HERE of all places...
...ESPECIALLY when you were a shoe-in for that robotics program at CMU.
C'mon dad, I'd rather spend the summer with April. Can't I just have ONE MORE YEAR where I don't have to worry about enriching my future?
I just want to see you continue to apply yourself. You've got so much potential.
I mean, you could really take the world by storm...if you keep your life plan on track...
Except we're not pressuring her, ARE WE? We will support her NO MATTER WHAT she wants to do.
OF COURSE we will and I'm NOT pressuring I'm just saying SHE'S SO SMART...

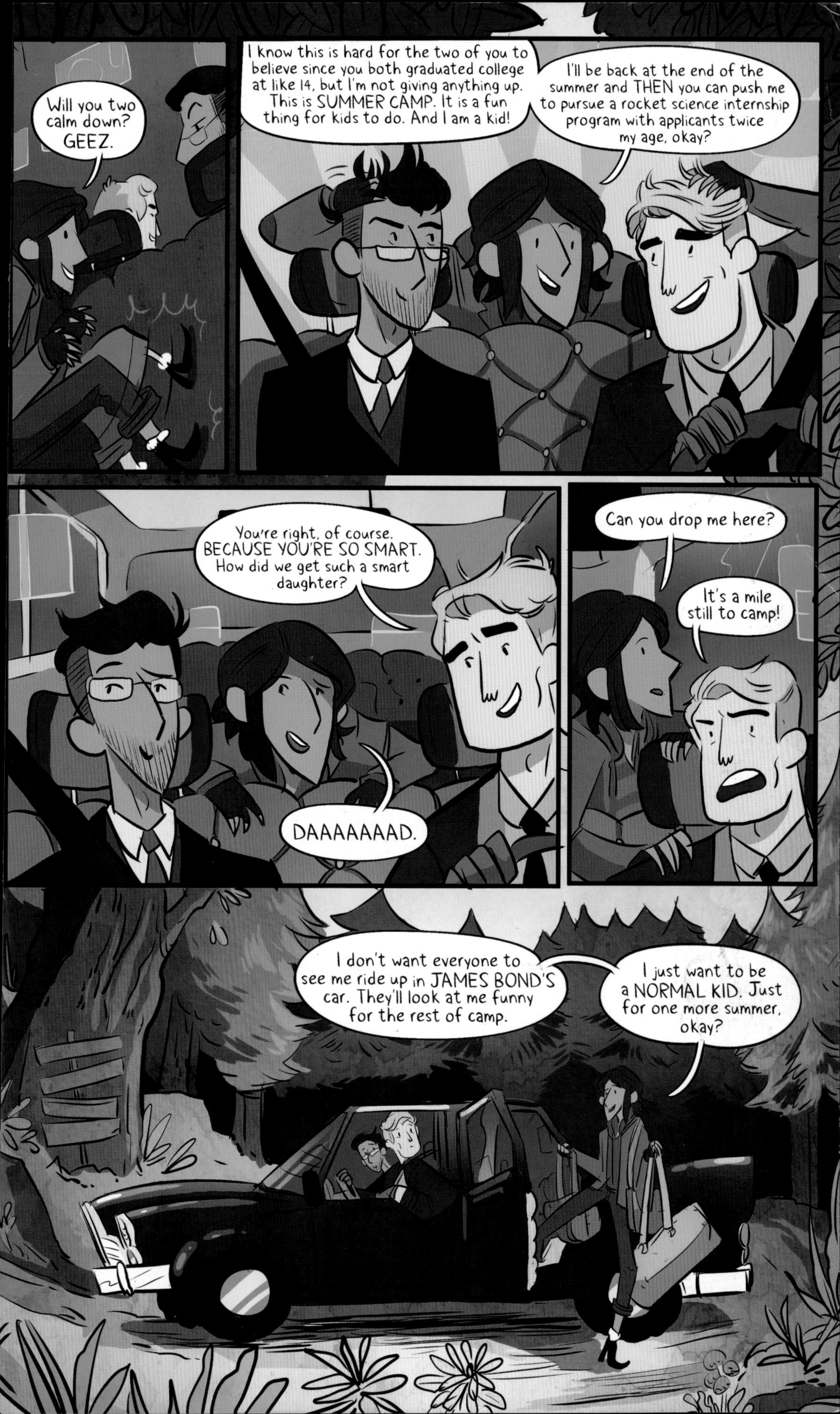
Will you two calm down? GEEZ.
I know this is hard for the two of you to believe since you both graduated college at like 14, but I'm not giving anything up. This is SUMMER CAMP. It is a fun thing for kids to do. And I am a kid!
I'll be back at the end of the summer and THEN you can push me to pursue a rocket science internship program with applicants twice my age, okay?
You're right, of course. BECAUSE YOU'RE SO SMART. How did we get such a smart daughter?
DAAAAAAAD.
Can you drop me here?
It's a mile still to camp!
I don't want everyone to see me ride up in JAMES BOND'S car. They'll look at me funny for the rest of camp.
I just want to be a NORMAL KID. Just for one more summer, okay?

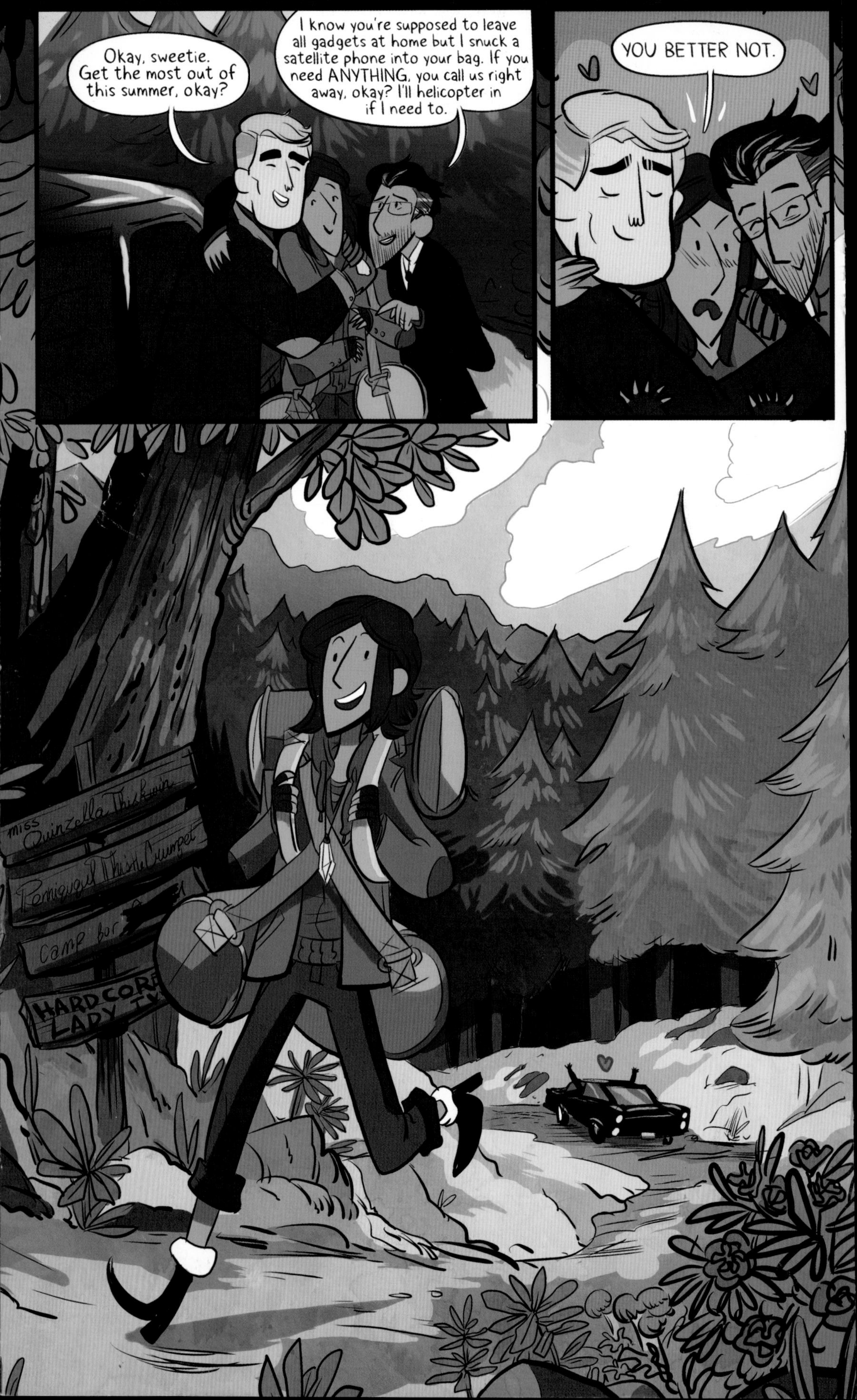
Okay, sweetie. Get the most out of this summer, okay?
I know you're supposed to leave all gadgets at home but I snuck a satellite phone into your bag. If you need ANYTHING, you call us right away, okay? I'll helicopter in if I need to.
YOU BETTER NOT.

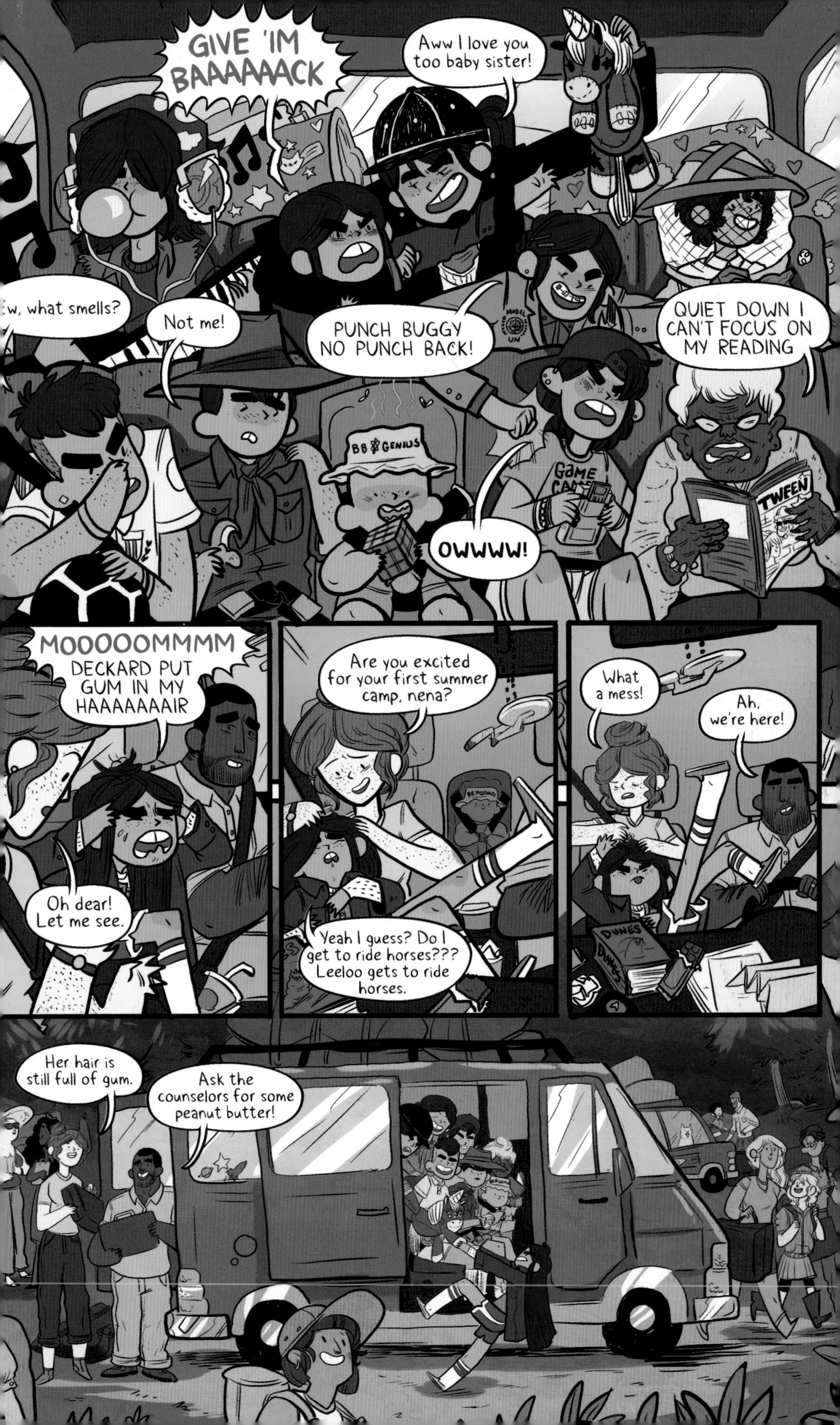
GIVE 'IM BAAAAAACK
Aww I love you too baby sister!
ew, what smells?
Not me!
PUNCH BUGGY NO PUNCH BACK!
QUIET DOWN I CAN'T FOCUS ON MY READING
BB GENIUS
MODEL UN
GAME
TWEEN
OWWWW!
MOOOOOMMMM DECKARD PUT GUM IN MY HAAAAAAAIR
Oh dear! Let me see.
Are you excited for your first summer camp, nena?
Yeah I guess? Do I get to ride horses??? Leeloo gets to ride horses.
What a mess!
Ah, we're here!
DUNES
Her hair is still full of gum.
Ask the counselors for some peanut butter!

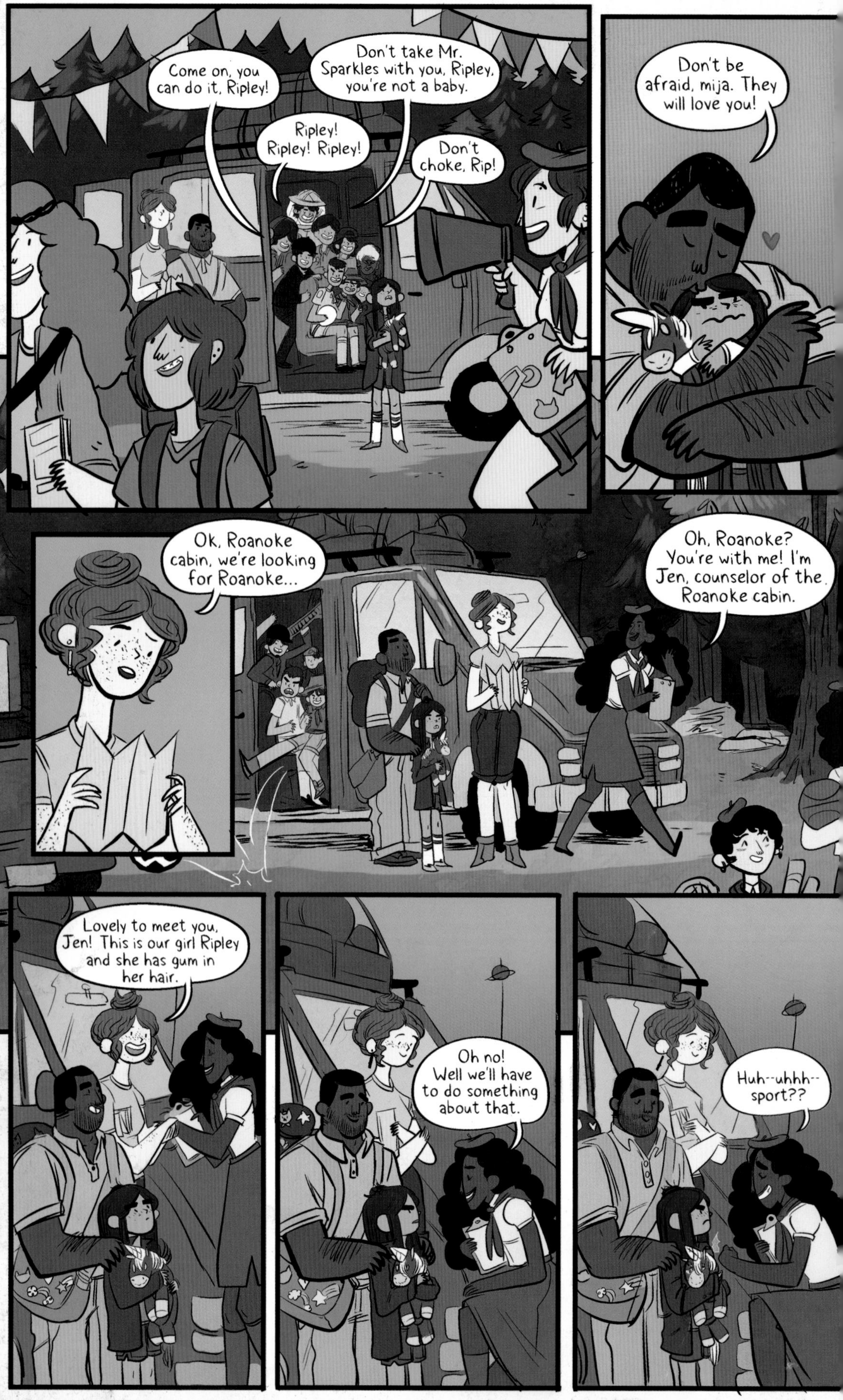
Come on, you can do it, Ripley!
Don't take Mr. Sparkles with you, Ripley, you're not a baby.
Ripley! Ripley! Ripley!
Don't choke, Rip!
Don't be afraid, mija. They will love you!
Ok, Roanoke cabin, we're looking for Roanoke...
Oh, Roanoke? You're with me! I'm Jen, counselor of the Roanoke cabin.
Lovely to meet you, Jen! This is our girl Ripley and she has gum in her hair.
Oh no! Well we'll have to do something about that.
Huh--uhhh--sport??

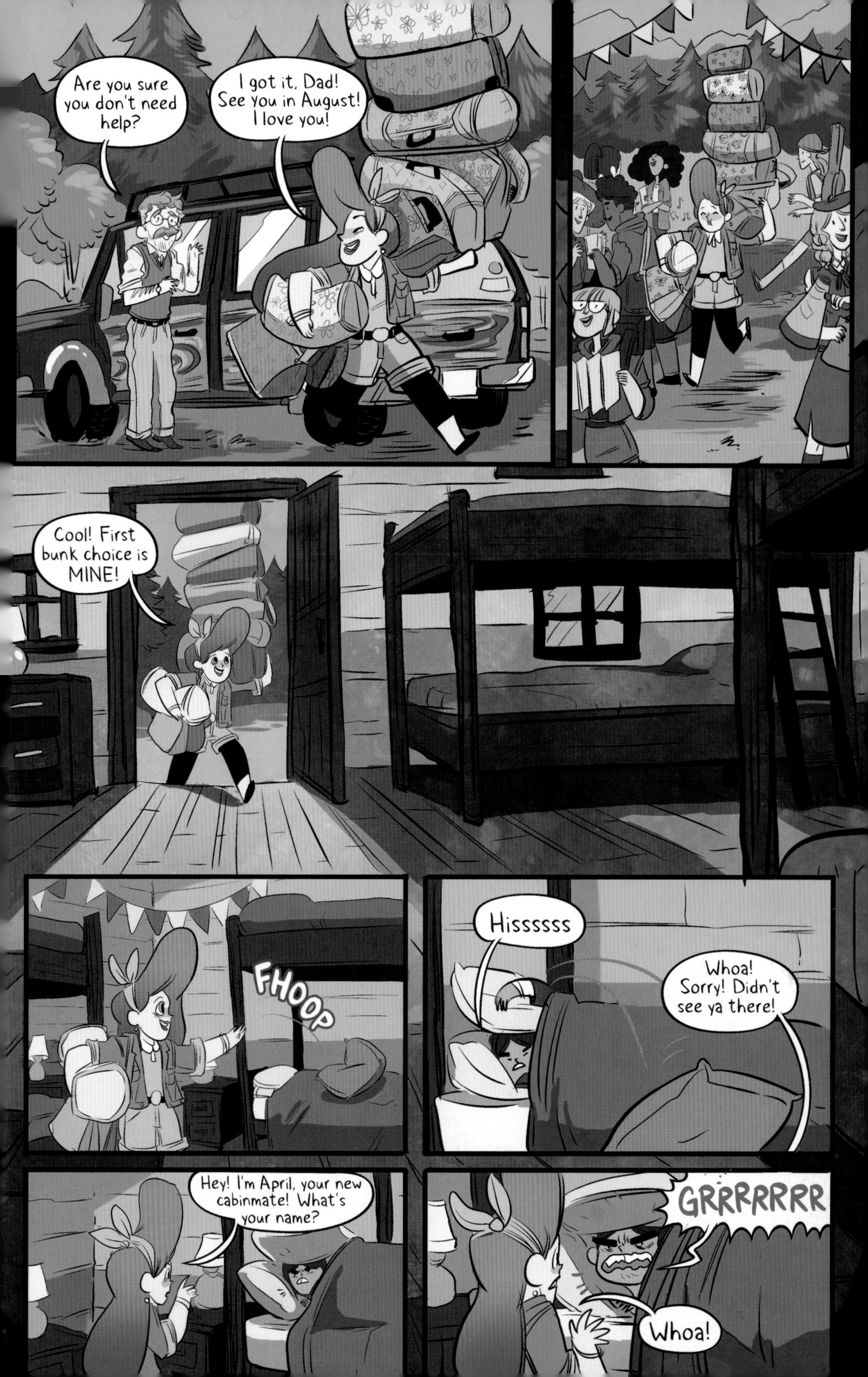

Are you sure you don't need help?
I got it, Dad! See you in August! I love you!
Cool! First bunk choice is MINE!
FHOOP
Hissssss
Whoa! Sorry! Didn't see ya there!
Hey! I'm April, your new cabinmate! What's your name?
GRRRRRRR
Whoa!

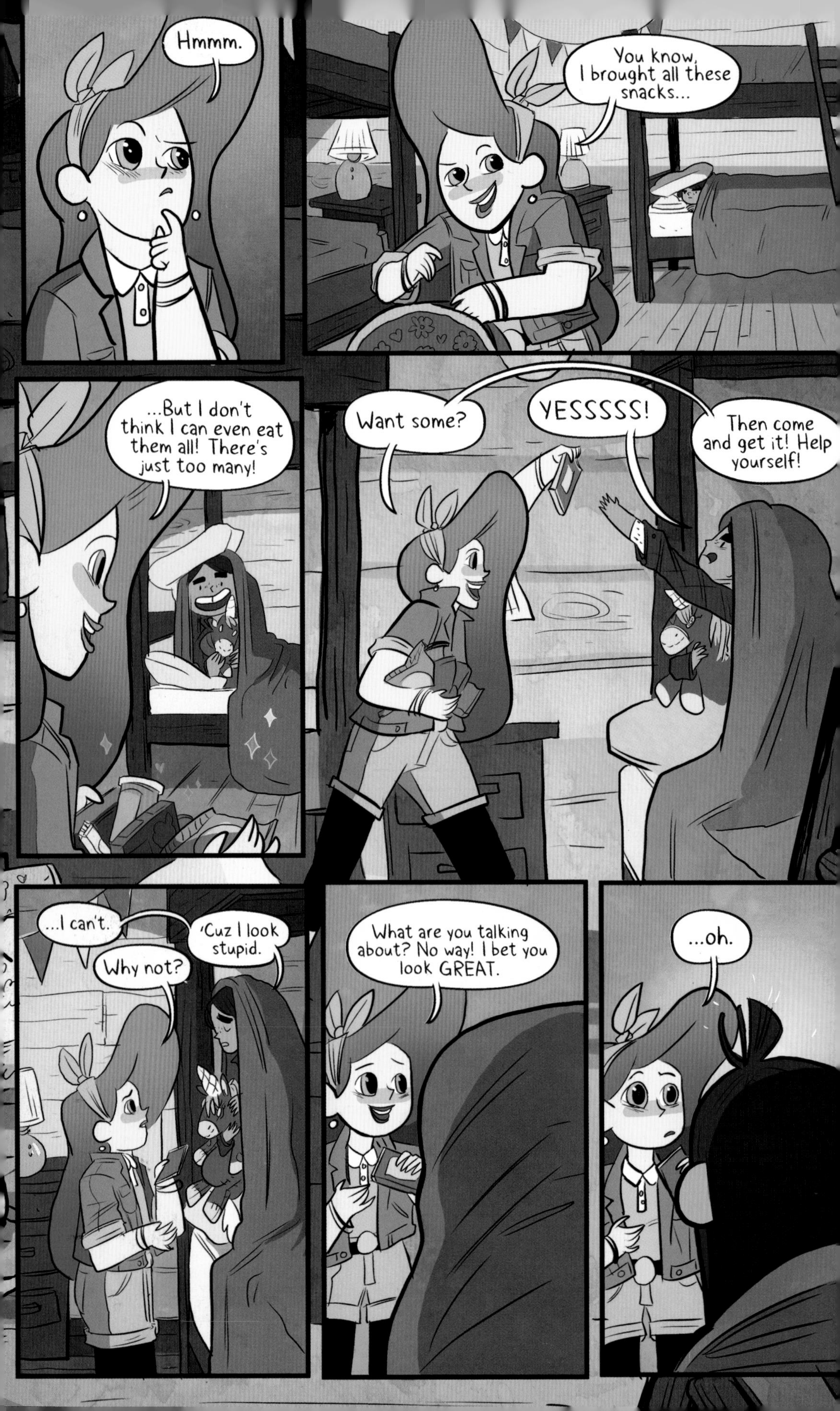
Hmmm.
You know, I brought all these snacks...
...But I don't think I can even eat them all! There's just too many!
Want some?
YESSSSS!
Then come and get it! Help yourself!
...I can't.
Why not?
'Cuz I look stupid.
What are you talking about? No way! I bet you look GREAT.
...oh.

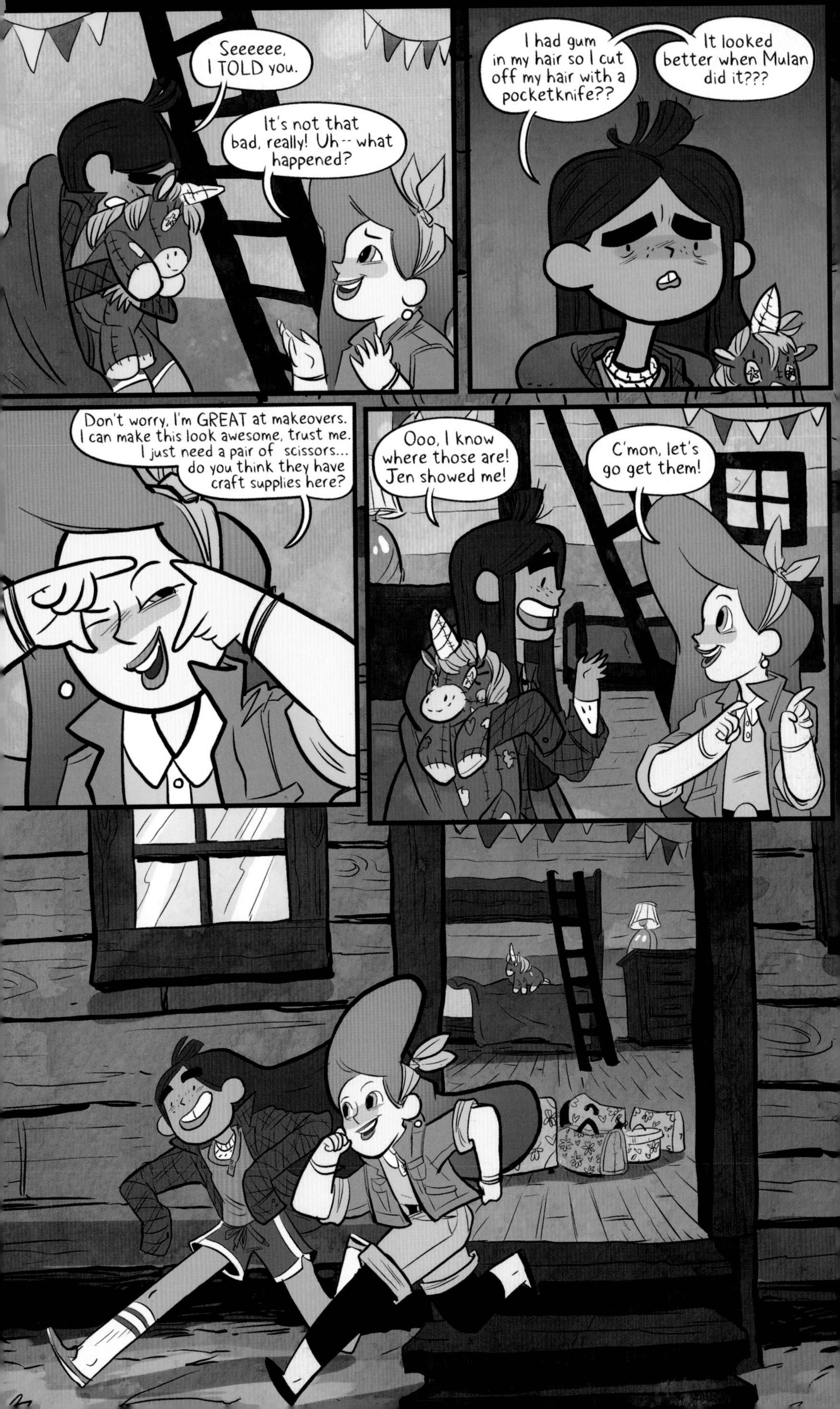
Seeeeee, I TOLD you.
It's not that bad, really! Uh-- what happened?
I had gum in my hair so I cut off my hair with a pocketknife??
It looked better when Mulan did it???
Don't worry, I'm GREAT at makeovers. I can make this look awesome, trust me. I just need a pair of scissors... do you think they have craft supplies here?
Ooo, I know where those are! Jen showed me!
C'mon, let's go get them!

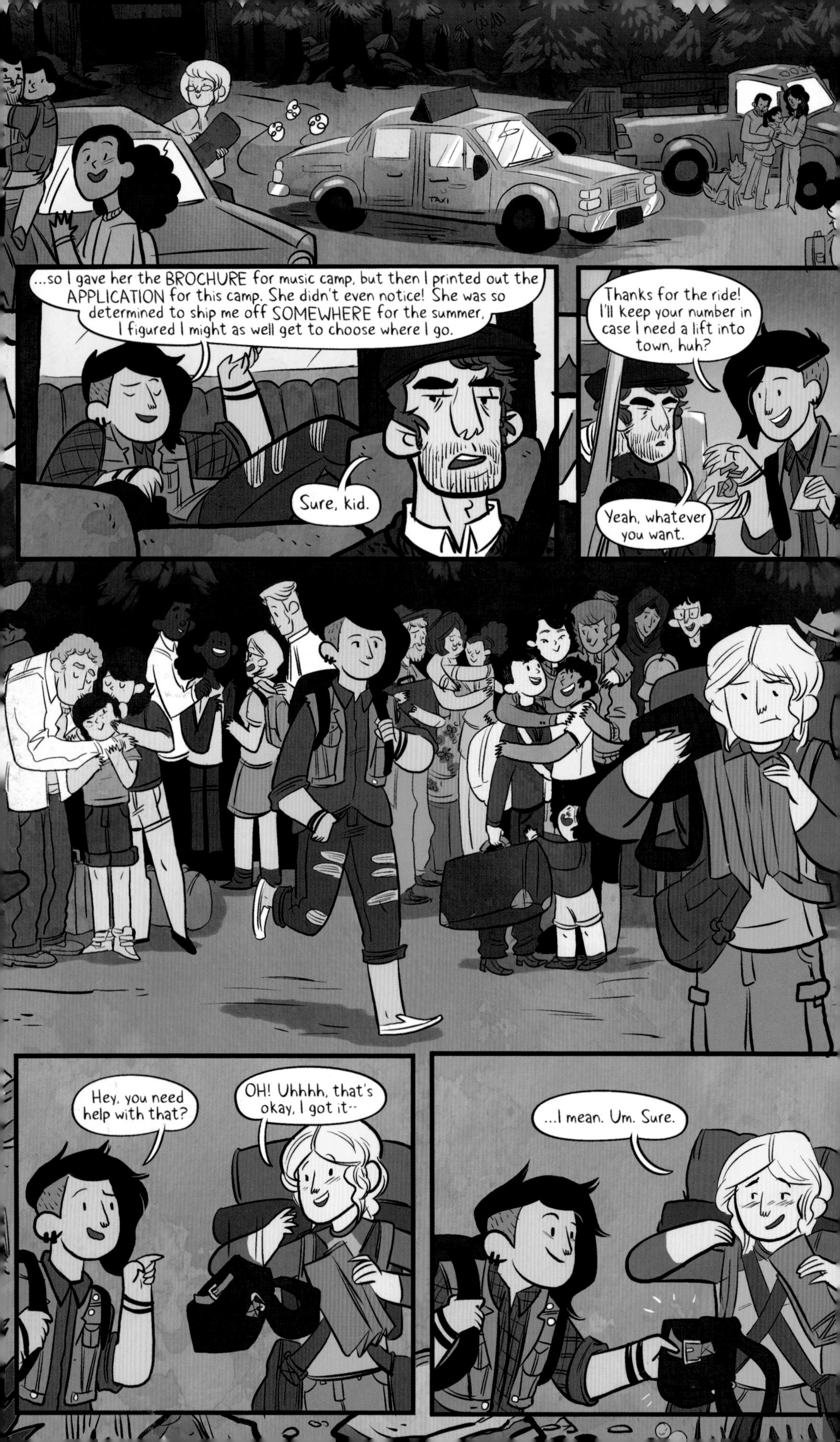
...so I gave her the BROCHURE for music camp, but then I printed out the APPLICATION for this camp. She didn't even notice! She was so determined to ship me off SOMEWHERE for the summer, I figured I might as well get to choose where I go.
Sure, kid.
Thanks for the ride! I'll keep your number in case I need a lift into town, huh?
Yeah, whatever you want.
TAXI
Hey, you need help with that?
OH! Uhhhh, that's okay, I got it--
...I mean. Um. Sure.

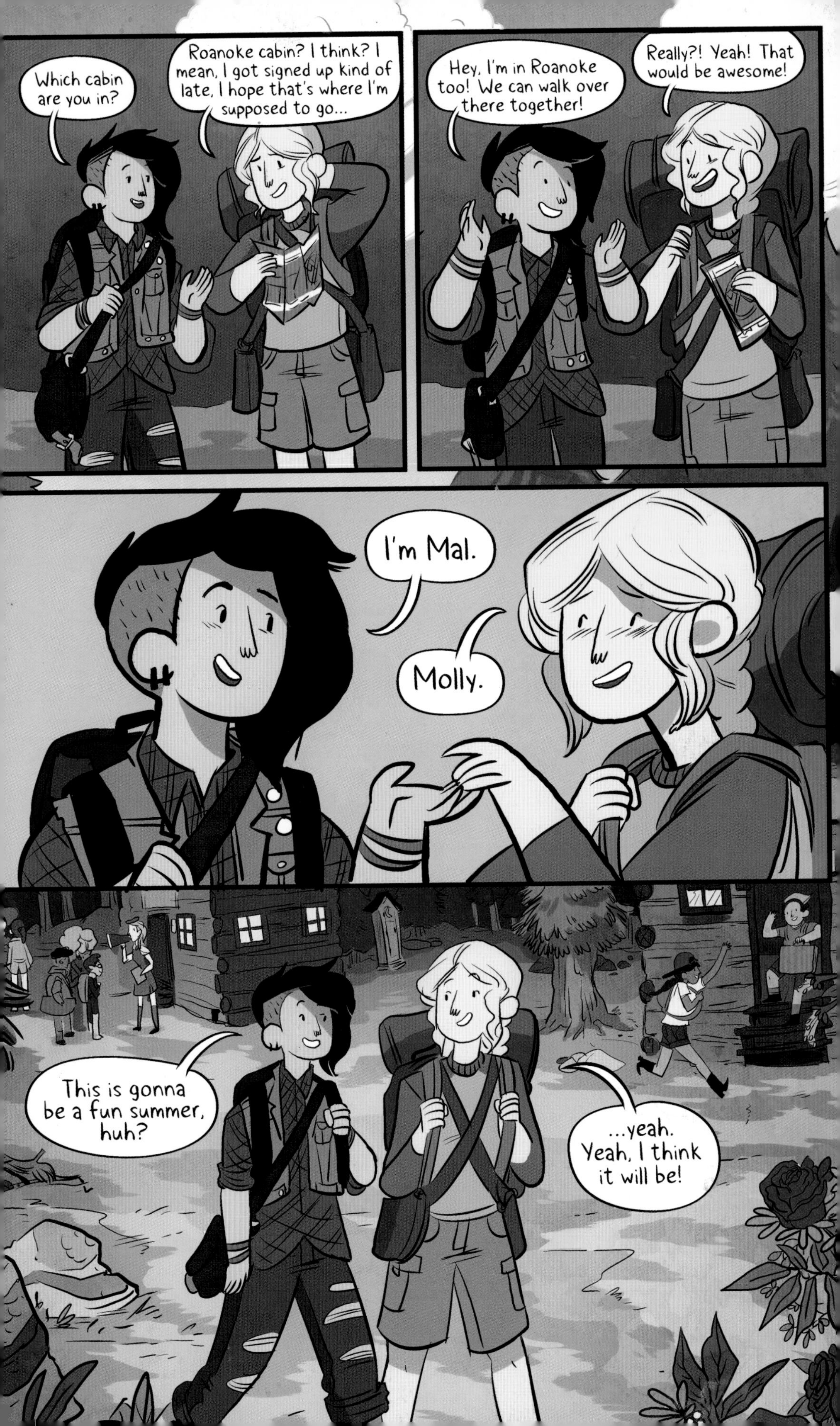
Which cabin are you in?
Roanoke cabin? I think? I mean, I got signed up kind of late, I hope that's where I'm supposed to go...
Hey, I'm in Roanoke too! We can walk over there together!
Really?! Yeah! That would be awesome!
I'm Mal.
Molly.
This is gonna be a fun summer, huh?
...yeah. Yeah, I think it will be!

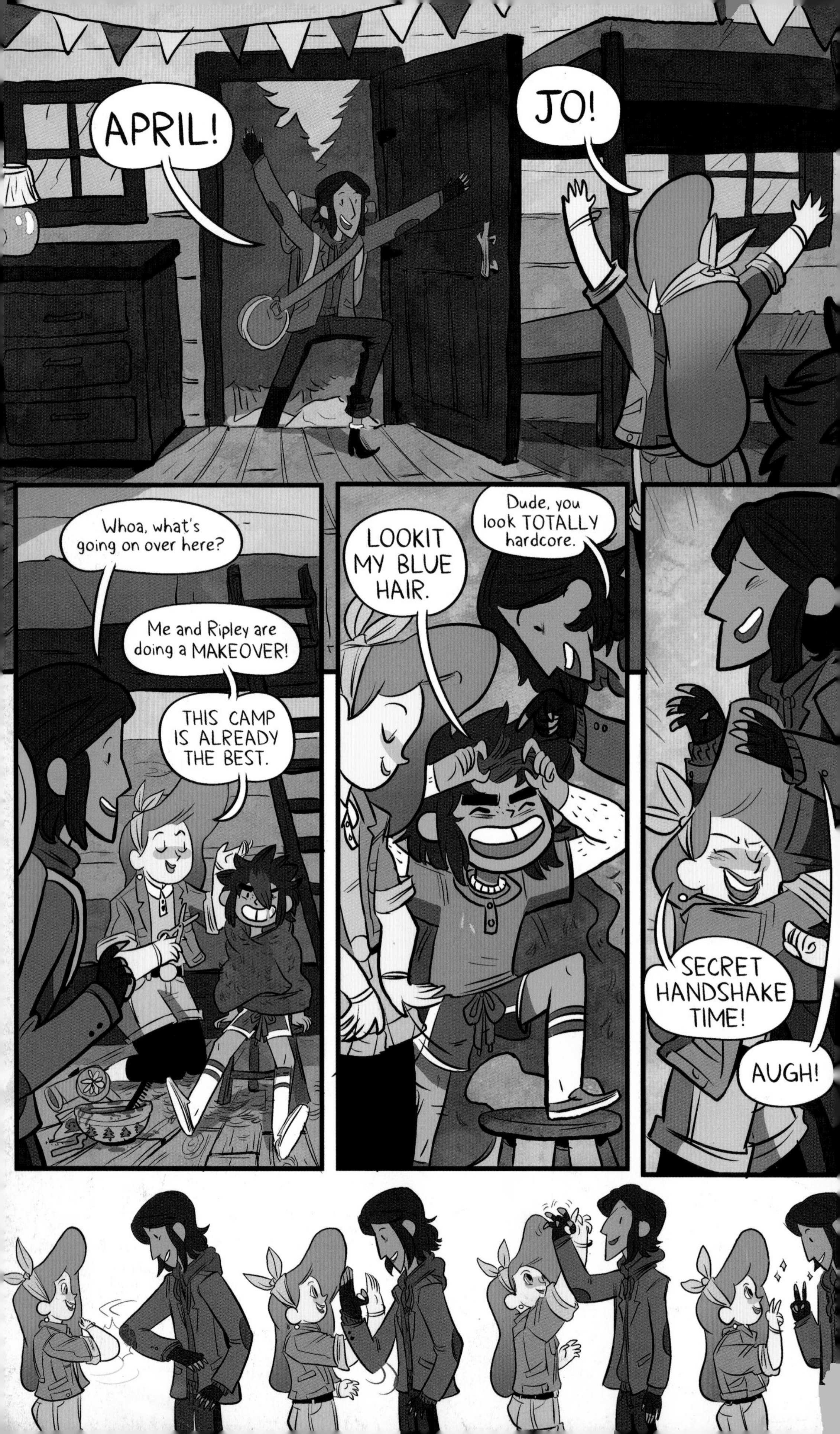
APRIL!
JO!
Whoa, what's going on over here?
Me and Ripley are doing a MAKEOVER!
THIS CAMP IS ALREADY THE BEST.
LOOKIT MY BLUE HAIR.
Dude, you look TOTALLY hardcore.
SECRET HANDSHAKE TIME!
AUGH!

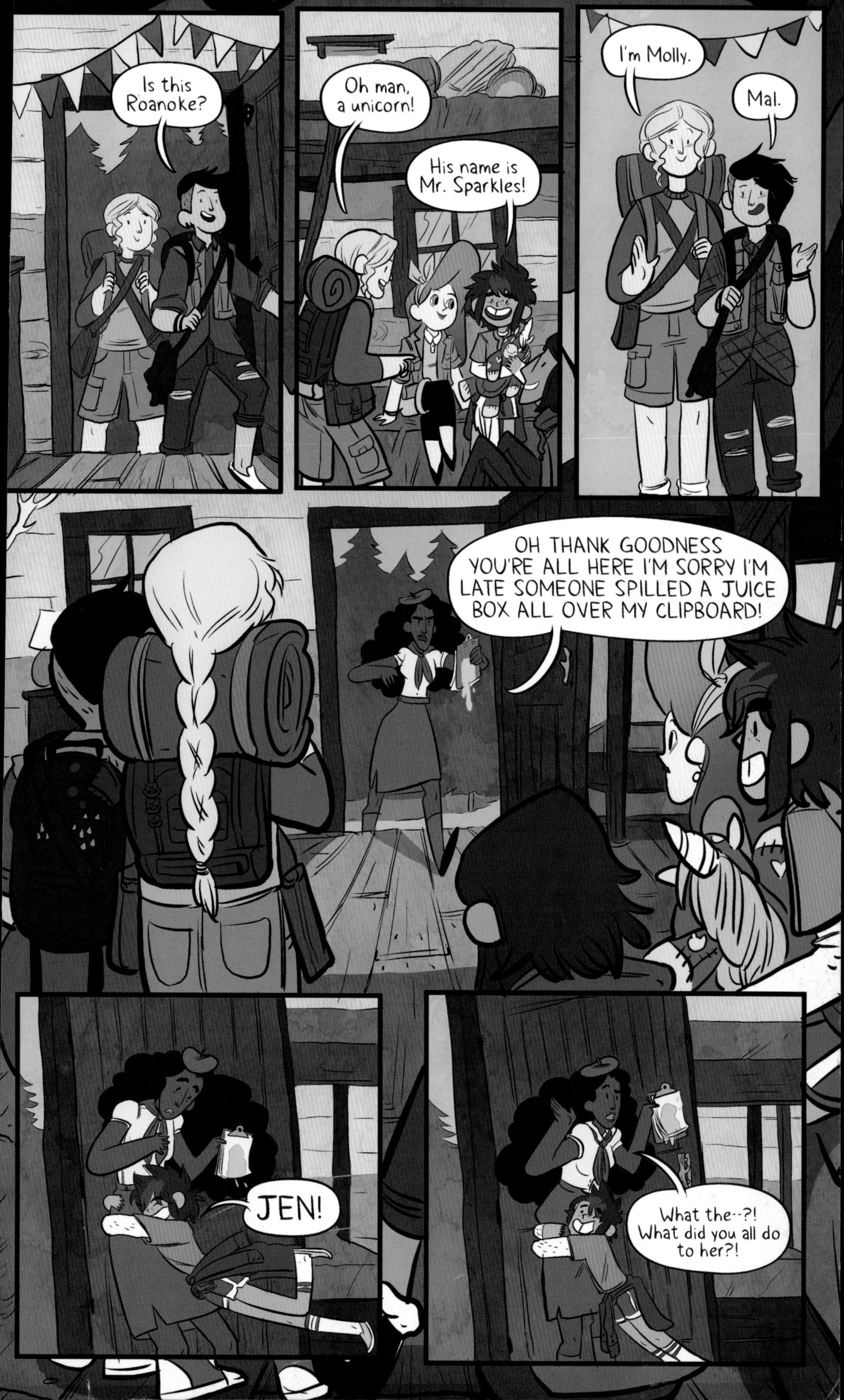
Is this Roanoke?
Oh man, a unicorn!
His name is Mr. Sparkles!
I'm Molly.
Mal.
OH THANK GOODNESS YOU'RE ALL HERE I'M SORRY I'M LATE SOMEONE SPILLED A JUICE BOX ALL OVER MY CLIPBOARD!
JEN!
What the--?! What did you all do to her?!

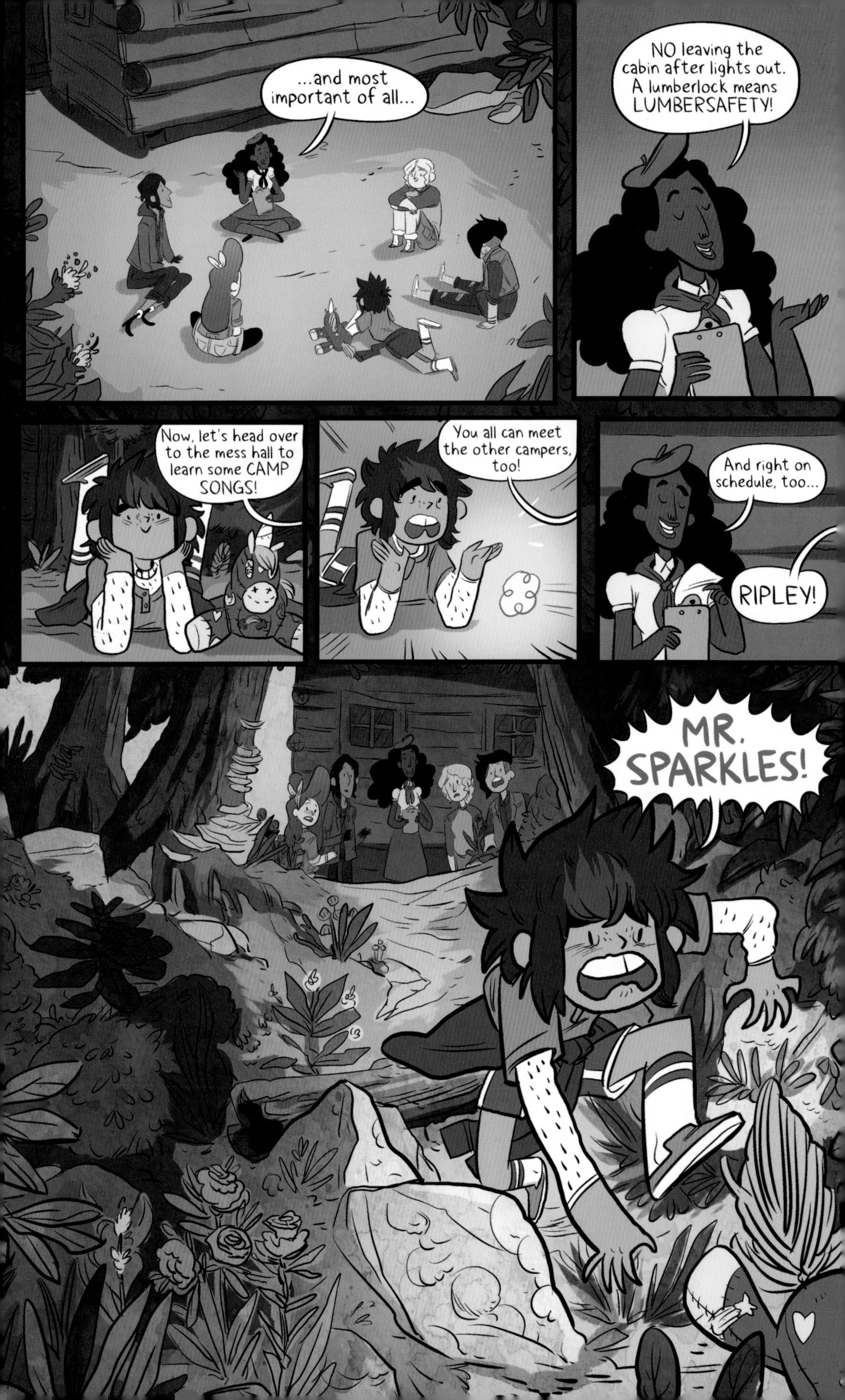
...and most important of all...
NO leaving the cabin after lights out. A lumberlock means LUMBERSAFETY!
Now, let's head over to the mess hall to learn some CAMP SONGS!
You all can meet the other campers, too!
And right on schedule, too...
RIPLEY!
MR. SPARKLES!

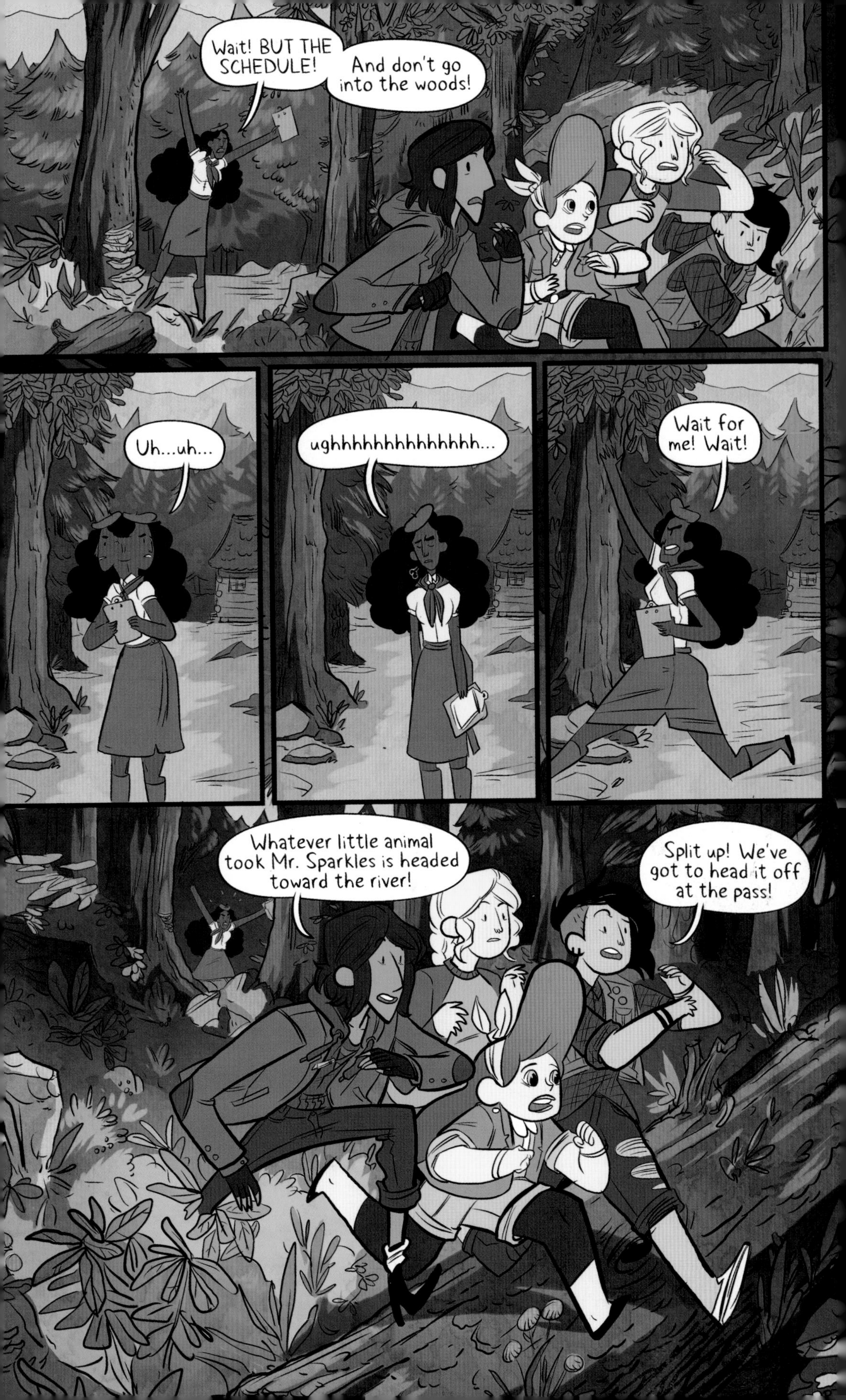
Wait! BUT THE SCHEDULE!
And don't go into the woods!
Uh...uh...
ughhhhhhhhhhhhhh...
Wait for me! Wait!
Whatever little animal took Mr. Sparkles is headed toward the river!
Split up! We've got to head it off at the pass!

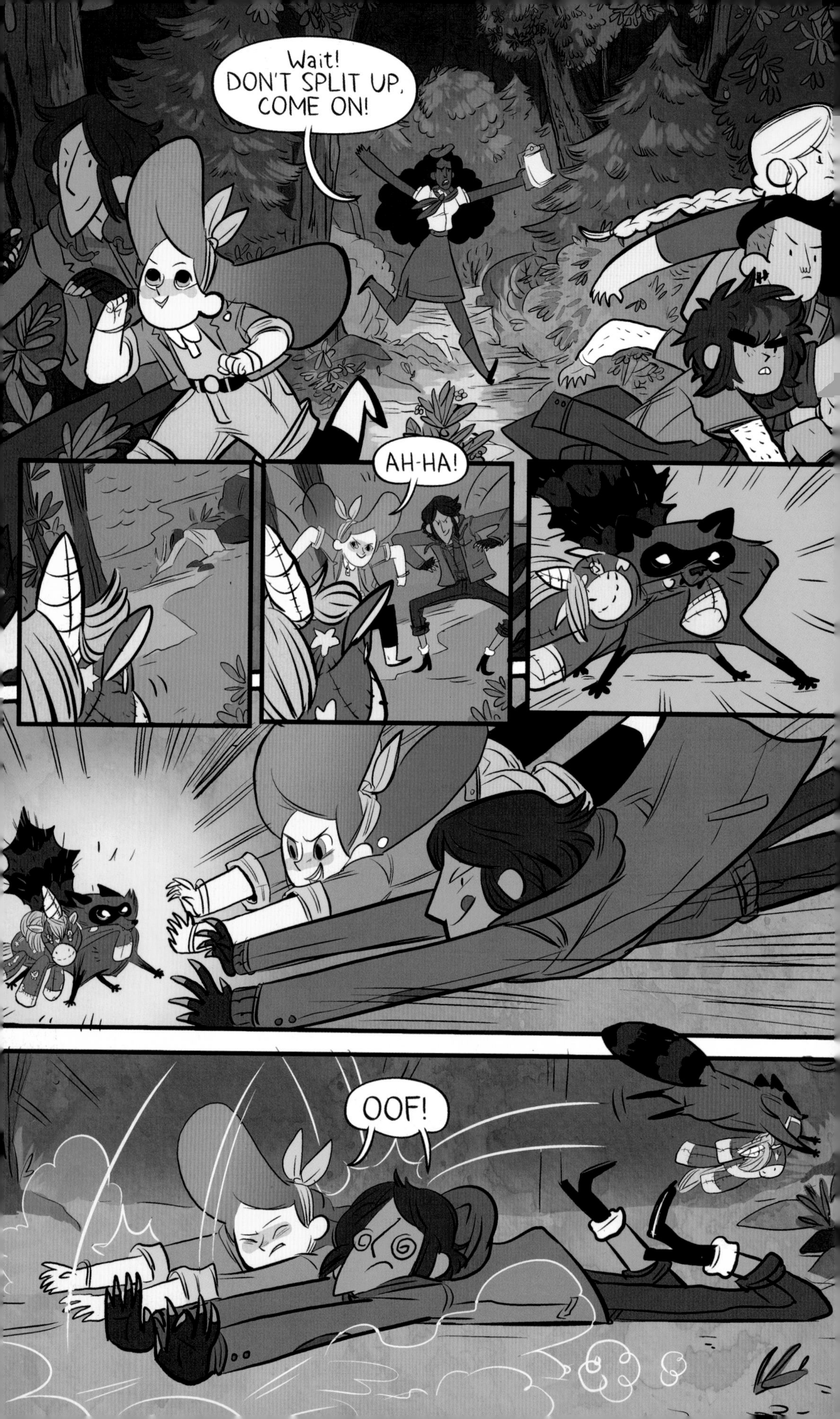
Wait! DON'T SPLIT UP, COME ON!
AH-HA!
OOF!

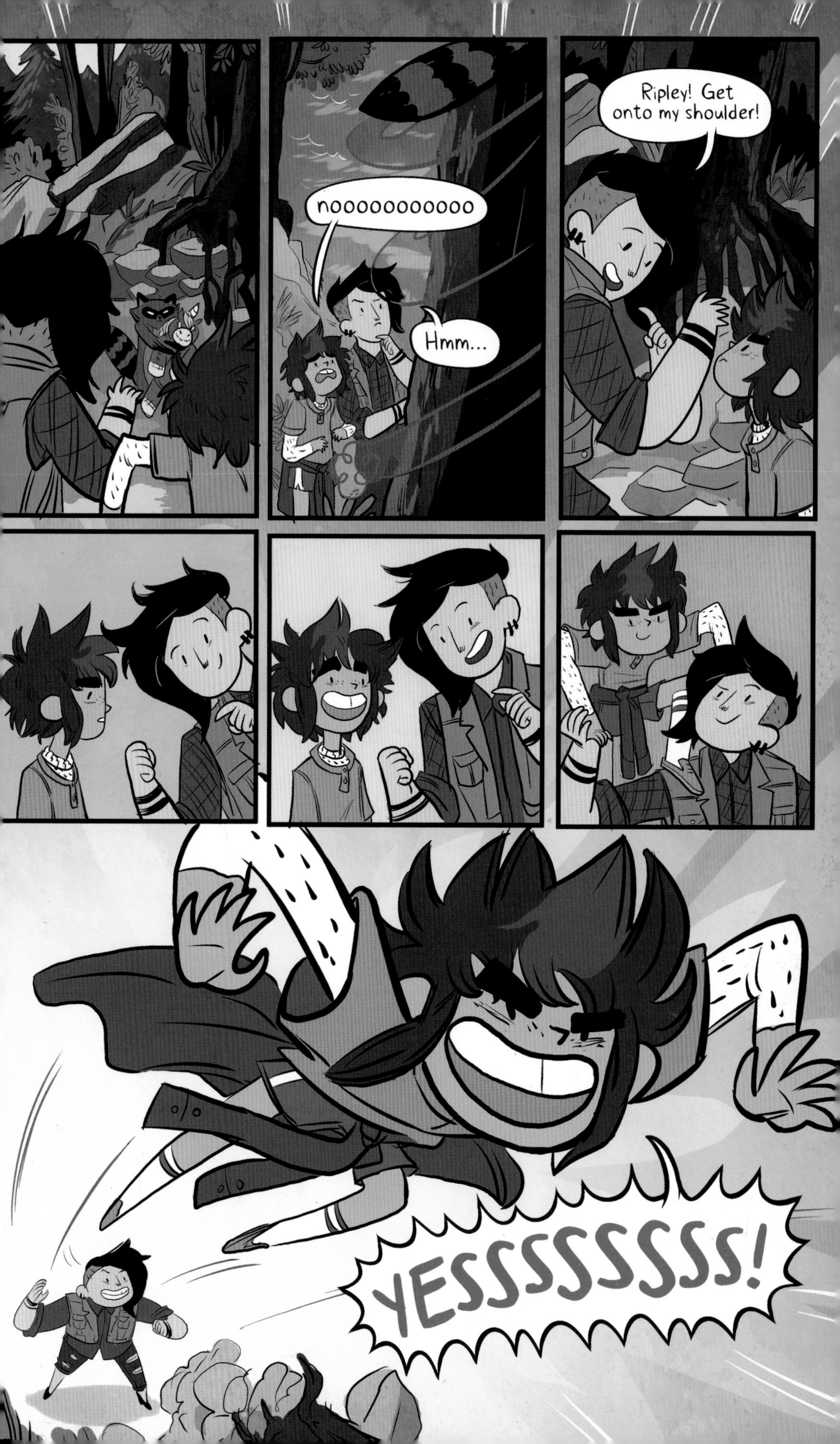
noooooooooooo
Hmm...
Ripley! Get onto my shoulder!
YESSSSSSSS!

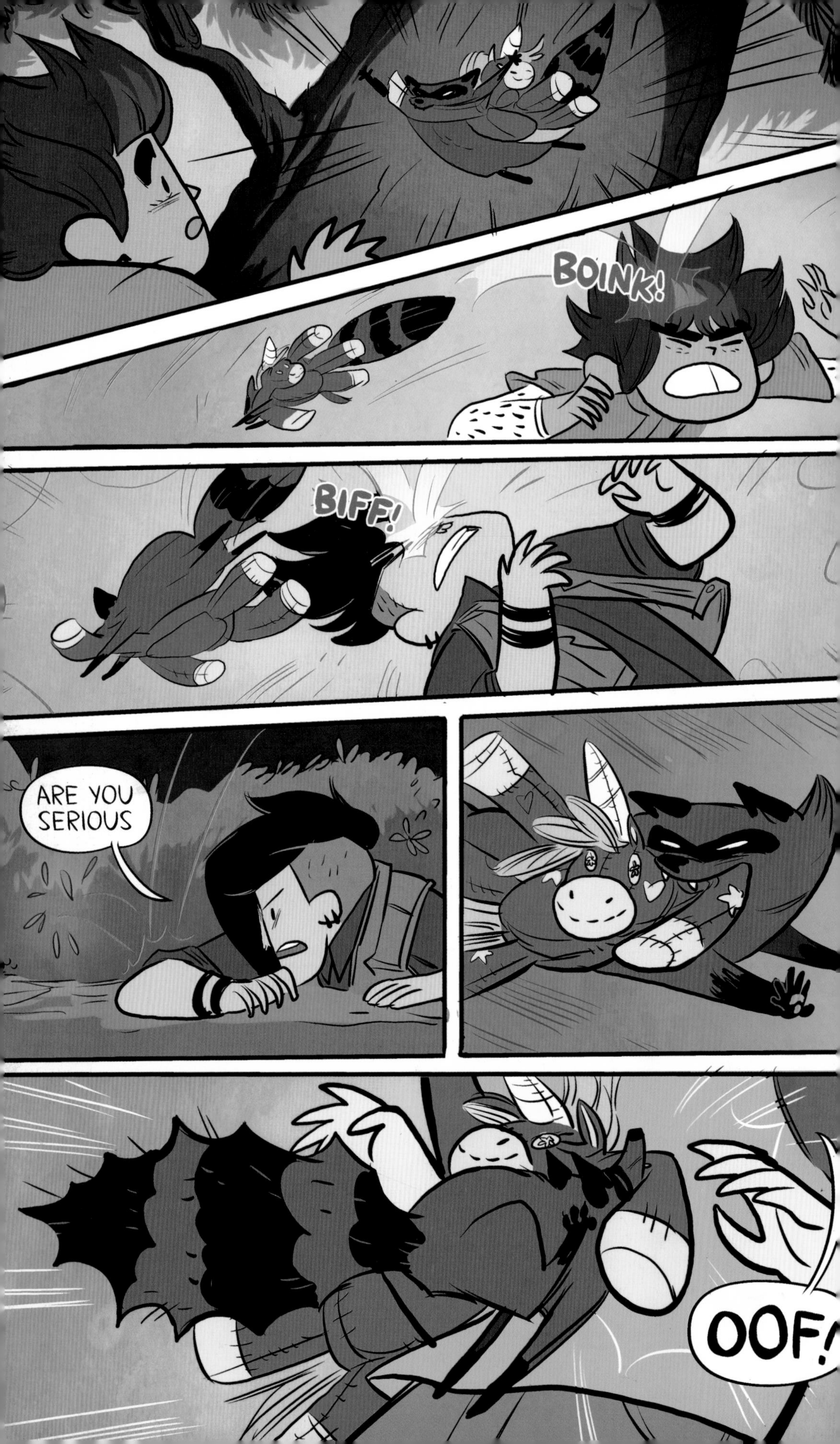
BOINK!
BIFF!
ARE YOU SERIOUS
OOF!

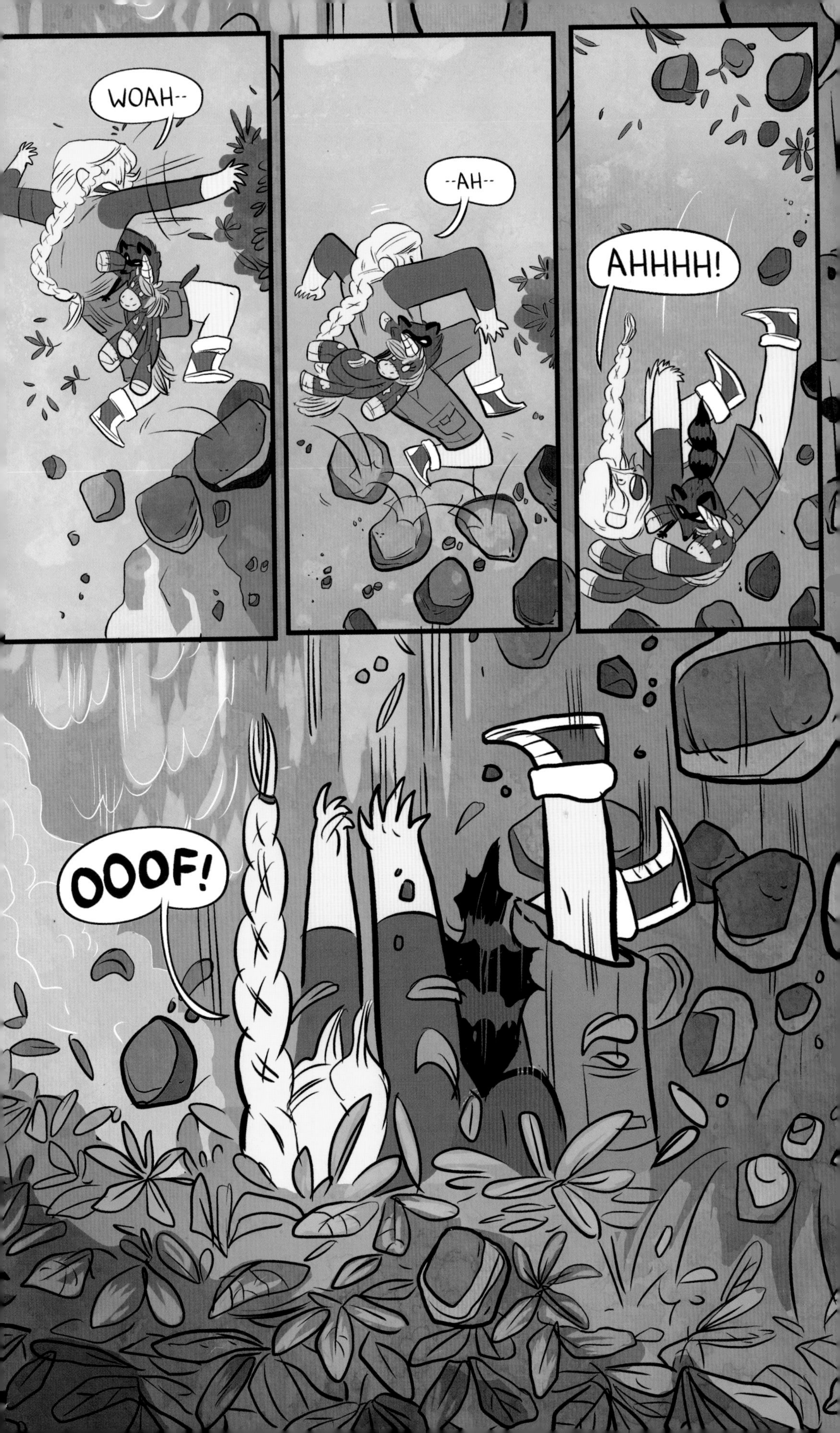
WOAH--
--AH--
AHHHH!
OOOF!

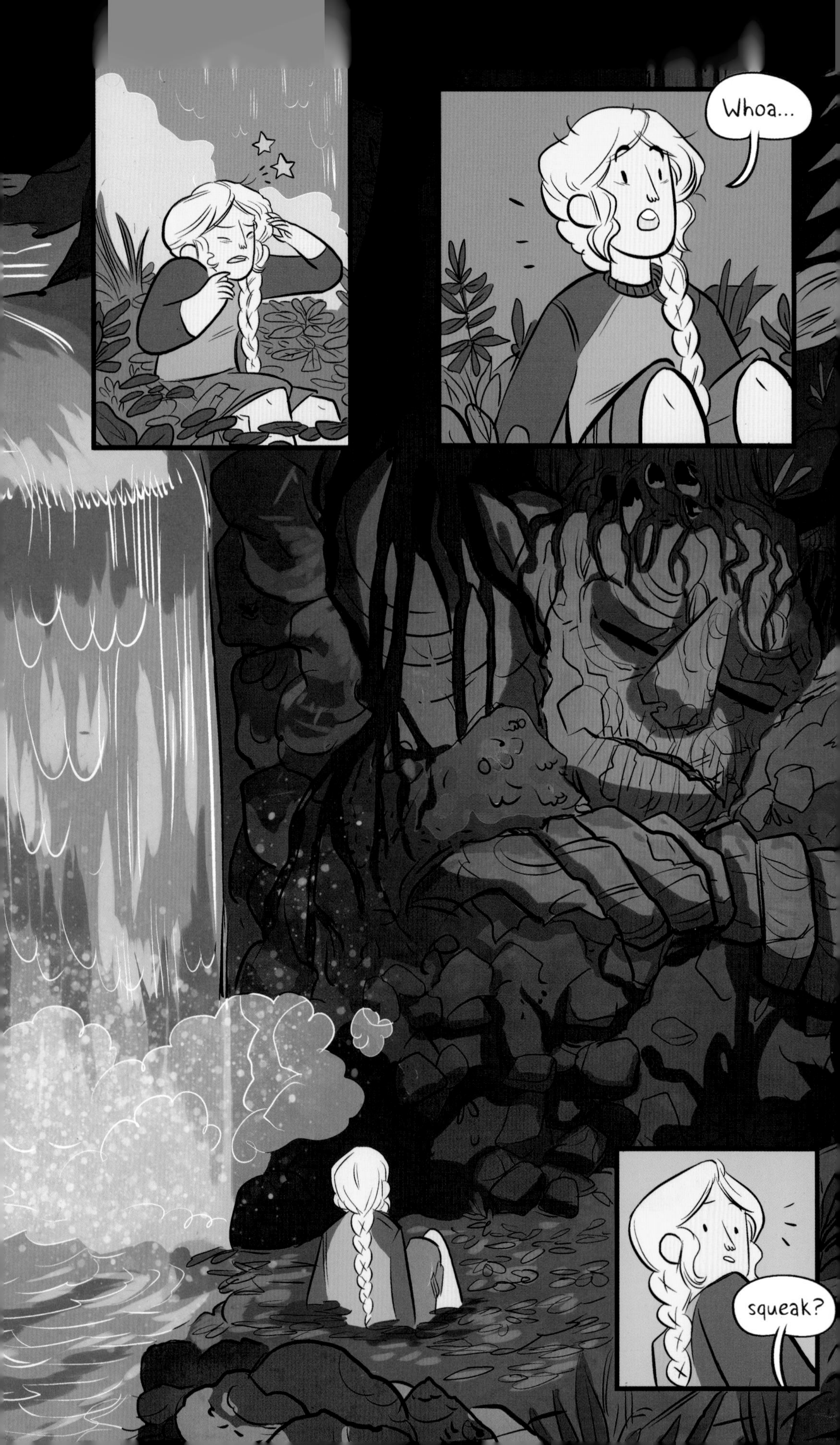
Whoa...
squeak?

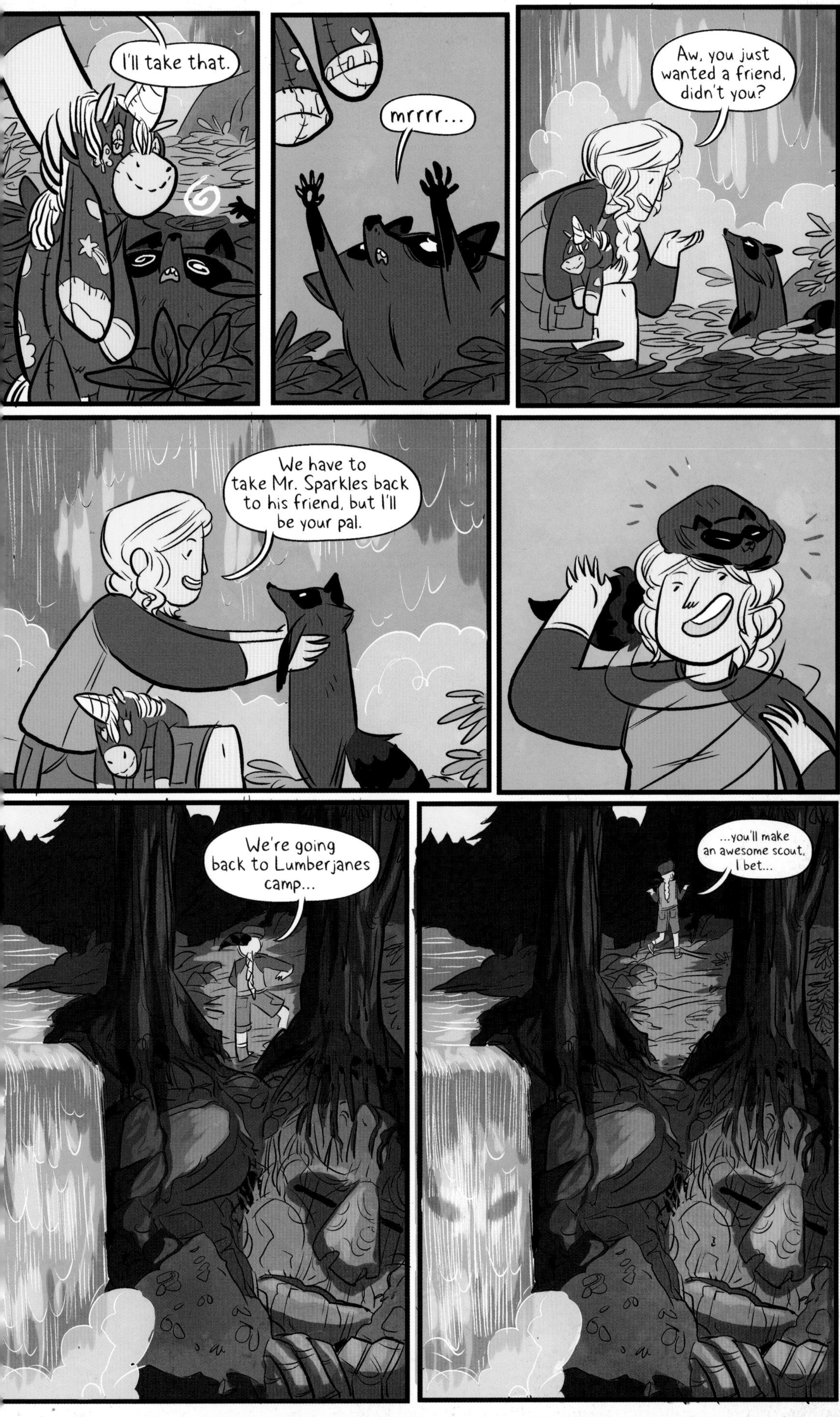
I'll take that.
mrrrr...
Aw, you just wanted a friend, didn't you?
We have to take Mr. Sparkles back to his friend, but I'll be your pal.
We're going back to Lumberjanes camp...
...you'll make an awesome scout, I bet...

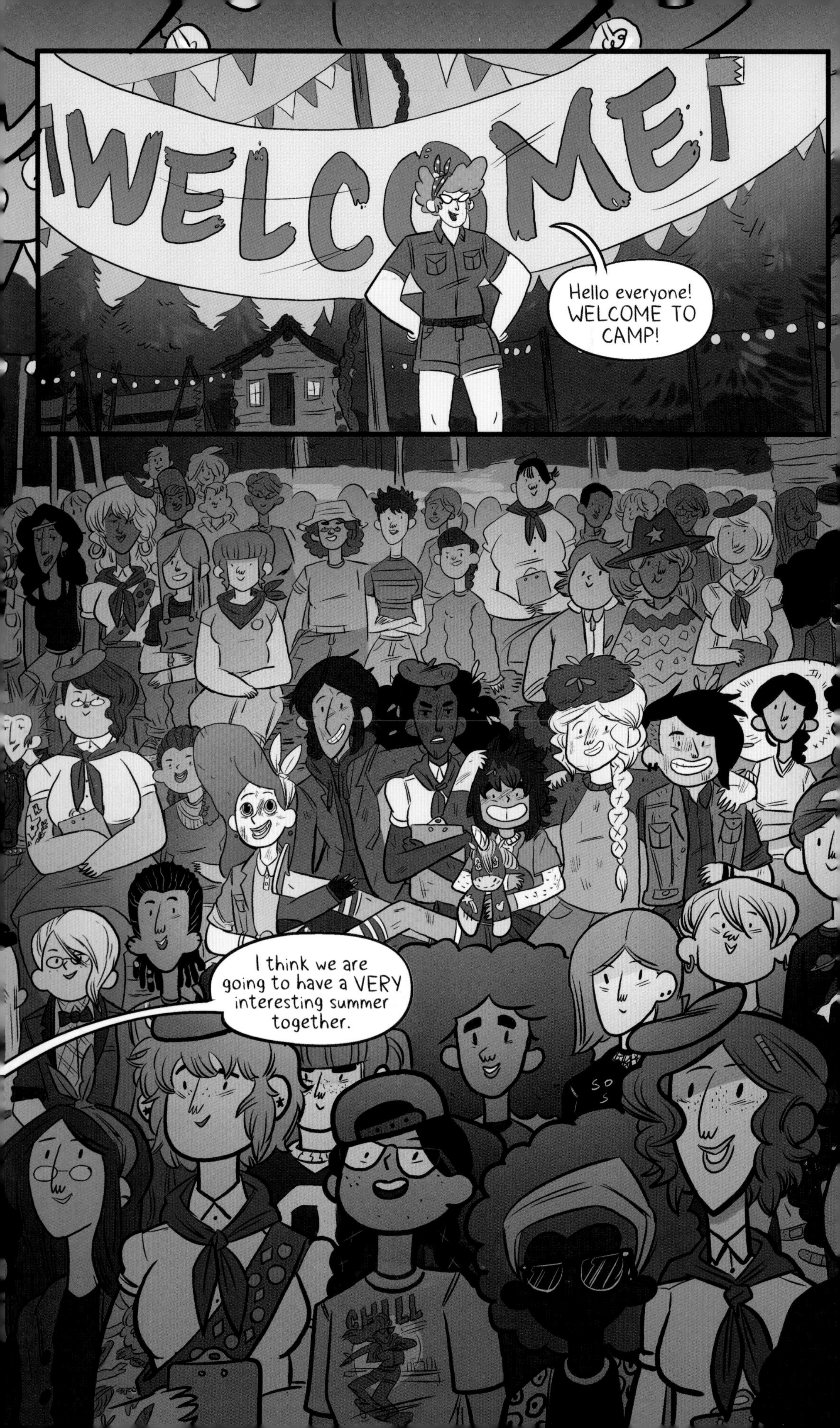
WELCOME!
Hello everyone! WELCOME TO CAMP!
I think we are going to have a VERY interesting summer together.
CHILL

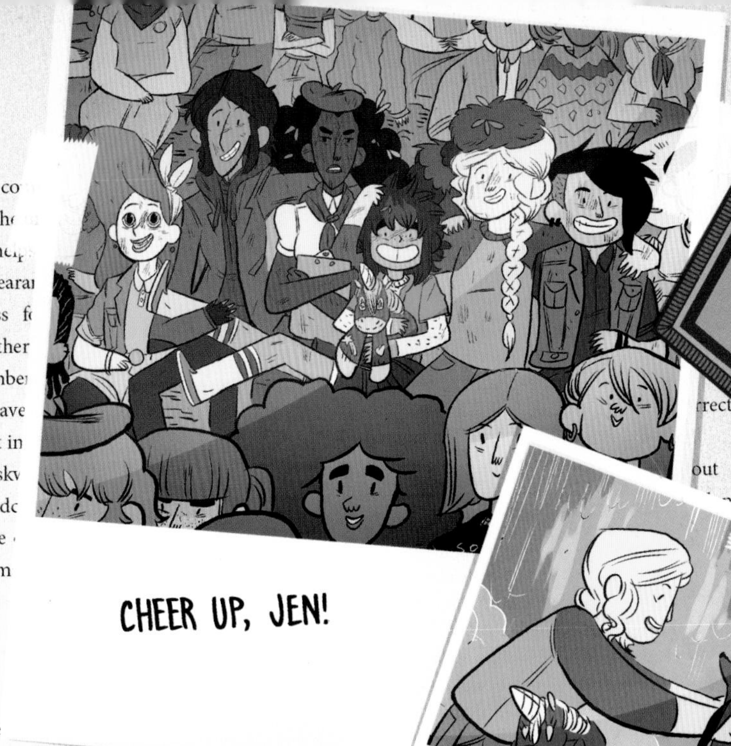
CHEER UP, JEN!

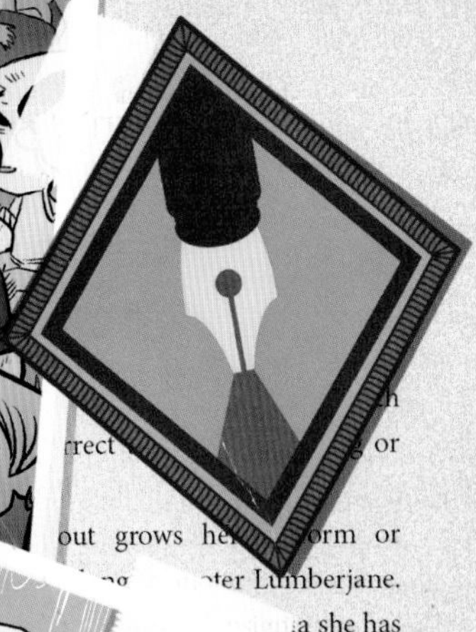

will co

The

It he

appeara

dress f

Further

Lumbe

to have ... rrect ... or

part in

Thiskv ... out grows her ... orm or

Hardc ... ter Lumberjane.

have ... a she has

them ... her

... her

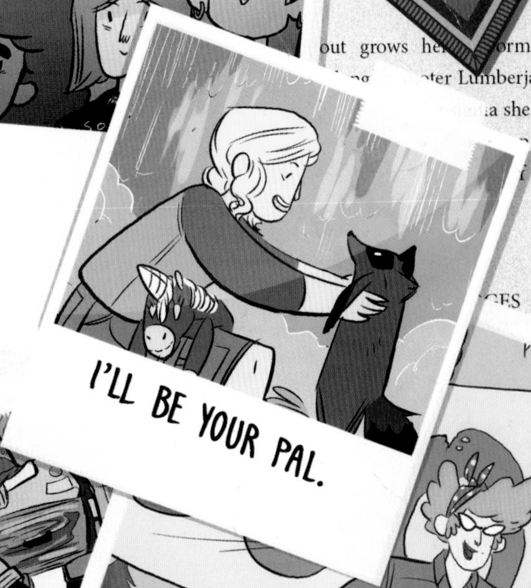
I'LL BE YOUR PAL.

The ... GES

yellow, short sl

emb

the w

choose

slacks,

made o

out-of-d

green bere

the colla

Shoes ma

heels, rou ... kings or

socks sho ... with the shoes or wi

the uniform. Ne ... ces, bracelets, or

belong with a Lumberjane unifo

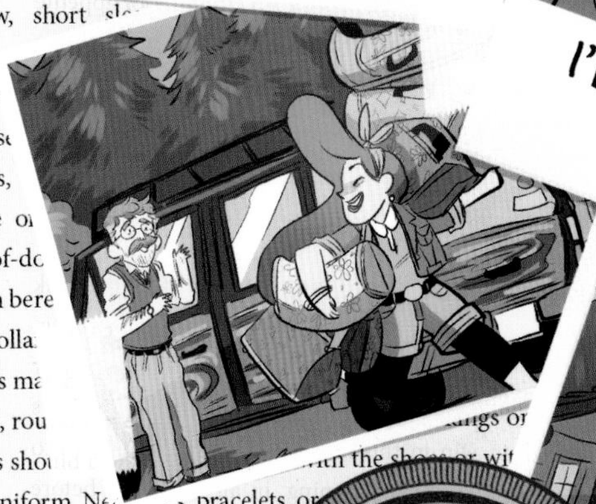

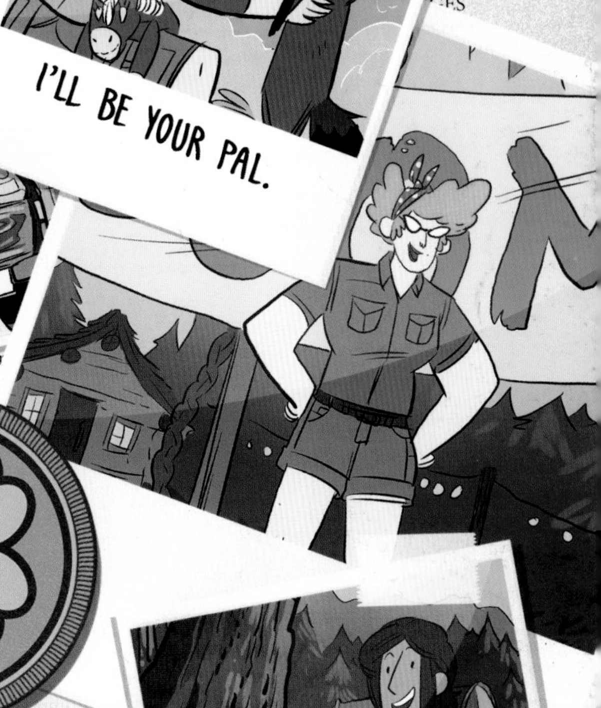

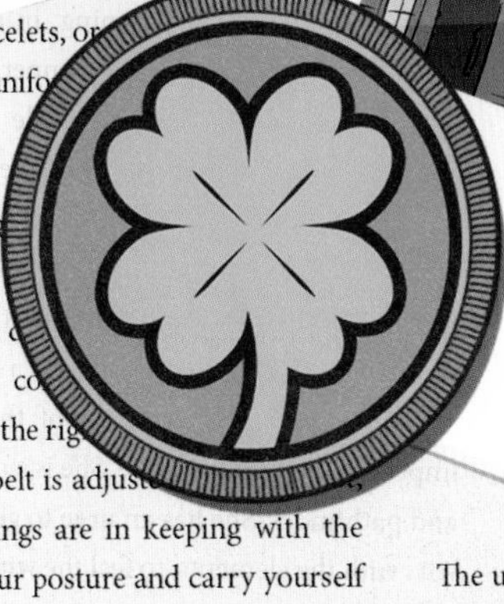

HOW TO WEAR

To look well in a uniform ... uniform be kept in good co ... pressed. See that the skirt is the rig ... height and build, that the belt is adjus ... that your shoes and stockings are in keeping with the uniform, that you watch your posture and carry yourself with dignity and grace. If the beret is removed indoors, be sure that your hair is neat and kept in place with an insonspicuous clip or ribbon. When you wear a Lumberjane uniform you are identified as a member of this organization and you should be doubly careful to conduct yourself in a way that will show everyone that courtesy and thoughtfullness are part of being a Lumberjane. People are likely to judge a whole nation by the selfishness of a few individuals, to criticize a whole family because of the misconduct of one member, and to feel unkindly toward and organization because of the

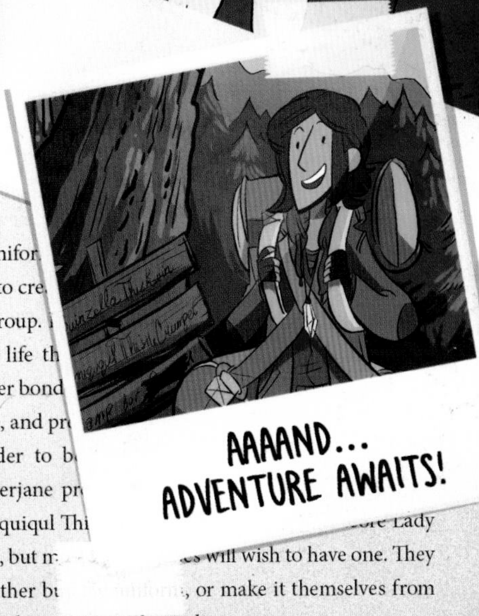
AAAAND...
ADVENTURE AWAITS!

The unifor ... helps to cre ... in a group. ... active life th ... another bond ... future, and pr ... in order to b ... Lumberjane pr ... Penniquiqul Thi ... ore Lady Types, but m ... es will wish to have one. They can either bu ... uniform, or make it themselves from materials available at the trading post.

LUMBERJANES FIELD MANUAL

CHAPTER EIGHTEEN

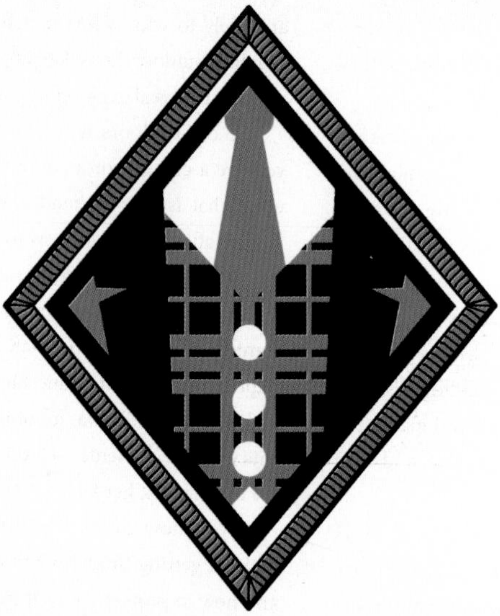

Lumberjanes "Literature" Program Field

DRESSIN' FOR SUCCESSIN' BADGE

"Plaid is a good way to go, always."

As a modern Lumberjane, you will be facing new and intriguing things out in the world outside of camp that we can only imagine as we put together this workbook. Time constantly changes, new trials and tribulations will face every Lumberjane, and at the same time, things don't always change. One of the concerns a Lumberjane will have in their day-to-day life from camp and even in the world beyond the camp, is how to represent themselves.

The *Dressin' for Successin'* badge is a point of pride for any Lumberjane, as they learn the importance of not only a functional wardrobe, but how to use every layer to the best of their ability. Does that sweater vest match with the preselected stockings that you brought to camp for a free day with your friends? Can it also serve as a rope and hold the weight of you and your cabin as you decide to climb the neverending tree? Perfect. Clothing looks nice, and there is nothing wrong with wanting to look nice. The best thing that we can ever teach you at this camp is to be able to dress like you want to dress, and at the end of the day, if bracelets also work as a projectile weapon, then even better.

To obtain the *Dressin' for Successin'* badge a Lumberjane must be able to put together three outfits for a hike through the night. They will come across multiple terrains that cannot be prepared for as the terrains like to move whenever they feel like it and it will be up to the Lumberjane to put together the perfect collection of clothing to help them through any possibility. The only advice that we give our young campers as they prepare to earn this badge would be to dress comfortably, and always know that plaid has never let us down. Once you've obtained the *Dressin' for Successin'* badge, then you'll be able to move on to the next badge with relative ease, depending on your foot wear choice of the day. Keep in mind, friends are always available to help you out when it comes to this badge.

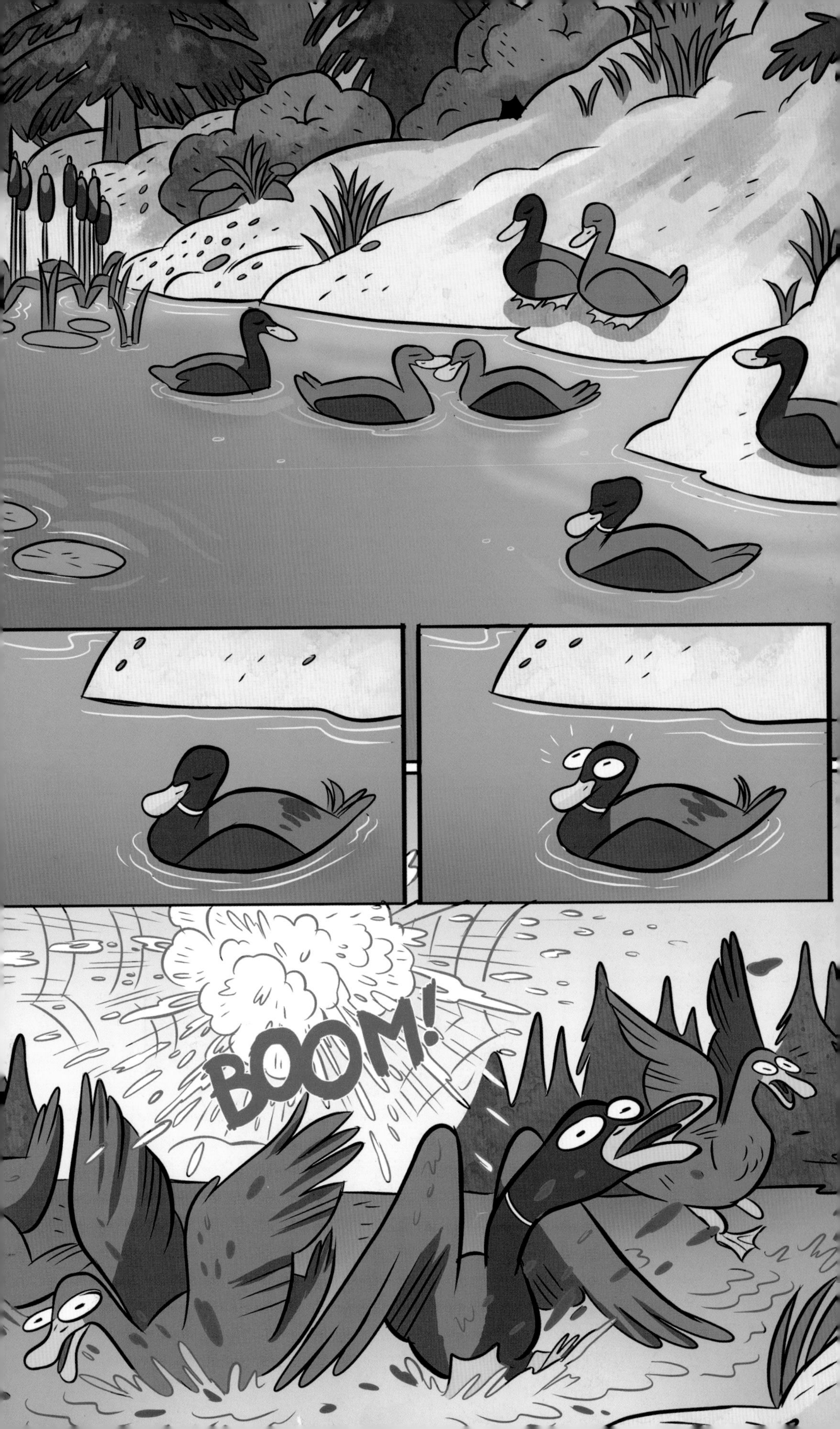
BOOM!

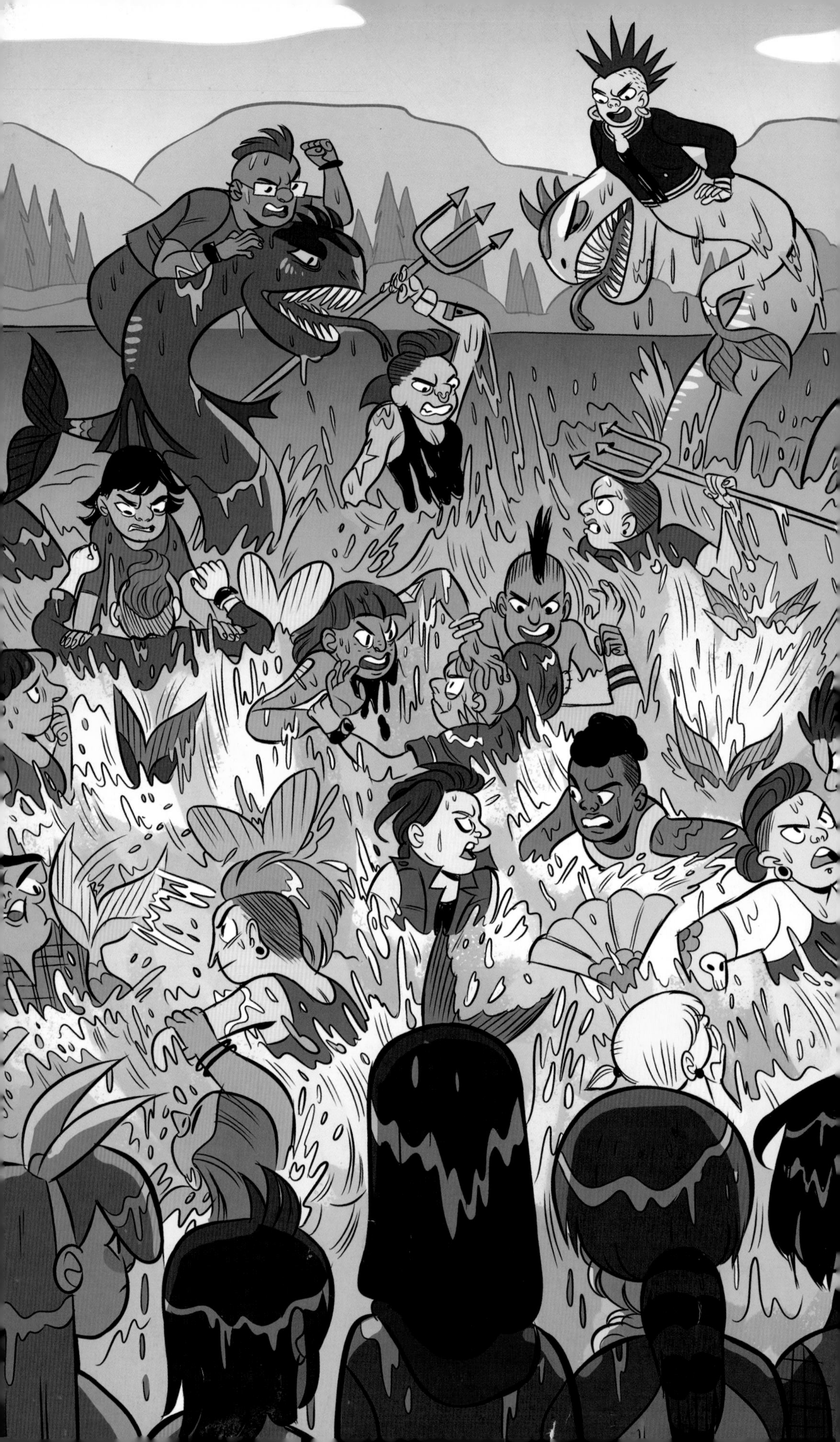

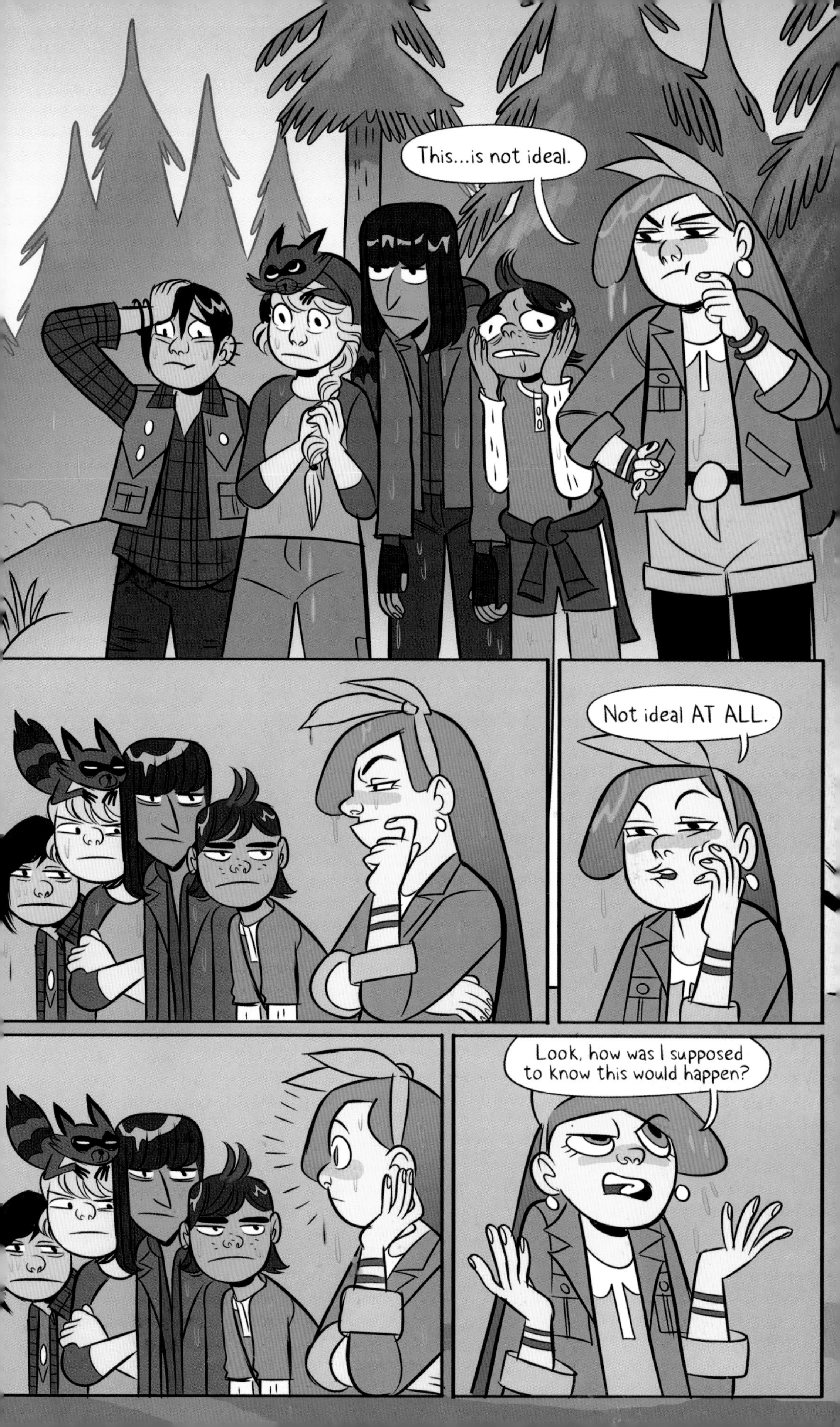
This...is not ideal.
Not ideal AT ALL.
Look, how was I supposed to know this would happen?

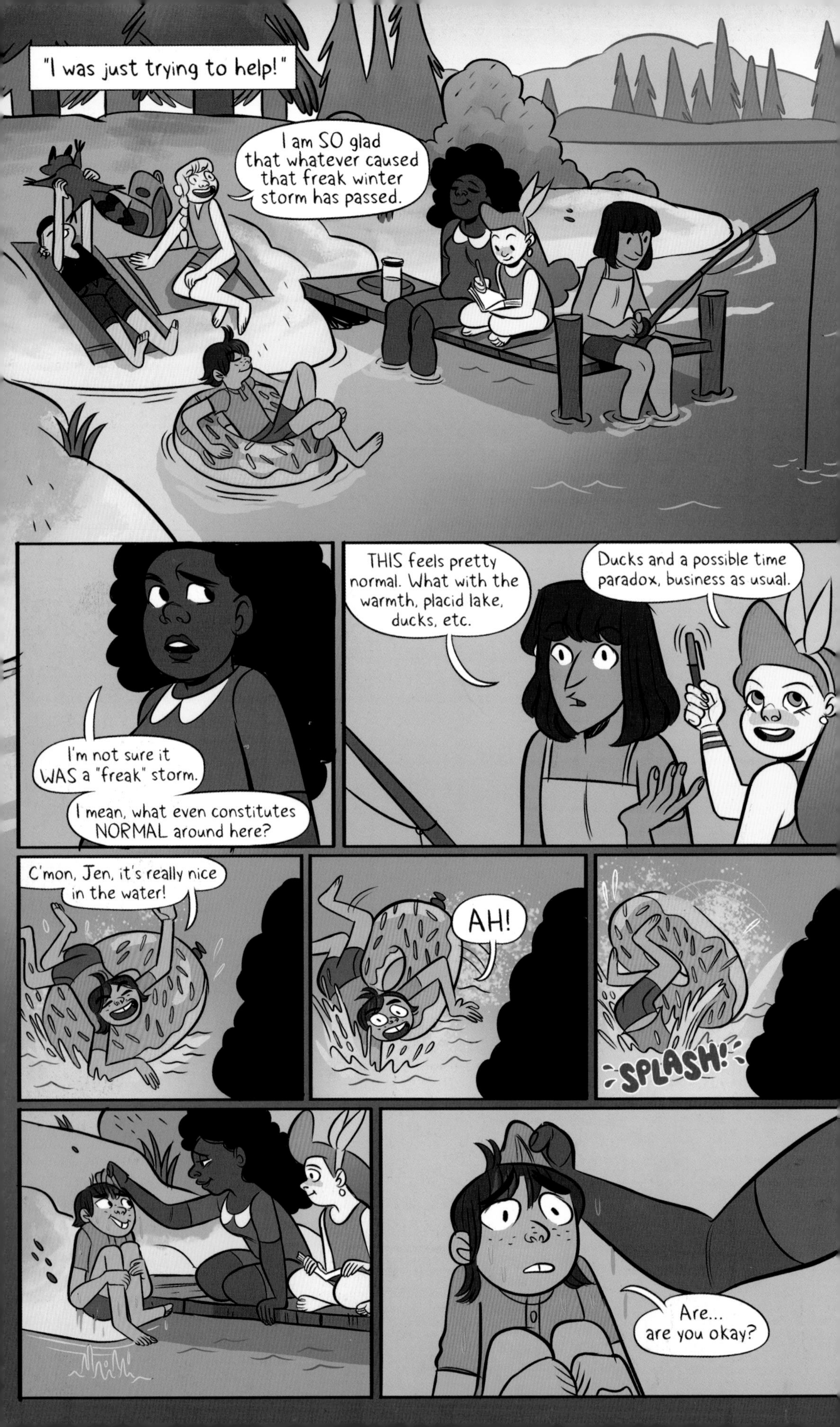
"I was just trying to help!"
I am SO glad that whatever caused that freak winter storm has passed.
I'm not sure it WAS a "freak" storm.
I mean, what even constitutes NORMAL around here?
THIS feels pretty normal. What with the warmth, placid lake, ducks, etc.
Ducks and a possible time paradox, business as usual.
C'mon, Jen, it's really nice in the water!
AH!
SPLASH!
Are... are you okay?

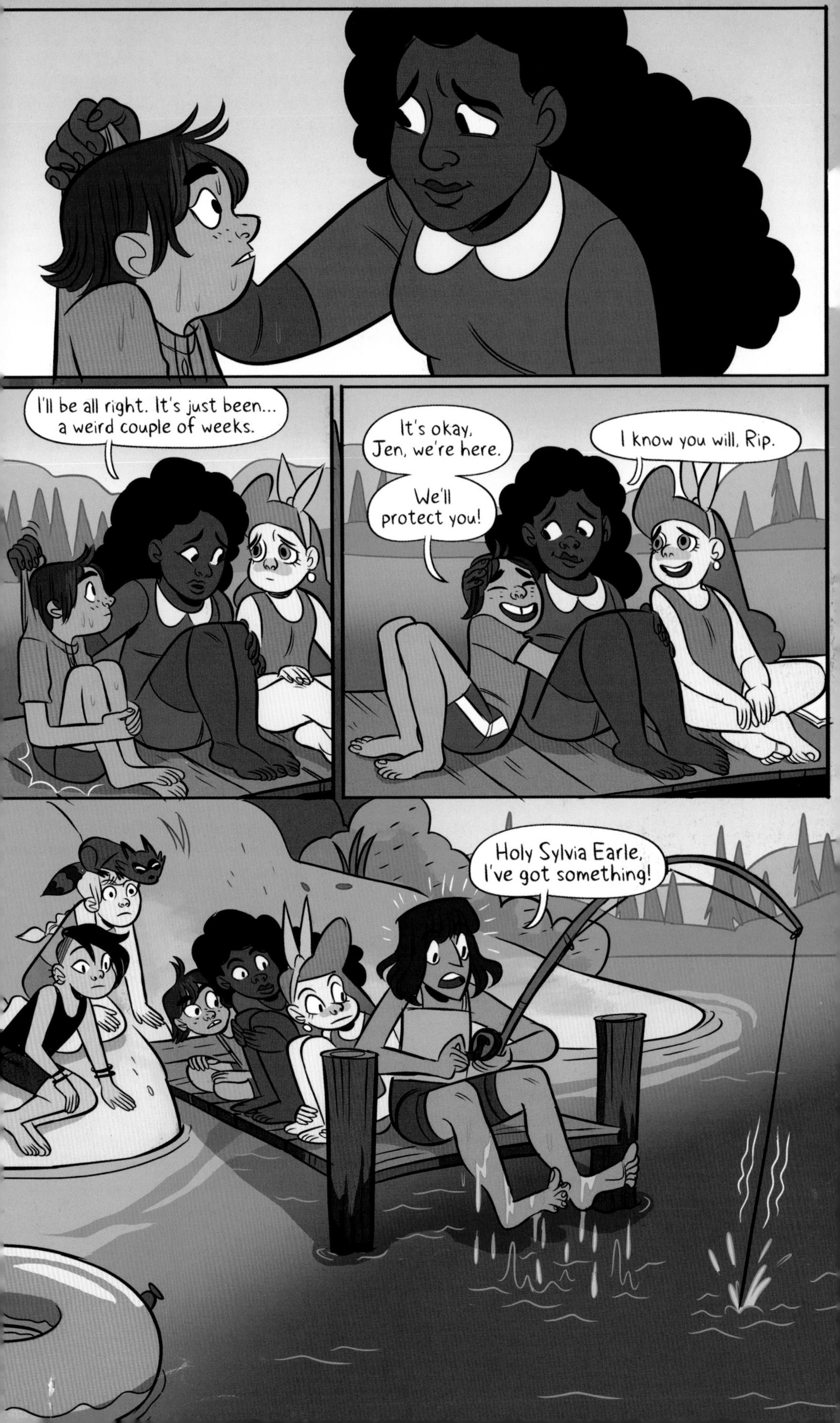
I'll be all right. It's just been... a weird couple of weeks.
It's okay, Jen, we're here.
We'll protect you!
I know you will, Rip.
Holy Sylvia Earle, I've got something!

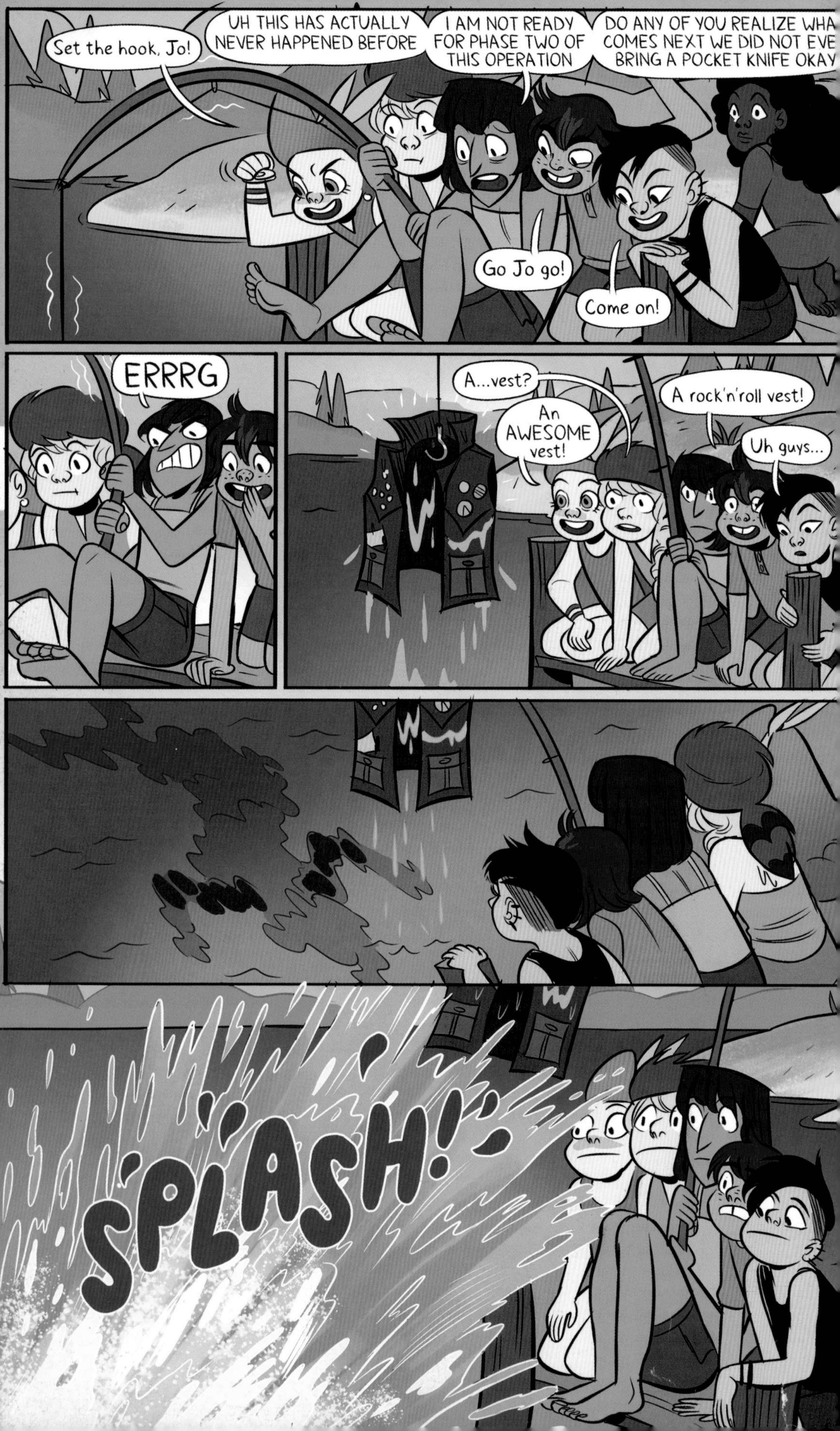
Set the hook, Jo!
UH THIS HAS ACTUALLY NEVER HAPPENED BEFORE
I AM NOT READY FOR PHASE TWO OF THIS OPERATION
DO ANY OF YOU REALIZE WHA COMES NEXT WE DID NOT EVE BRING A POCKET KNIFE OKAY
Go Jo go!
Come on!
ERRRG
A...vest?
An AWESOME vest!
A rock'n'roll vest!
Uh guys...
SPLASH!

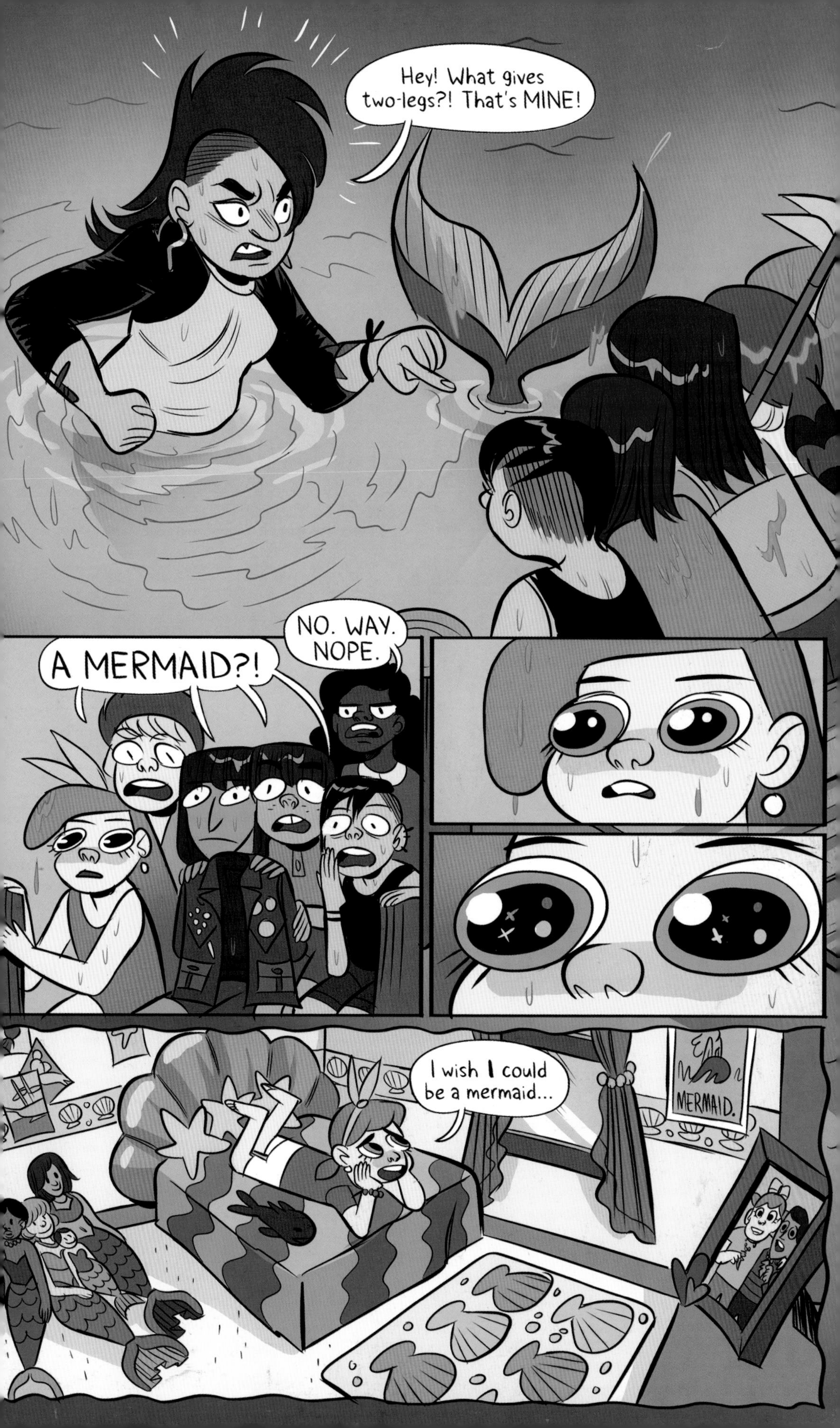
Hey! What gives two-legs?! That's MINE!
A MERMAID?!
NO. WAY. NOPE.
I wish I could be a mermaid...
MERMAID.

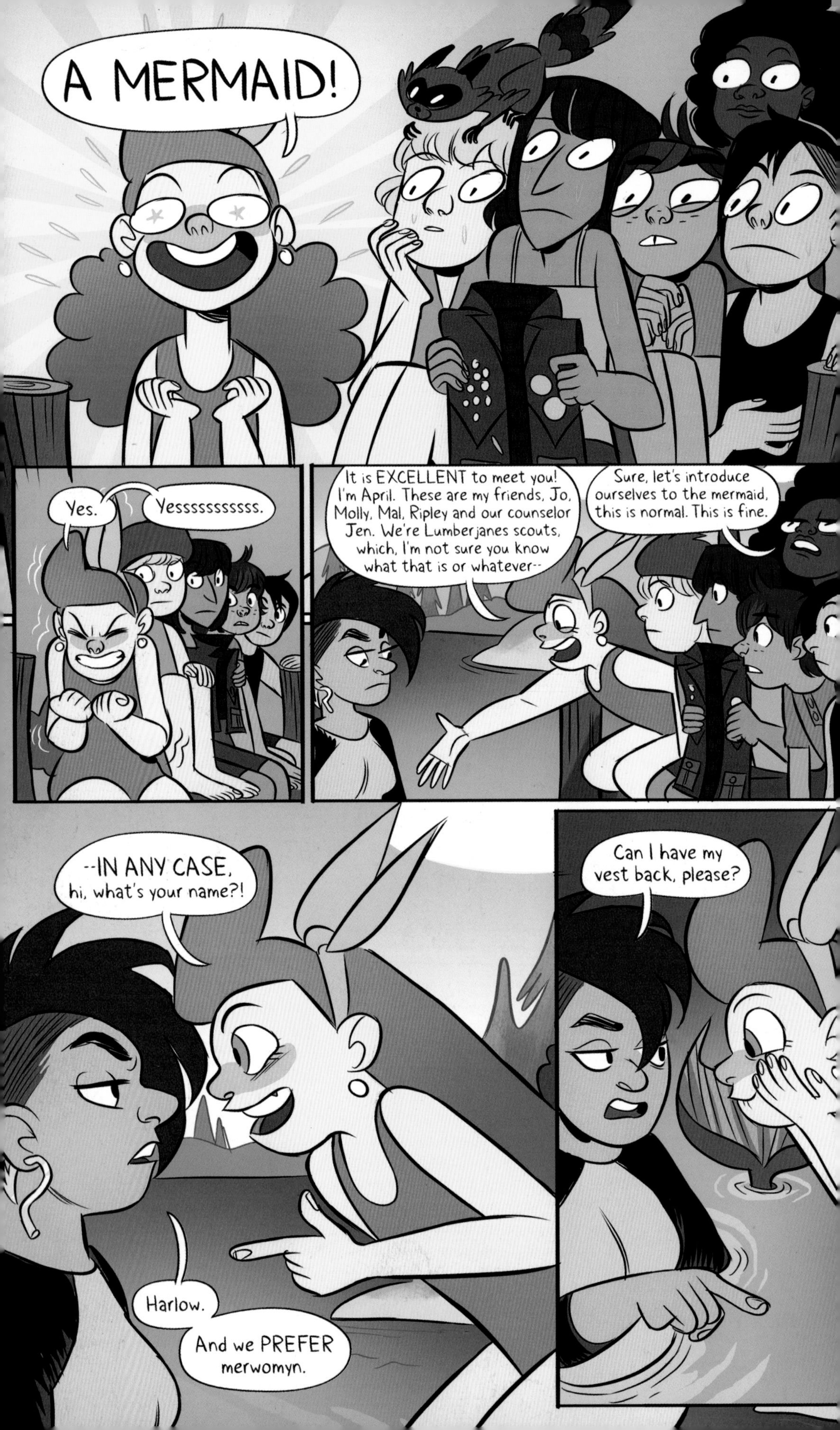
A MERMAID!
Yes.
Yessssssssssss.
It is EXCELLENT to meet you! I'm April. These are my friends, Jo, Molly, Mal, Ripley and our counselor Jen. We're Lumberjanes scouts, which, I'm not sure you know what that is or whatever--
Sure, let's introduce ourselves to the mermaid, this is normal. This is fine.
--IN ANY CASE, hi, what's your name?!
Harlow.
And we PREFER merwomyn.
Can I have my vest back, please?

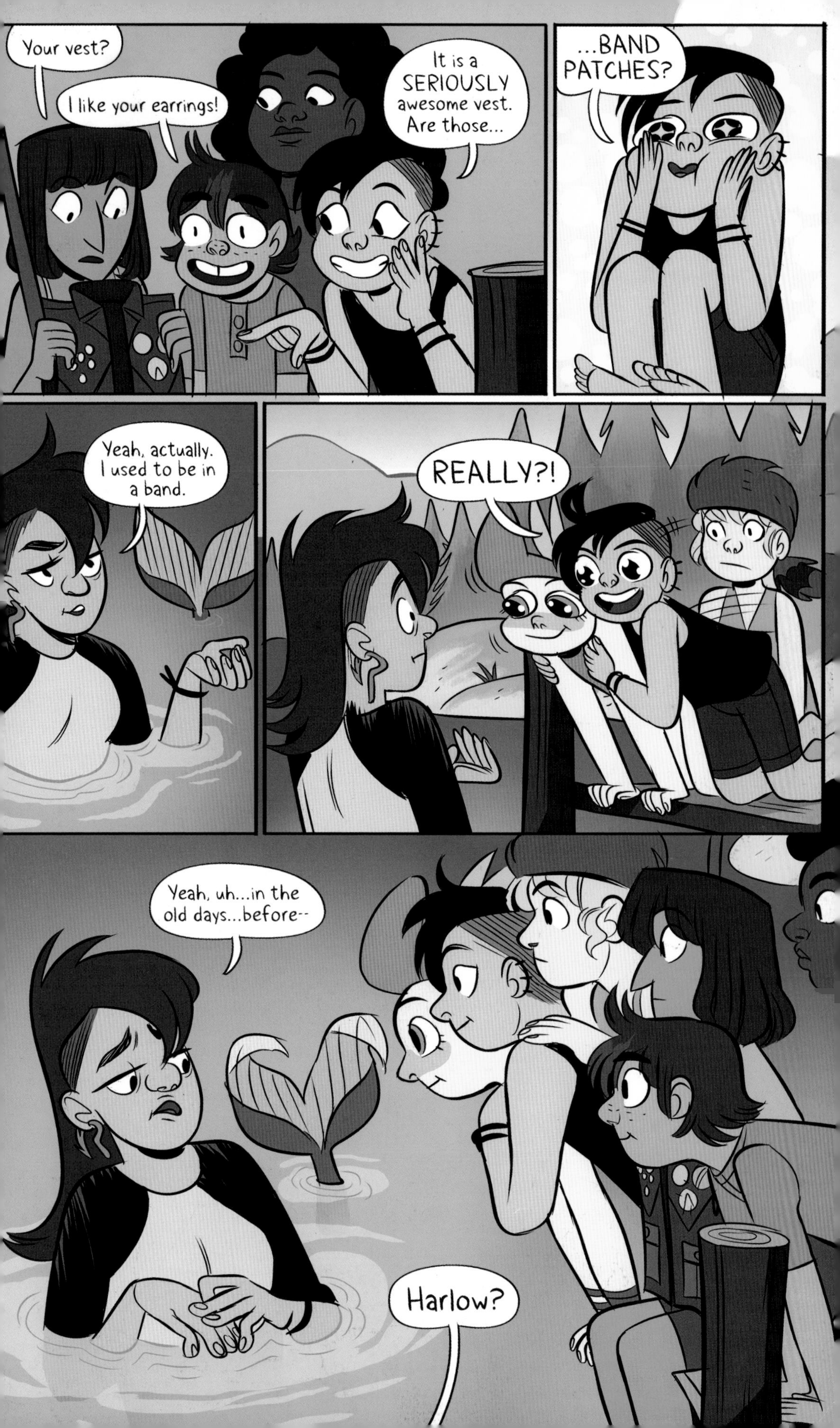
Your vest?
I like your earrings!
It is a SERIOUSLY awesome vest. Are those...
...BAND PATCHES?
Yeah, actually. I used to be in a band.
REALLY?!
Yeah, uh...in the old days...before--
Harlow?

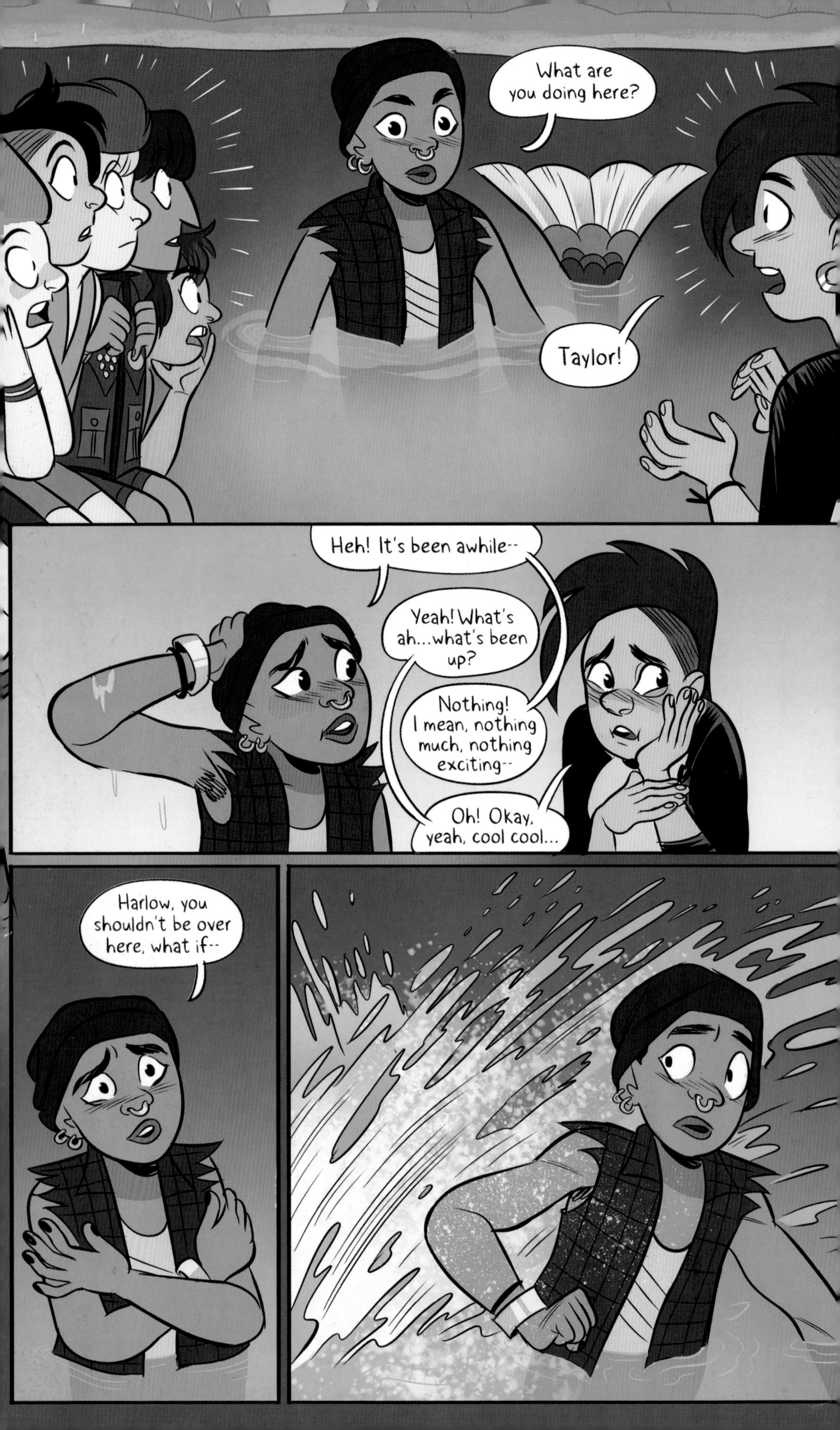
What are you doing here?
Taylor!
Heh! It's been awhile--
Yeah! What's ah...what's been up?
Nothing! I mean, nothing much, nothing exciting--
Oh! Okay, yeah, cool cool...
Harlow, you shouldn't be over here, what if--

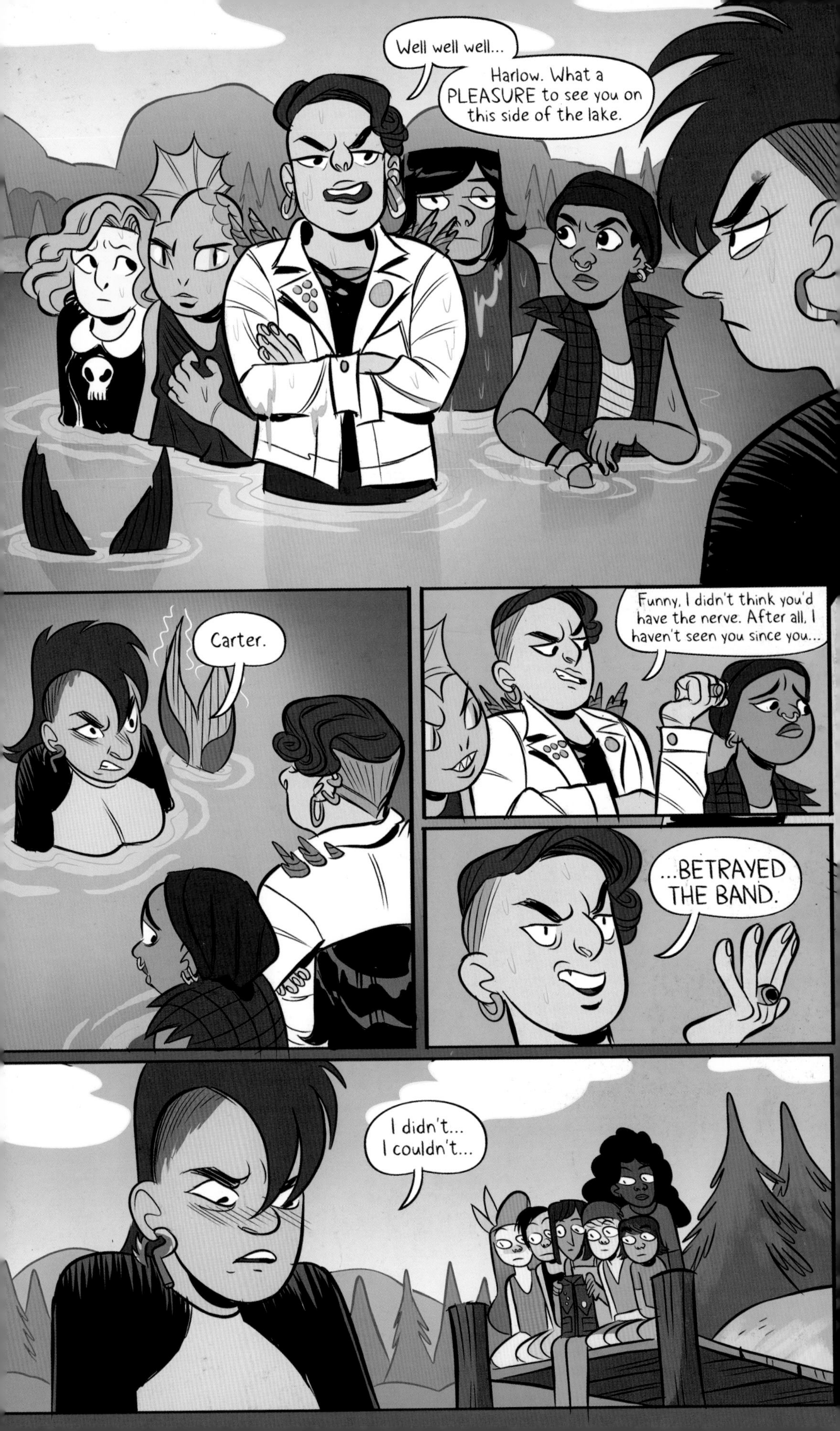
Well well well...
Harlow. What a PLEASURE to see you on this side of the lake.
Carter.
Funny, I didn't think you'd have the nerve. After all, I haven't seen you since you...
...BETRAYED THE BAND.
I didn't... I couldn't...

This...

...was a mistake.

Just a mistake.

One I won't make again. Don't worry...

...I know where I belong.

See you around, Taylor.

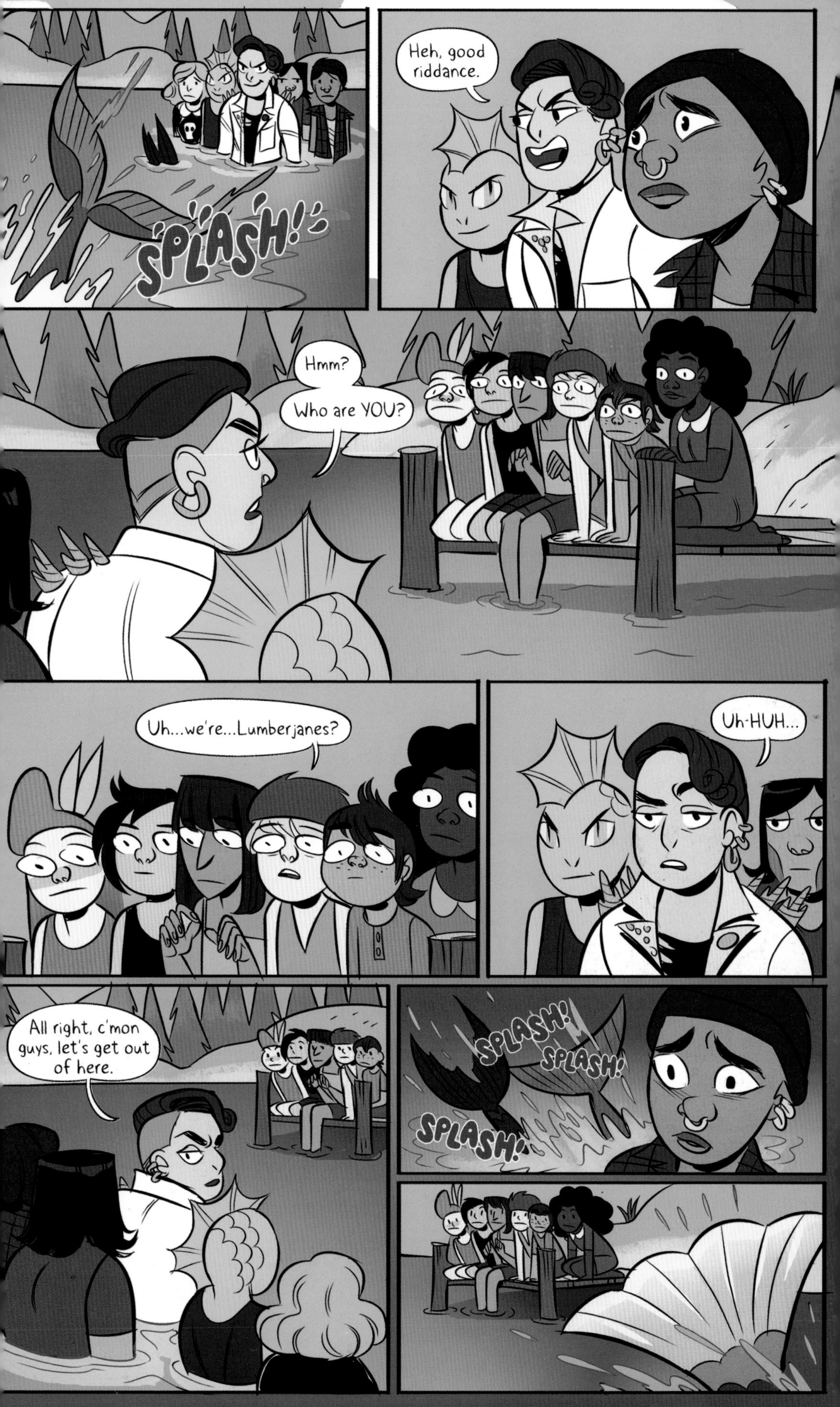
SPLASH!
Heh, good riddance.
Hmm?
Who are YOU?
Uh...we're...Lumberjanes?
Uh-HUH...
All right, c'mon guys, let's get out of here.
SPLASH!
SPLASH!
SPLASH!

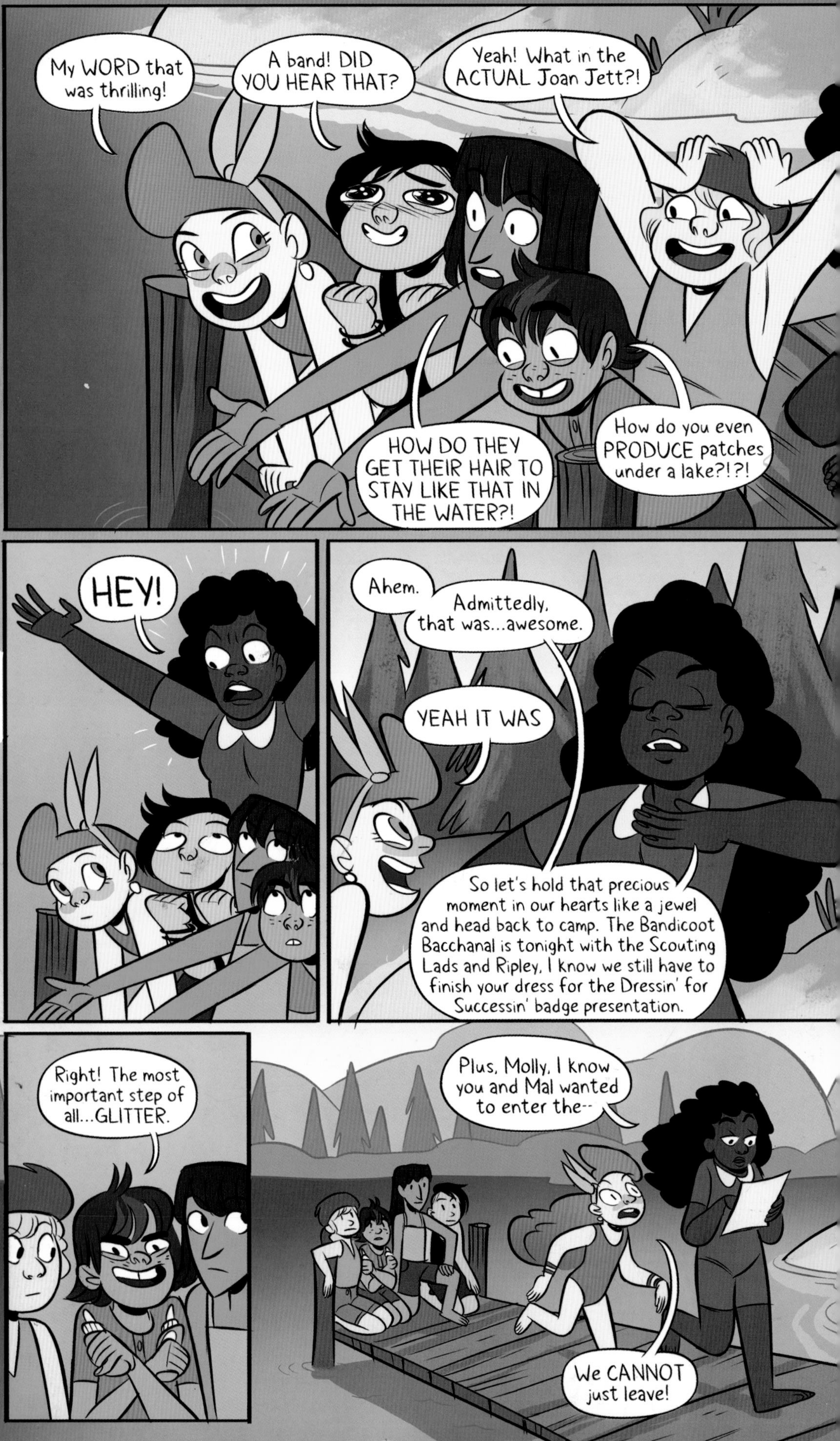
My WORD that was thrilling!
A band! DID YOU HEAR THAT?
Yeah! What in the ACTUAL Joan Jett?!
HOW DO THEY GET THEIR HAIR TO STAY LIKE THAT IN THE WATER?!
How do you even PRODUCE patches under a lake?!?!
HEY!
Ahem.
Admittedly, that was...awesome.
YEAH IT WAS
So let's hold that precious moment in our hearts like a jewel and head back to camp. The Bandicoot Bacchanal is tonight with the Scouting Lads and Ripley. I know we still have to finish your dress for the Dressin' for Successin' badge presentation.
Right! The most important step of all...GLITTER.
Plus, Molly, I know you and Mal wanted to enter the--
We CANNOT just leave!

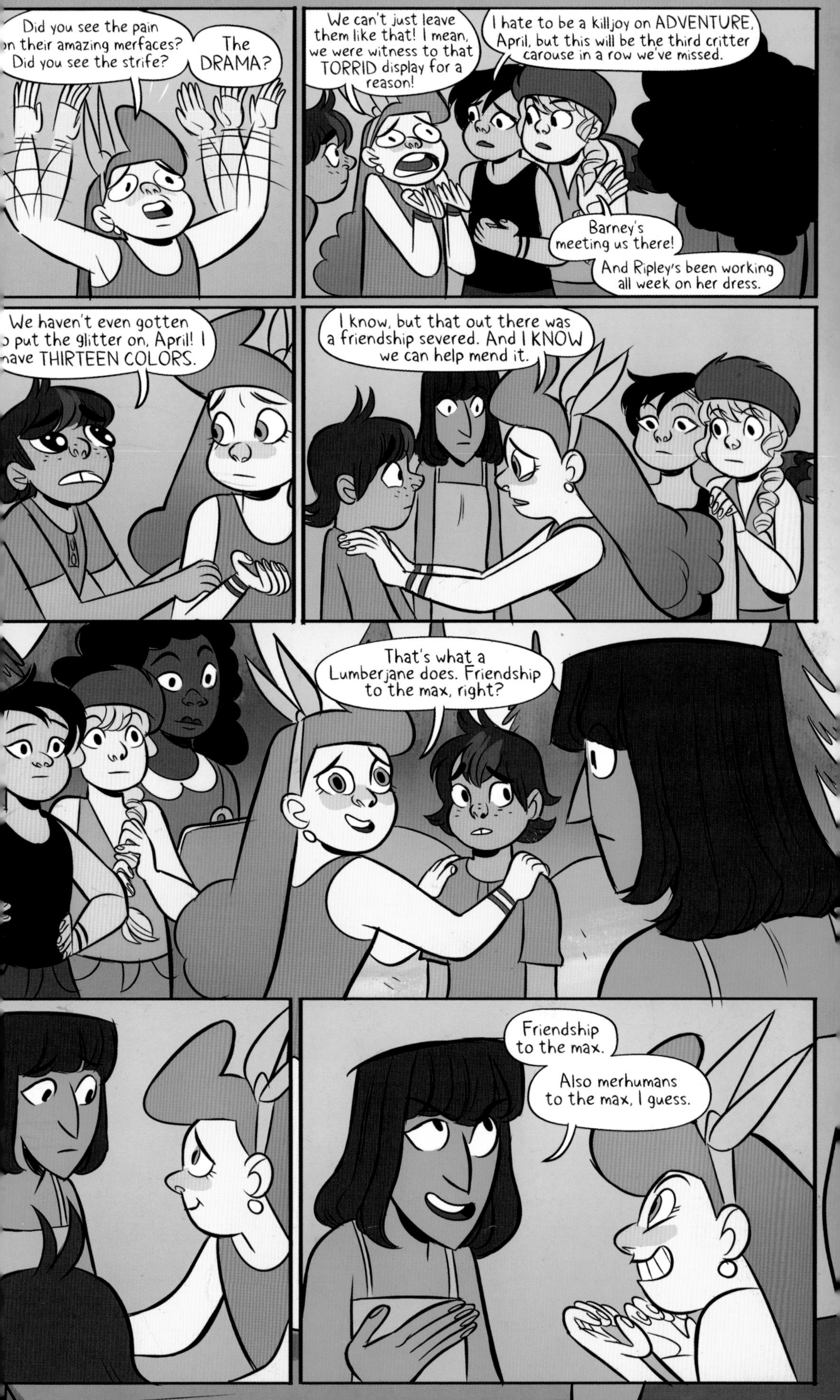
Did you see the pain on their amazing merfaces? Did you see the strife?
The DRAMA?
We can't just leave them like that! I mean, we were witness to that TORRID display for a reason!
I hate to be a killjoy on ADVENTURE, April, but this will be the third critter carouse in a row we've missed.
Barney's meeting us there!
And Ripley's been working all week on her dress.
We haven't even gotten to put the glitter on, April! I have THIRTEEN COLORS.
I know, but that out there was a friendship severed. And I KNOW we can help mend it.
That's what a Lumberjane does. Friendship to the max, right?
Friendship to the max.
Also merhumans to the max, I guess.

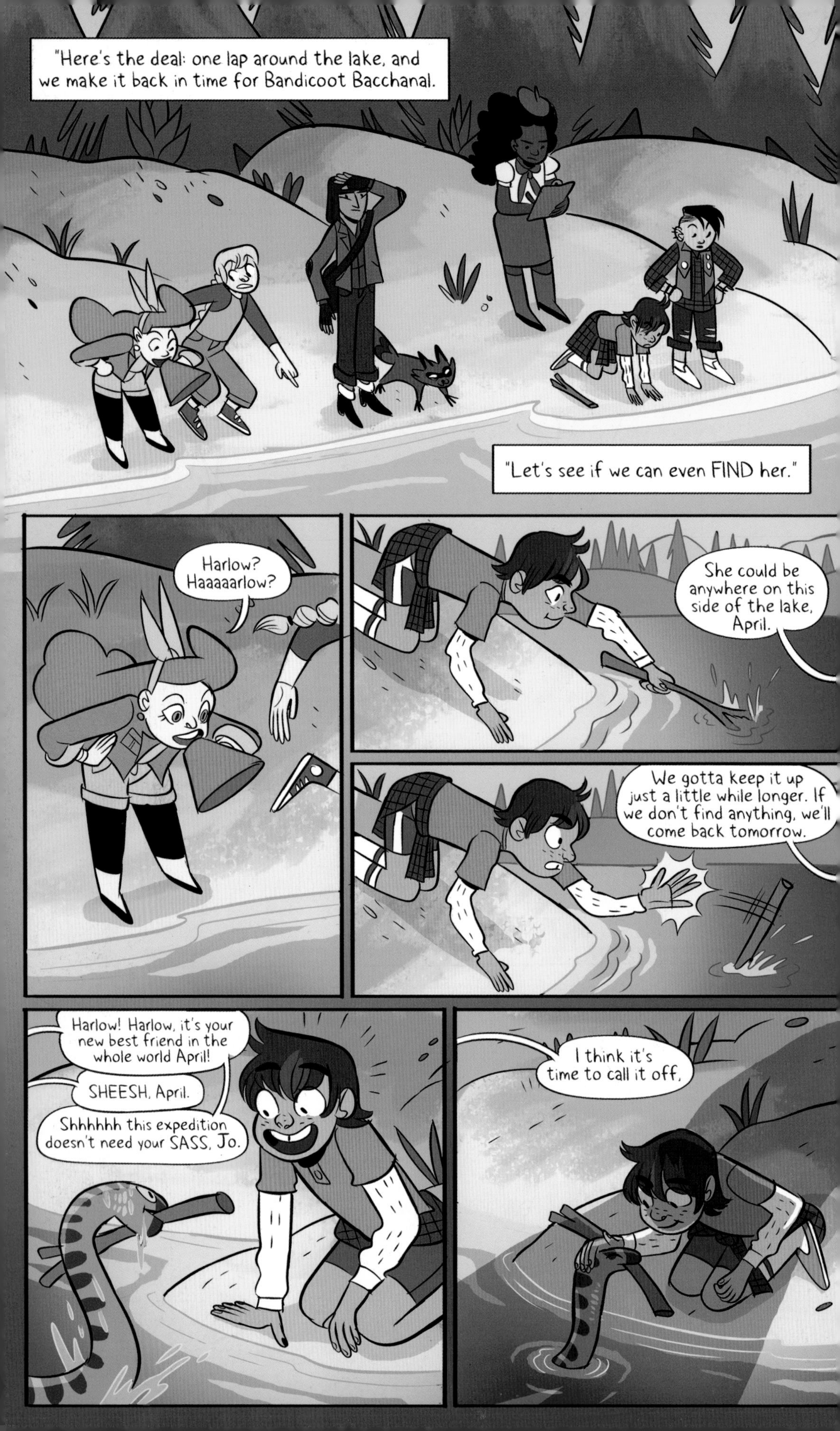
"Here's the deal: one lap around the lake, and we make it back in time for Bandicoot Bacchanal.
"Let's see if we can even FIND her."
Harlow? Haaaaarlow?
She could be anywhere on this side of the lake, April.
We gotta keep it up just a little while longer. If we don't find anything, we'll come back tomorrow.
Harlow! Harlow, it's your new best friend in the whole world April!
SHEESH, April.
Shhhhhh this expedition doesn't need your SASS, Jo.
I think it's time to call it off.

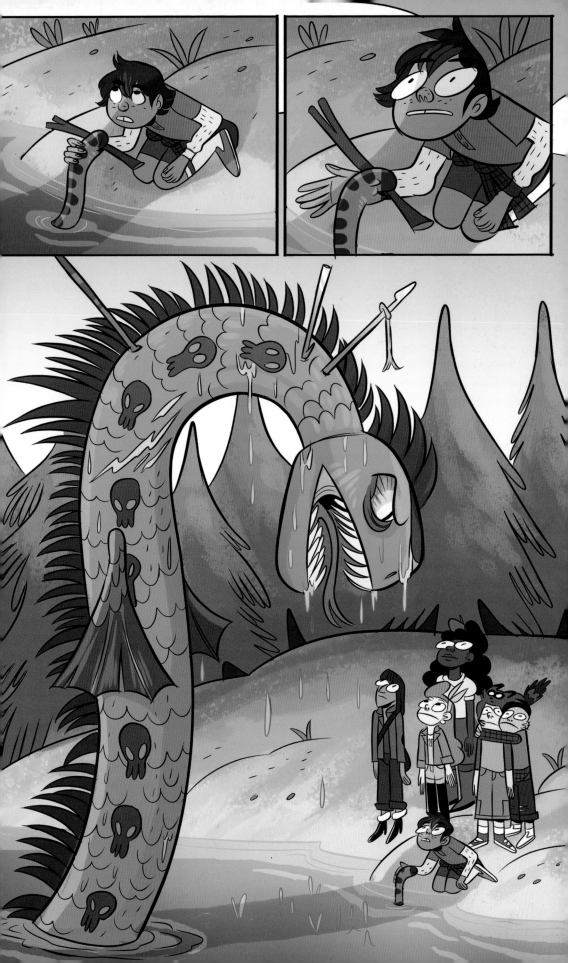

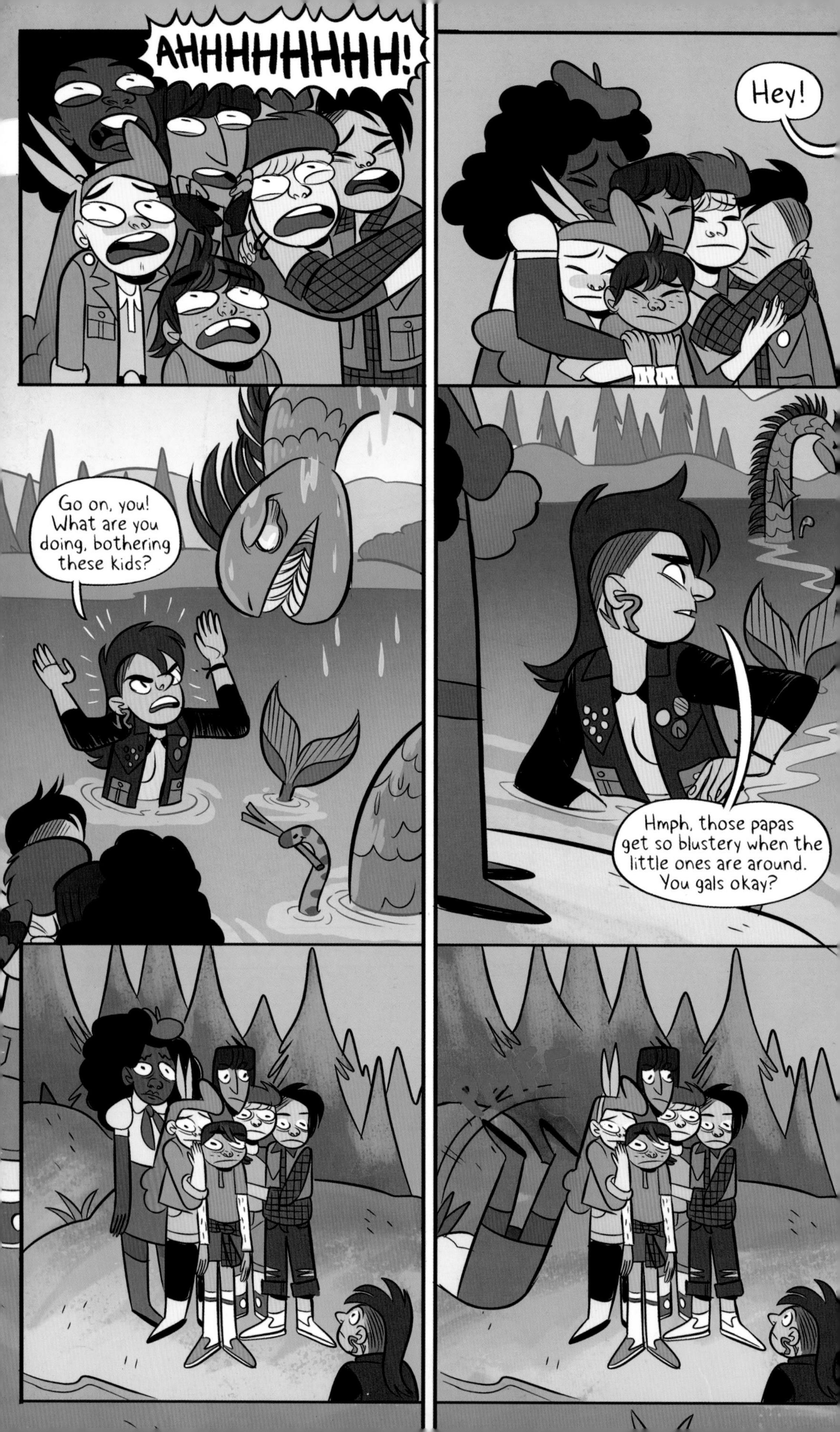
AHHHHHHHHH!
Hey!
Go on, you! What are you doing, bothering these kids?
Hmph, those papas get so blustery when the little ones are around. You gals okay?

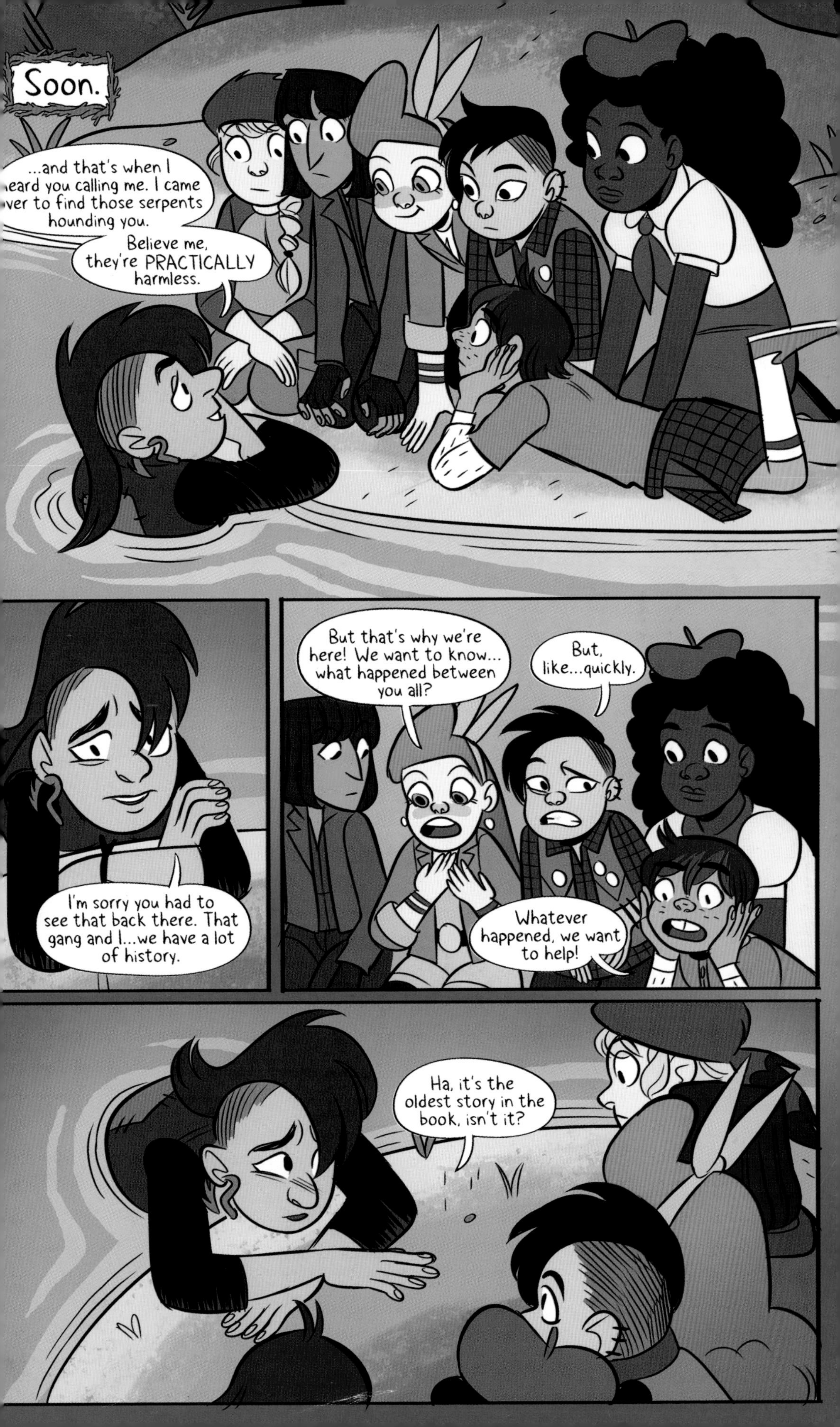
Soon.
...and that's when I heard you calling me. I came over to find those serpents hounding you.
Believe me, they're PRACTICALLY harmless.
I'm sorry you had to see that back there. That gang and I...we have a lot of history.
But that's why we're here! We want to know... what happened between you all?
But, like...quickly.
Whatever happened, we want to help!
Ha, it's the oldest story in the book, isn't it?

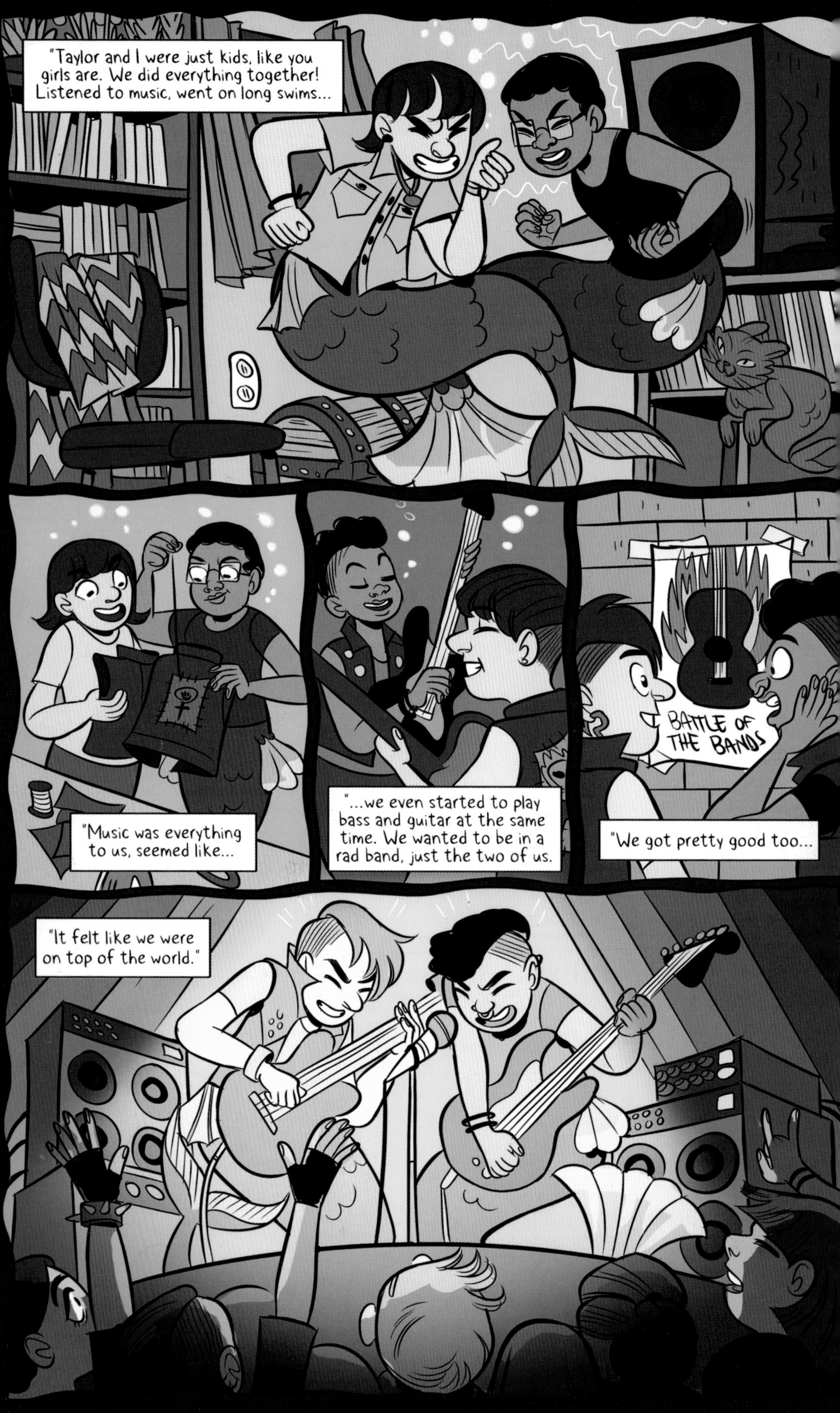
"Taylor and I were just kids, like you girls are. We did everything together! Listened to music, went on long swims...
"Music was everything to us, seemed like...
"...we even started to play bass and guitar at the same time. We wanted to be in a rad band, just the two of us.
BATTLE OF THE BANDS
"We got pretty good too...
"It felt like we were on top of the world."

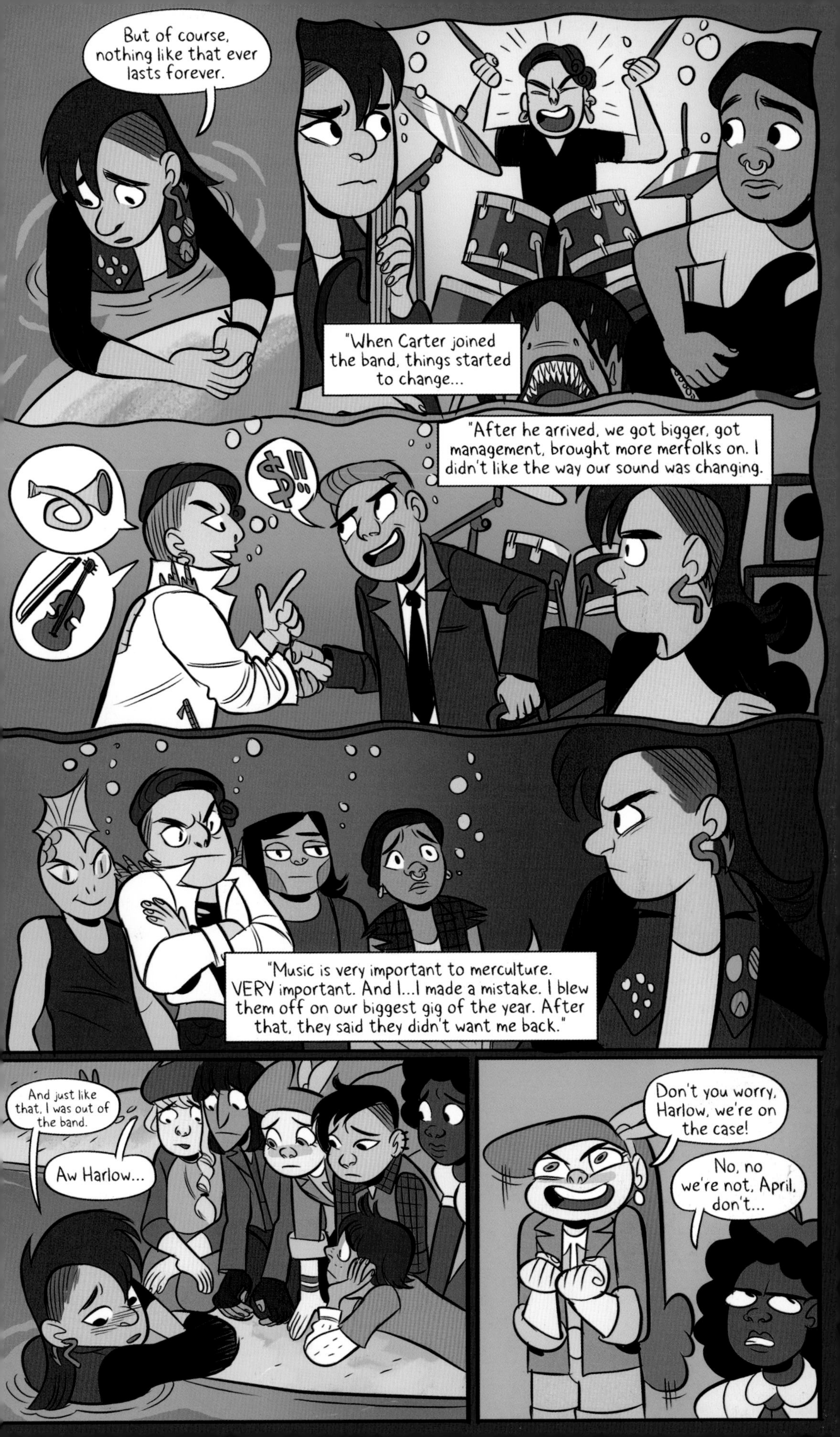
But of course, nothing like that ever lasts forever.
"When Carter joined the band, things started to change...
"After he arrived, we got bigger, got management, brought more merfolks on. I didn't like the way our sound was changing.
$!!
"Music is very important to merculture. VERY important. And I...I made a mistake. I blew them off on our biggest gig of the year. After that, they said they didn't want me back."
And just like that, I was out of the band.
Aw Harlow...
Don't you worry, Harlow, we're on the case!
No, no we're not, April, don't...

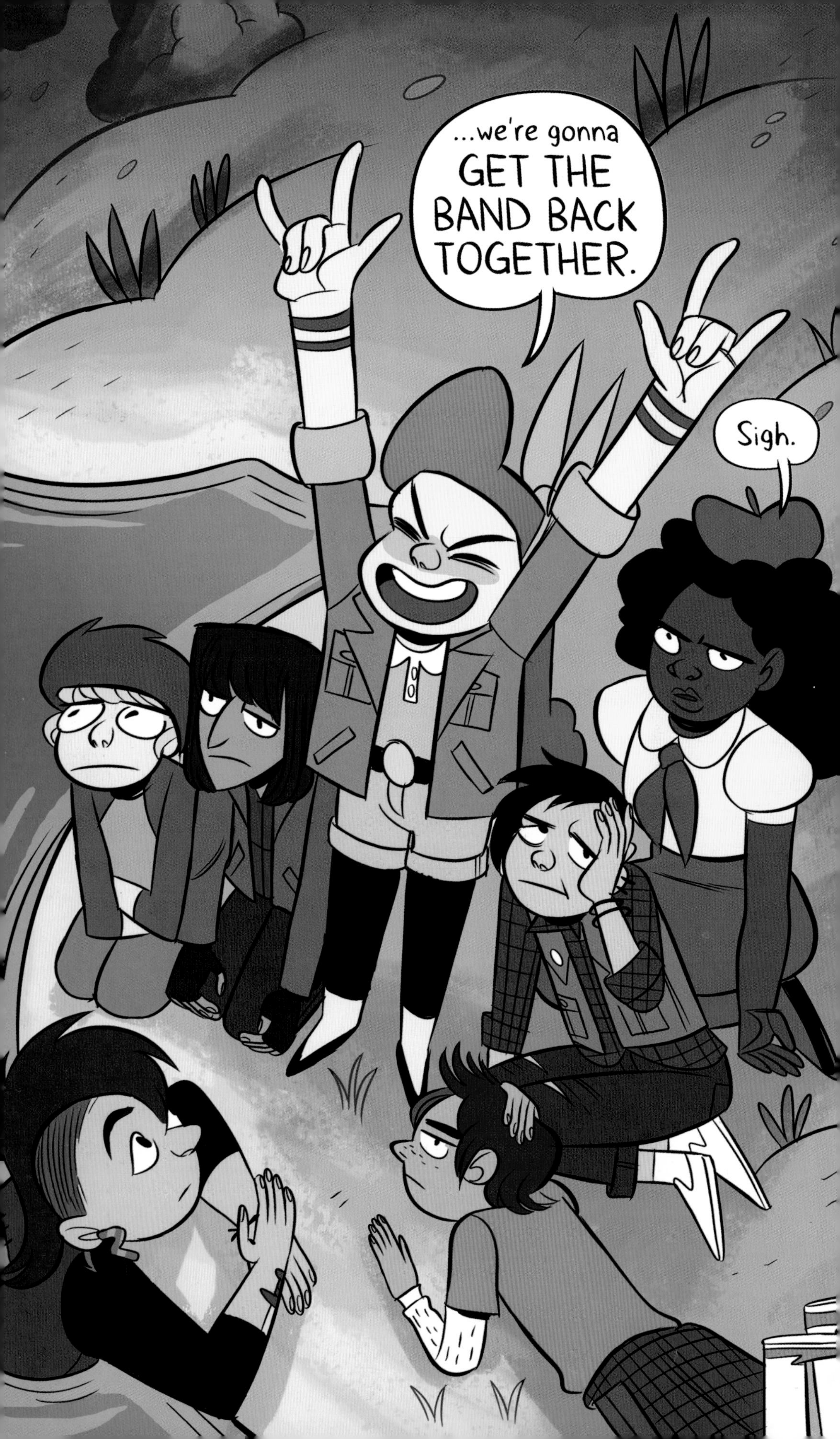
...we're gonna GET THE BAND BACK TOGETHER.
Sigh.

will co

The

It hel

appeara

dress f

Further

Lumbe

to have

part in

Thiskv

Hardc

have

them

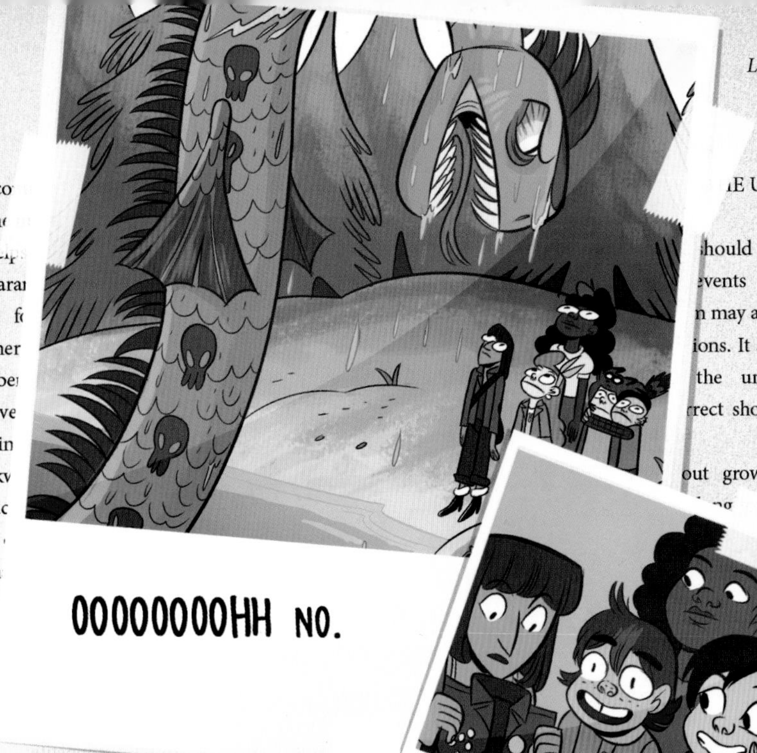
OOOOOOOOHH NO.

...E UNIFORM

...hould be worn at camp ...events when Lumberjanes ...n may also be worn at other ...ions. It should be worn as a ... the uniform dress with ...rrect shoes, and stocking or

... out grows her uniform or ...ter Lumberjane. ...a she has ... her ...f her

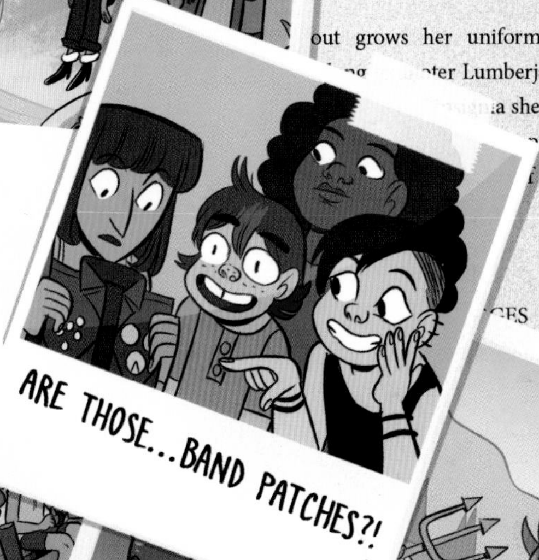
ARE THOSE...BAND PATCHES?!

...GES

The yellow, short sl... emb... the w... choose slacks, made o... out-of-do... green bere... the colla... Shoes ma... heels, rou... ...kings or socks shou... ...with the shoes or wi... the uniform. Ne...es, bracelets, or other jewelry do... belong with a Lumberjane uniform.

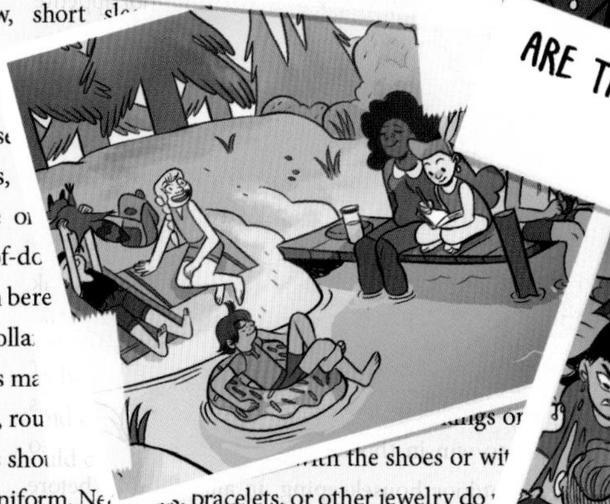

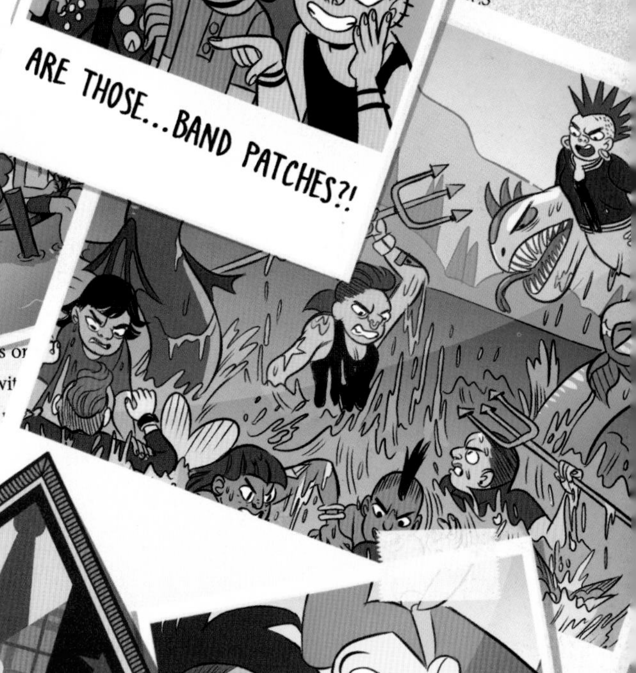

HOW TO WEAR THE UNIFOR...

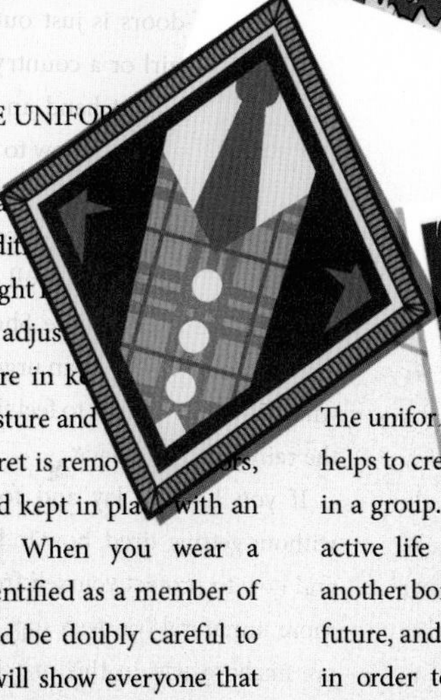

To look well in a uniform dema... uniform be kept in good condit... pressed. See that the skirt is the right ... height and build, that the belt is adjus... that your shoes and stockings are in k... uniform, that you watch your posture and ... with dignity and grace. If the beret is remo... ...ors, be sure that your hair is neat and kept in pla... with an insonspicuous clip or ribbon. When you wear a Lumberjane uniform you are identified as a member of this organization and you should be doubly careful to conduct yourself in a way that will show everyone that courtesy and thoughtfullness are part of being a Lumberjane. People are likely to judge a whole nation by the selfishness of a few individuals, to criticize a whole family because of the misconduct of one member, and to feel unkindly toward and organization because of the

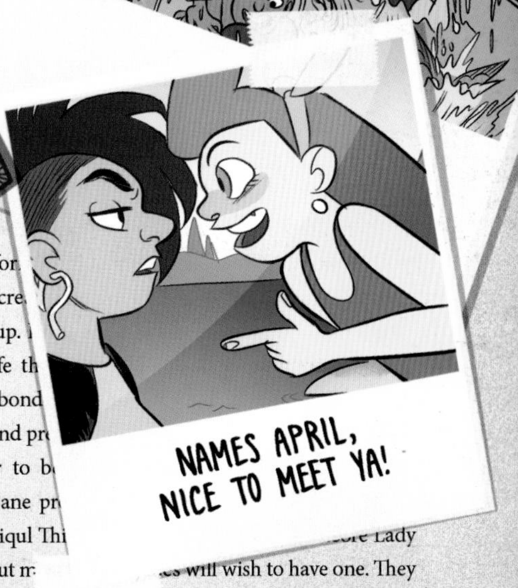
NAMES APRIL,
NICE TO MEET YA!

The unifor... helps to cre... in a group. ... active life th... another bond ... future, and pr... in order to b... Lumberjane pr... Penniquiqul Thi... ...ore Lady Types, but m... ...es will wish to have one. They can either bu... uniform, or make it themselves from materials available at the trading post.

LUMBERJANES FIELD MANUAL

CHAPTER NINETEEN

Lumberjanes "Cooking" Program Field

ENSEMBLE ASSEMBLE! BADGE

"Some instructions may be required."

While music is an important subject that should have more focus in schools, a Lumberjane will learn the commonplace use of music in everyday situations, as well as not so everyday, from knowing the proper tone need to help your fellow camp mate out with their song to knowing the proper pitch needed in order to get everyone's attention. A Lumberjane recognizes how basic understanding of music can not only help their understanding of the flow of the world around them but how furthering that knowledge can also lead to a really good time. The human experience can be boiled down to patterns and it is with this understanding that a Lumberjane sees their importance not only in the lives that she directly influences but those outside her known friend group.

To obtain the *Ensemble Assemble!* badge, a Lumberjane must be able to play an instrument. Not only that, a Lumberjanes must be able to gather a group of their fellow campers together to form their own band in order to create unique musical treats as a group. A focus of camp is and will always be the power of friendship and teamwork and this badge is no different. The goal of this badge is to take a variety of campers at different levels in their musical growth and get them to work together to help each other grow while at the same time learning to work in tandem to create a unique sound just for that group.

With an *Ensemble Assemble!* badge, a Lumberjane will be able to read and write music. They will be able to have the basic knowledge of keys and notes, as well as how to handle an instrument of their choosing. More advanced scouts will be allowed to bring their instrument from home and use their knowledge to help their campmates earn this badge. Every cabin will be asked to play one song at the mid-camp festival every term, and each cabin will be judged by their peers. The winning cabin will receive the badge as well as a lesson from the Scout Master.

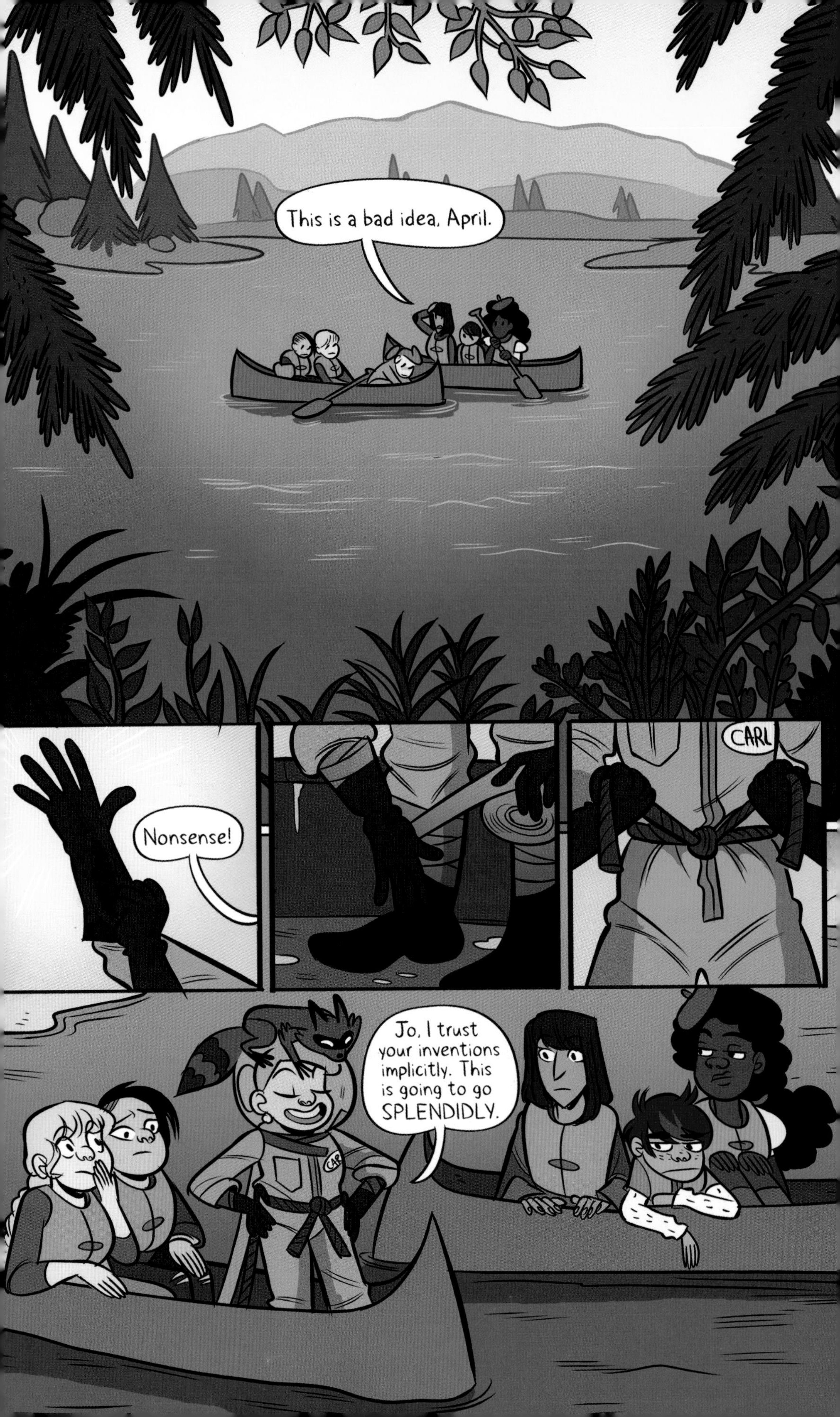

This is a bad idea, April.
Nonsense!
CARL
Jo, I trust your inventions implicitly. This is going to go SPLENDIDLY.

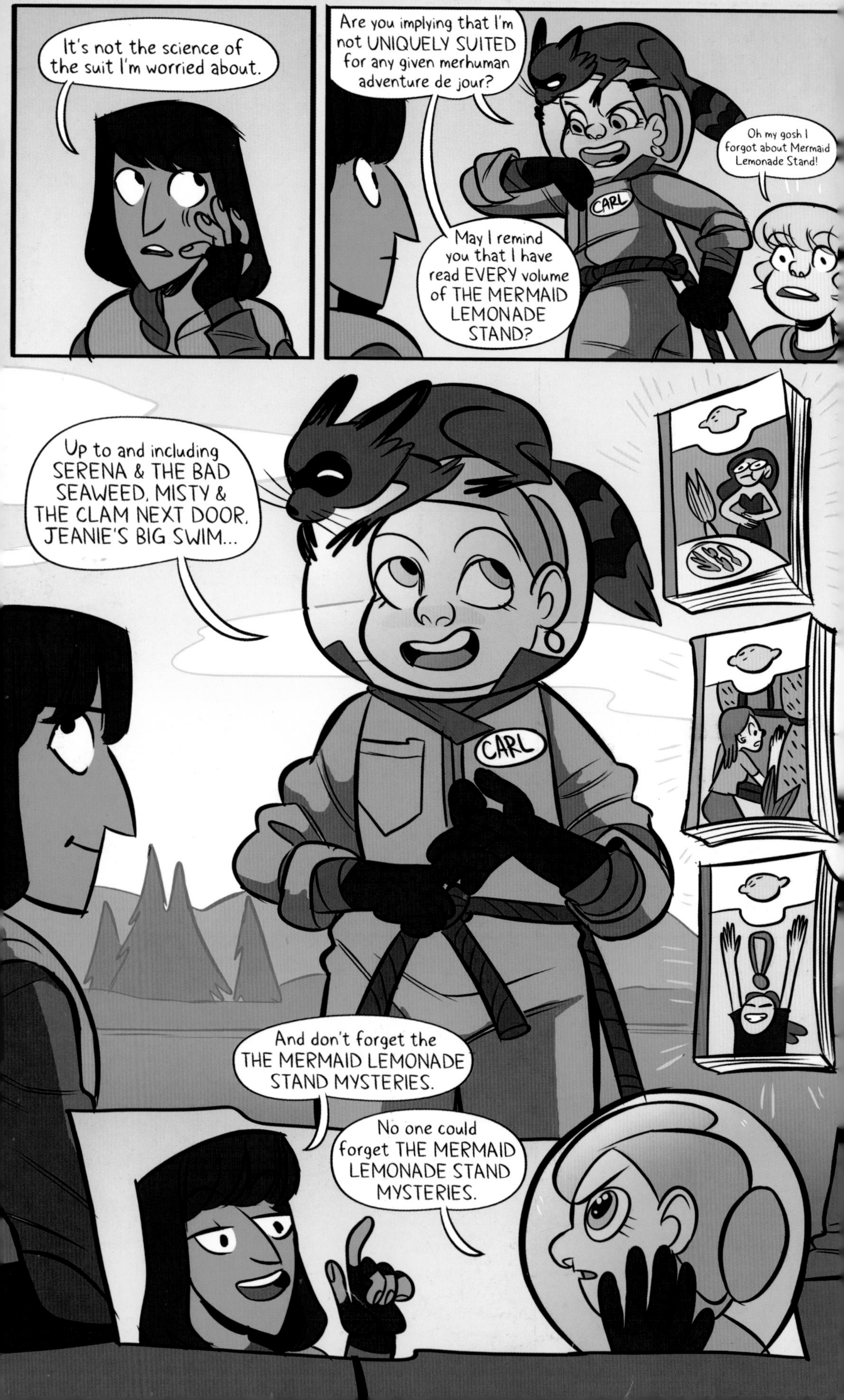
It's not the science of the suit I'm worried about.
Are you implying that I'm not UNIQUELY SUITED for any given merhuman adventure de jour?
May I remind you that I have read EVERY volume of THE MERMAID LEMONADE STAND?
Oh my gosh I forgot about Mermaid Lemonade Stand!
CARL
Up to and including SERENA & THE BAD SEAWEED, MISTY & THE CLAM NEXT DOOR, JEANIE'S BIG SWIM...
CARL
And don't forget the THE MERMAID LEMONADE STAND MYSTERIES.
No one could forget THE MERMAID LEMONADE STAND MYSTERIES.

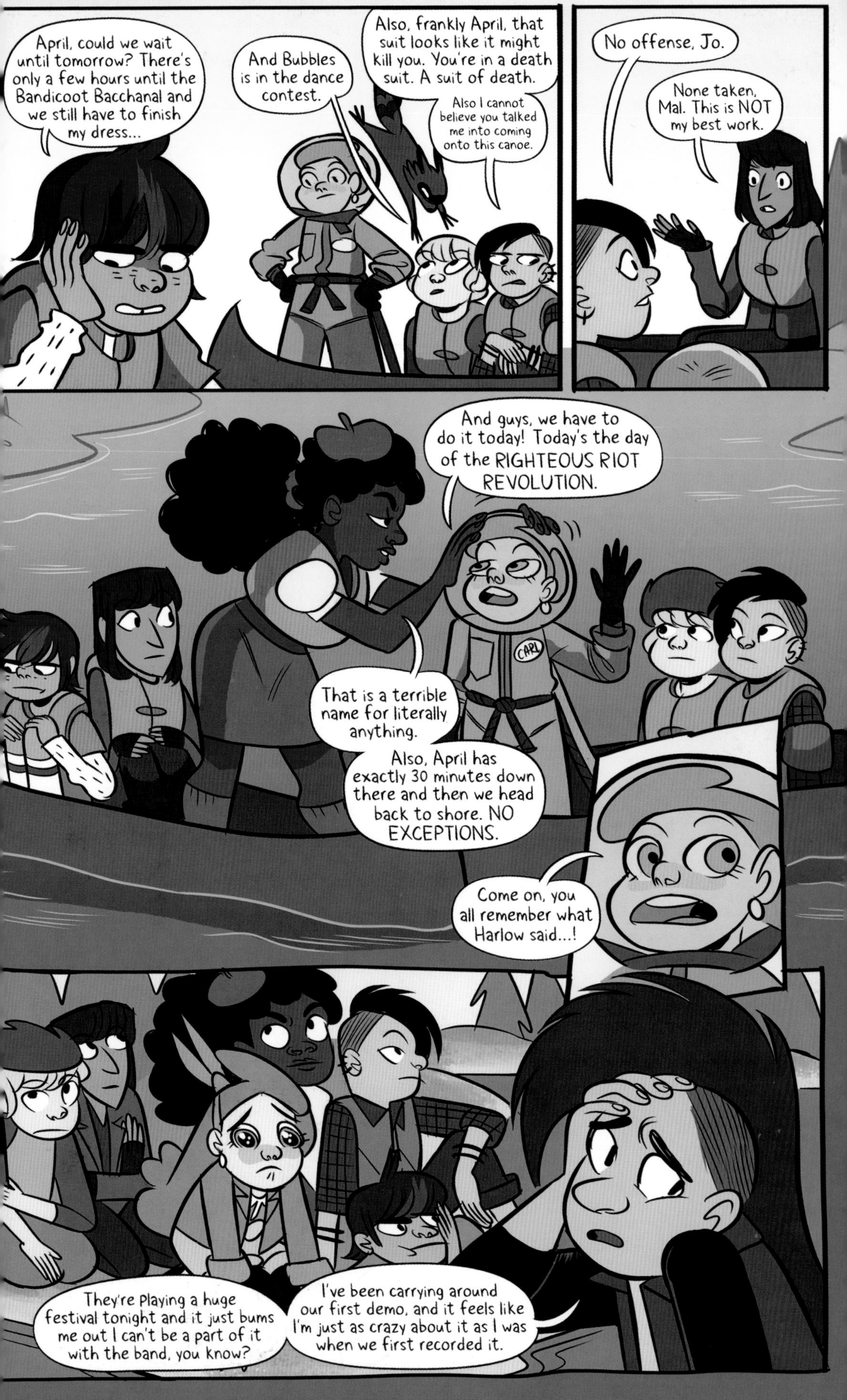
April, could we wait until tomorrow? There's only a few hours until the Bandicoot Bacchanal and we still have to finish my dress...
And Bubbles is in the dance contest.
Also, frankly April, that suit looks like it might kill you. You're in a death suit. A suit of death.
Also I cannot believe you talked me into coming onto this canoe.
No offense, Jo.
None taken, Mal. This is NOT my best work.
And guys, we have to do it today! Today's the day of the RIGHTEOUS RIOT REVOLUTION.
CARL
That is a terrible name for literally anything.
Also, April has exactly 30 minutes down there and then we head back to shore. NO EXCEPTIONS.
Come on, you all remember what Harlow said...!
They're playing a huge festival tonight and it just bums me out I can't be a part of it with the band, you know?
I've been carrying around our first demo, and it feels like I'm just as crazy about it as I was when we first recorded it.

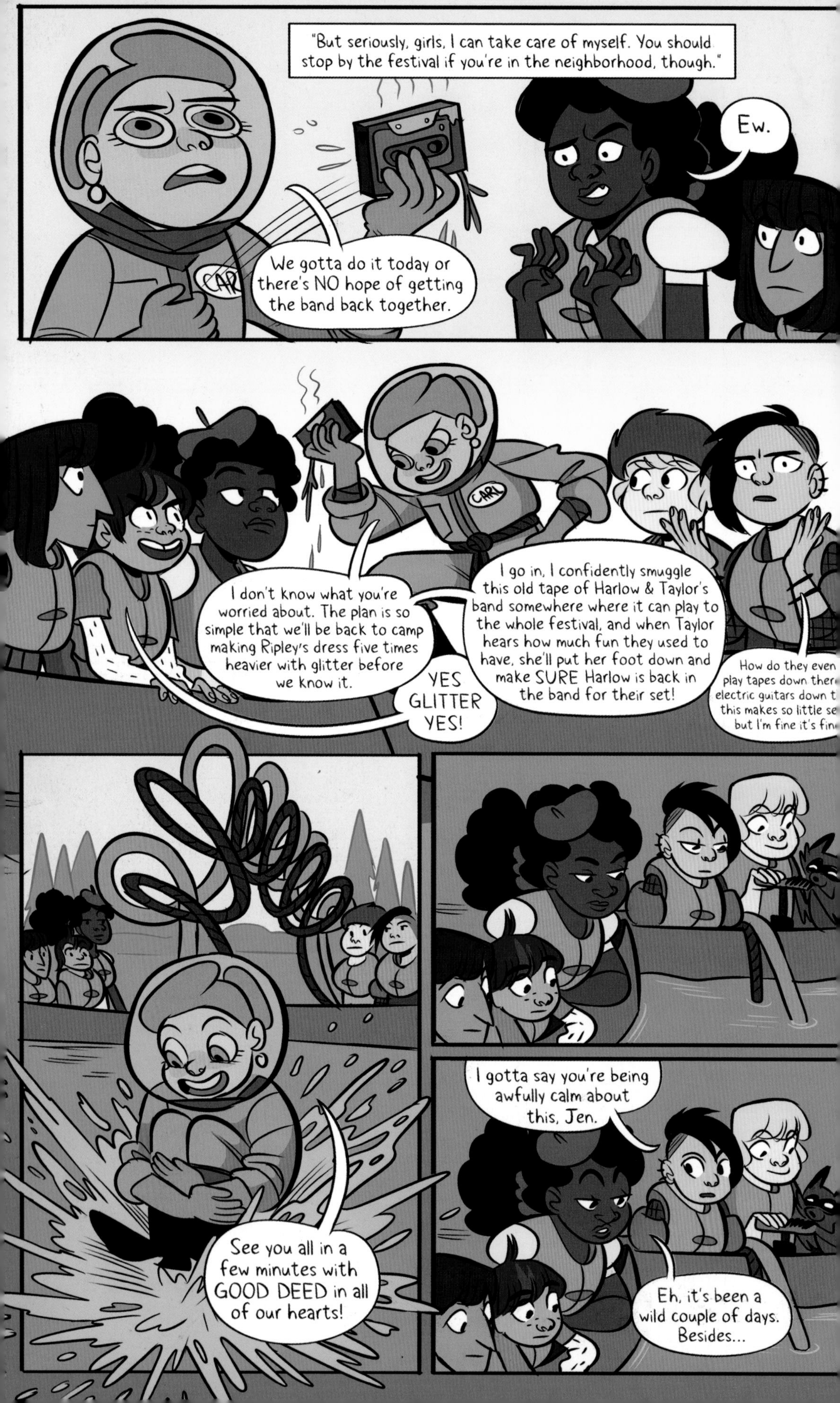
"But seriously, girls, I can take care of myself. You should stop by the festival if you're in the neighborhood, though."
We gotta do it today or there's NO hope of getting the band back together.
Ew.
I don't know what you're worried about. The plan is so simple that we'll be back to camp making Ripley's dress five times heavier with glitter before we know it.
I go in, I confidently smuggle this old tape of Harlow & Taylor's band somewhere where it can play to the whole festival, and when Taylor hears how much fun they used to have, she'll put her foot down and make SURE Harlow is back in the band for their set!
YES GLITTER YES!
See you all in a few minutes with GOOD DEED in all of our hearts!
I gotta say you're being awfully calm about this, Jen.
Eh, it's been a wild couple of days. Besides...

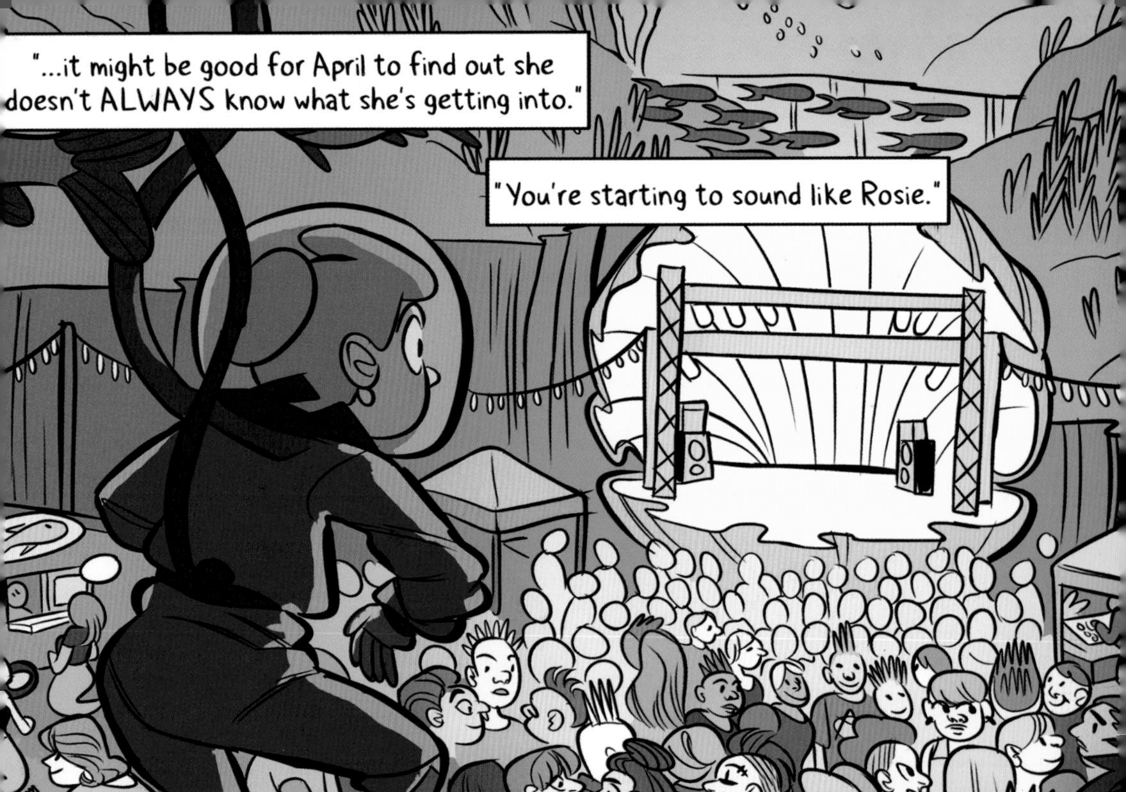
"...it might be good for April to find out she doesn't ALWAYS know what she's getting into."
"You're starting to sound like Rosie."

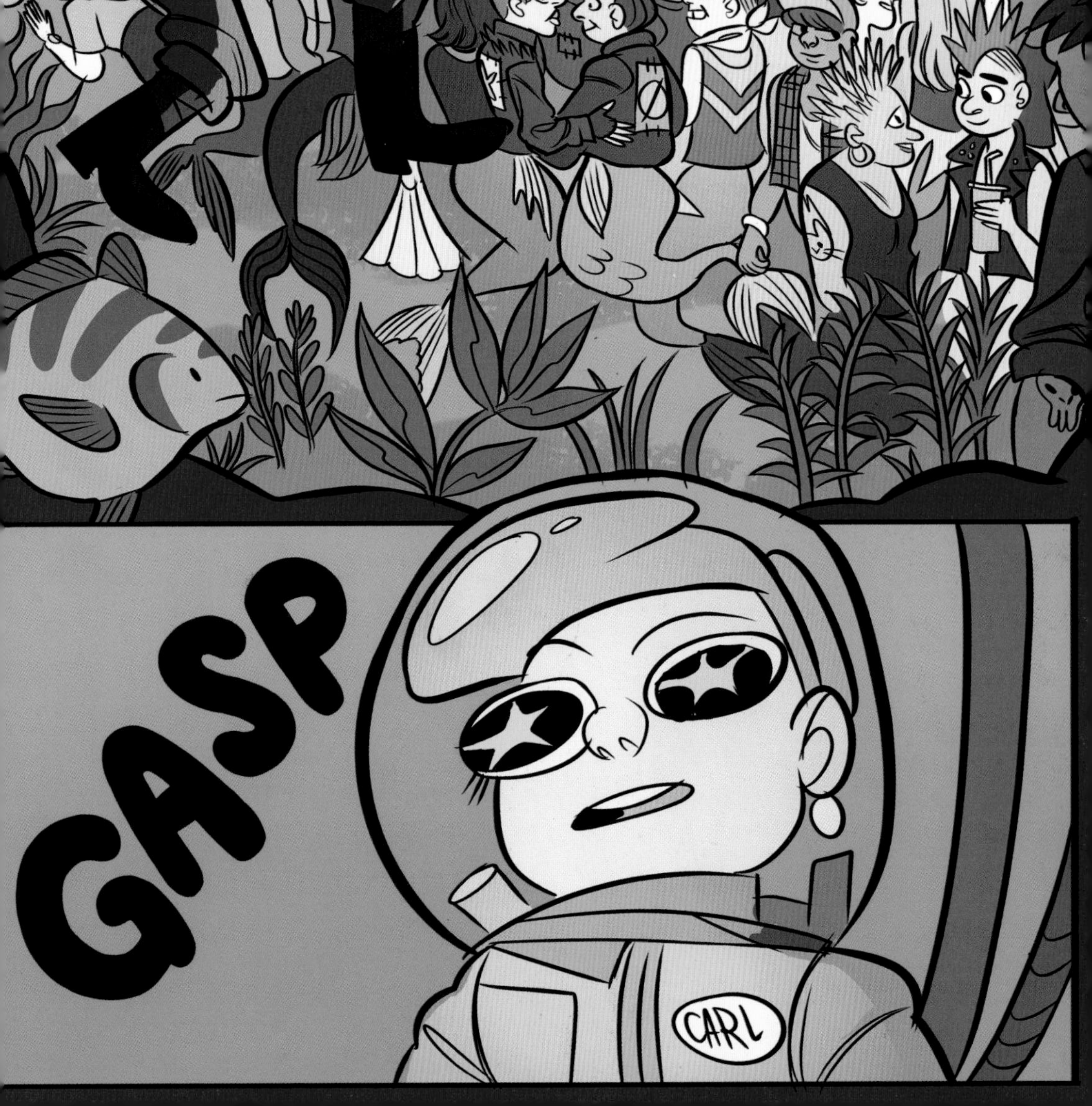
GASP
CARL

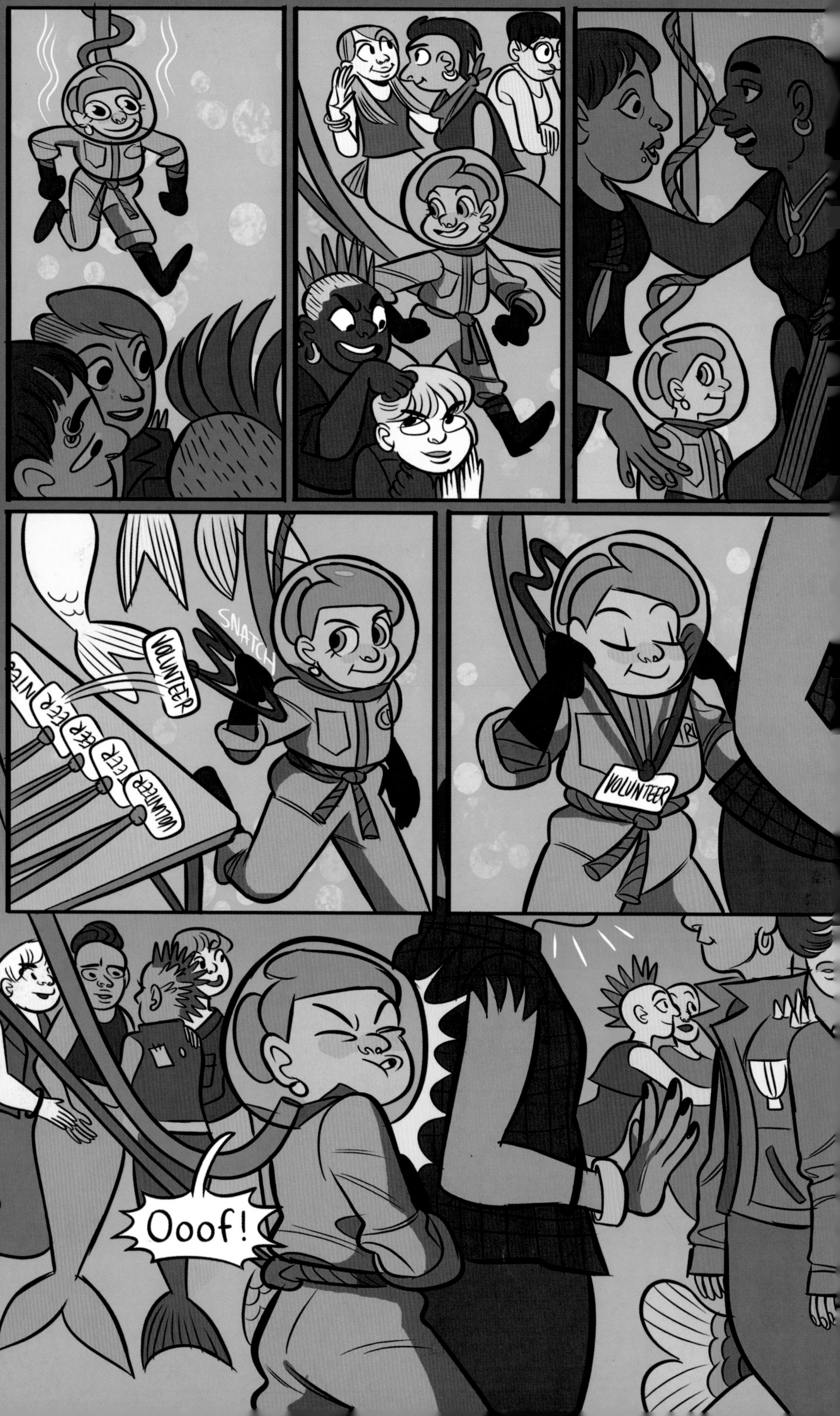
SNATCH
VOLUNTEER
VOLUNTEER
VOLUNTEER
Ooof!

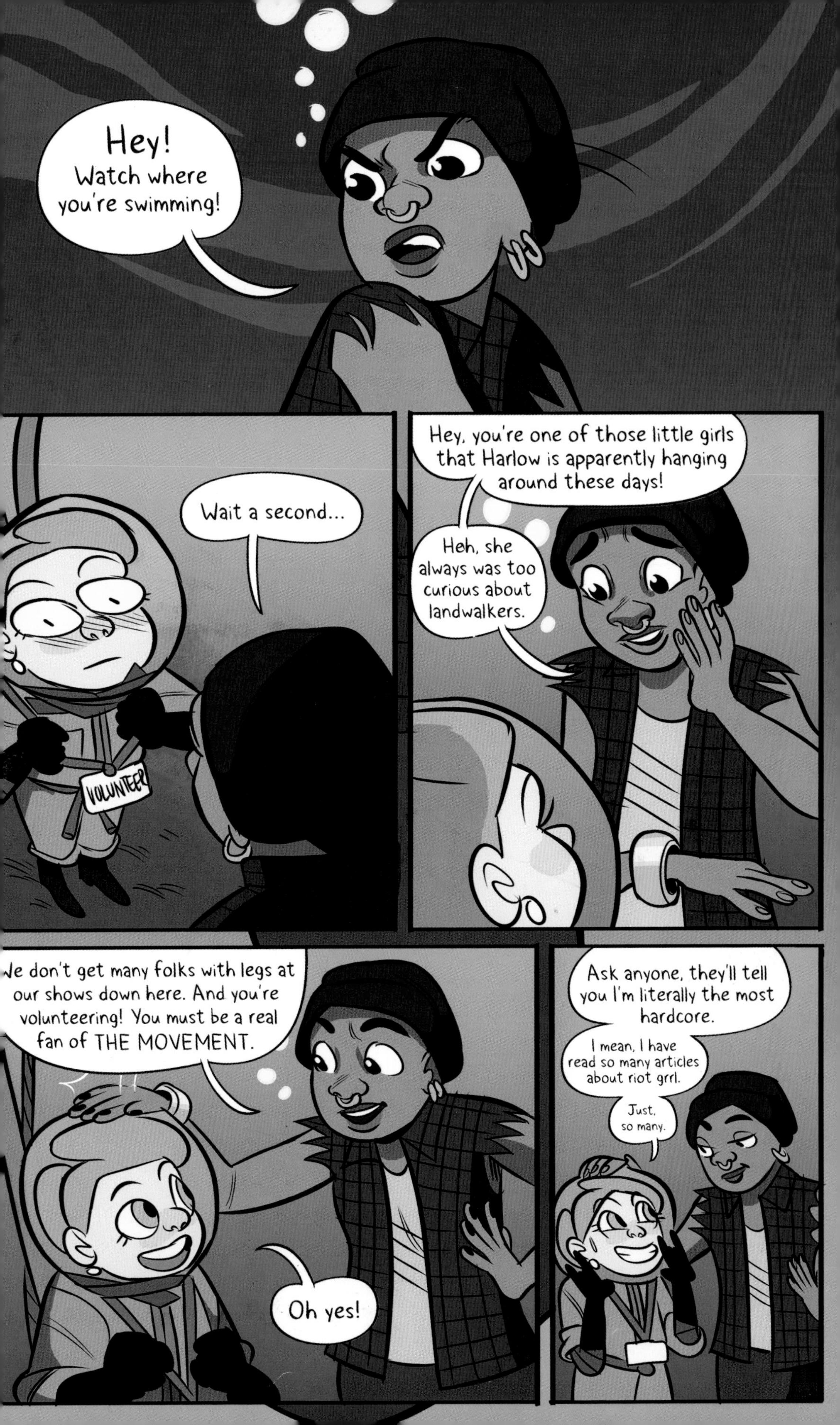
Hey!
Watch where you're swimming!
Wait a second...
VOLUNTEER
Hey, you're one of those little girls that Harlow is apparently hanging around these days!
Heh, she always was too curious about landwalkers.
We don't get many folks with legs at our shows down here. And you're volunteering! You must be a real fan of THE MOVEMENT.
Oh yes!
Ask anyone, they'll tell you I'm literally the most hardcore.
I mean, I have read so many articles about riot grrl.
Just, so many.

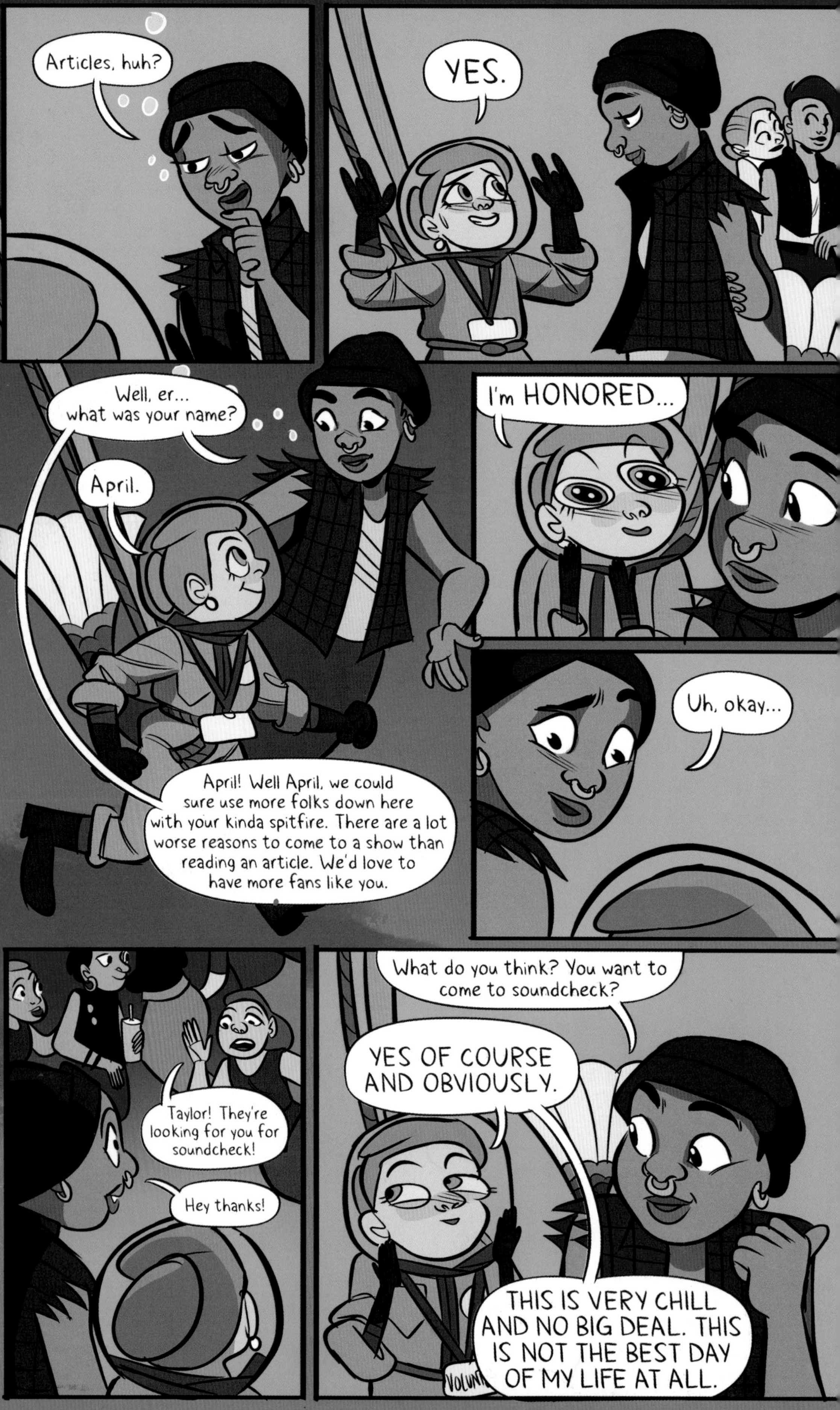
Articles, huh?
YES.
Well, er... what was your name?
April.
April! Well April, we could sure use more folks down here with your kinda spitfire. There are a lot worse reasons to come to a show than reading an article. We'd love to have more fans like you.
I'm HONORED...
Uh, okay...
Taylor! They're looking for you for soundcheck!
Hey thanks!
What do you think? You want to come to soundcheck?
YES OF COURSE AND OBVIOUSLY.
THIS IS VERY CHILL AND NO BIG DEAL. THIS IS NOT THE BEST DAY OF MY LIFE AT ALL.

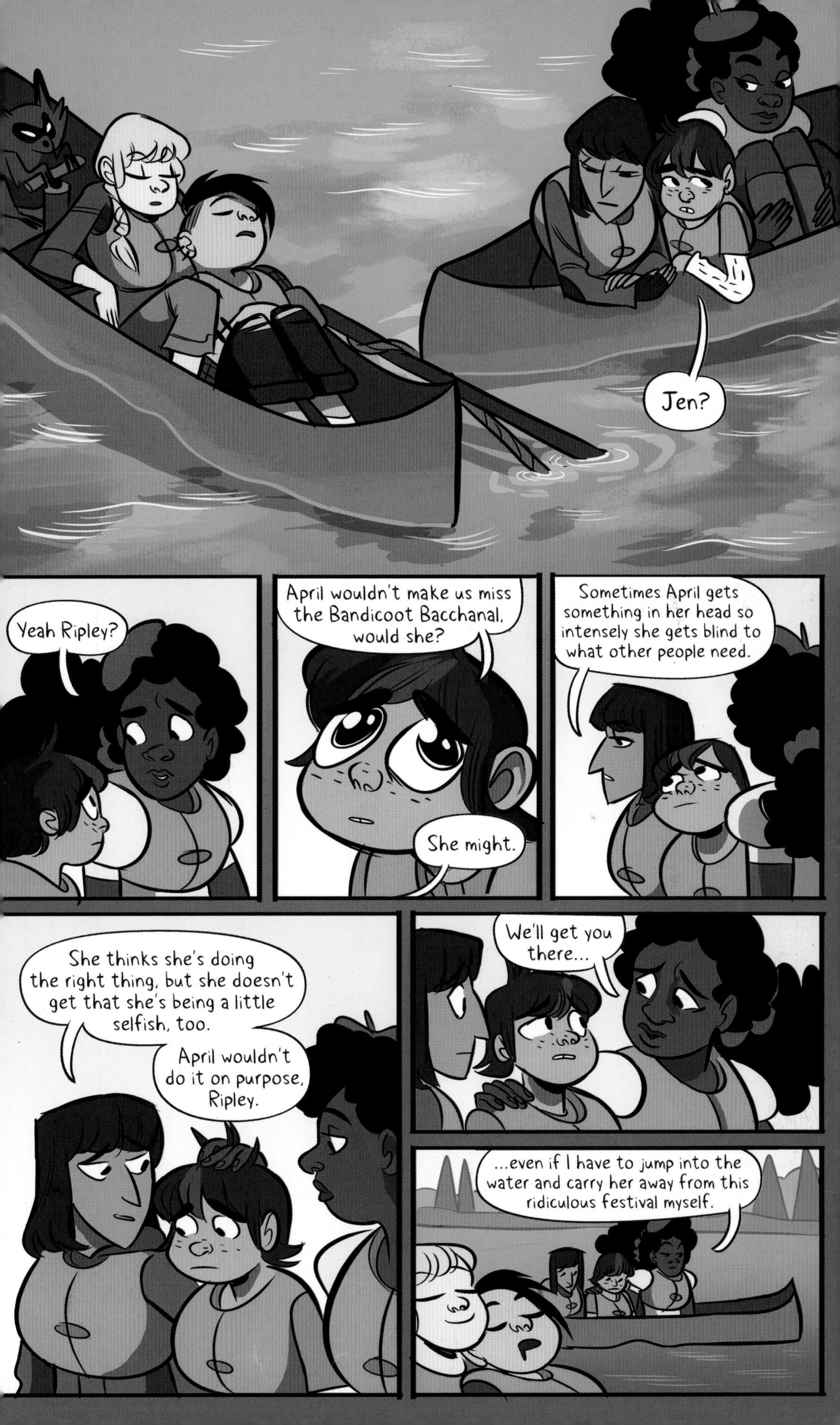
Jen?
Yeah Ripley?
April wouldn't make us miss the Bandicoot Bacchanal, would she?
She might.
Sometimes April gets something in her head so intensely she gets blind to what other people need.
She thinks she's doing the right thing, but she doesn't get that she's being a little selfish, too.
April wouldn't do it on purpose, Ripley.
We'll get you there...
...even if I have to jump into the water and carry her away from this ridiculous festival myself.

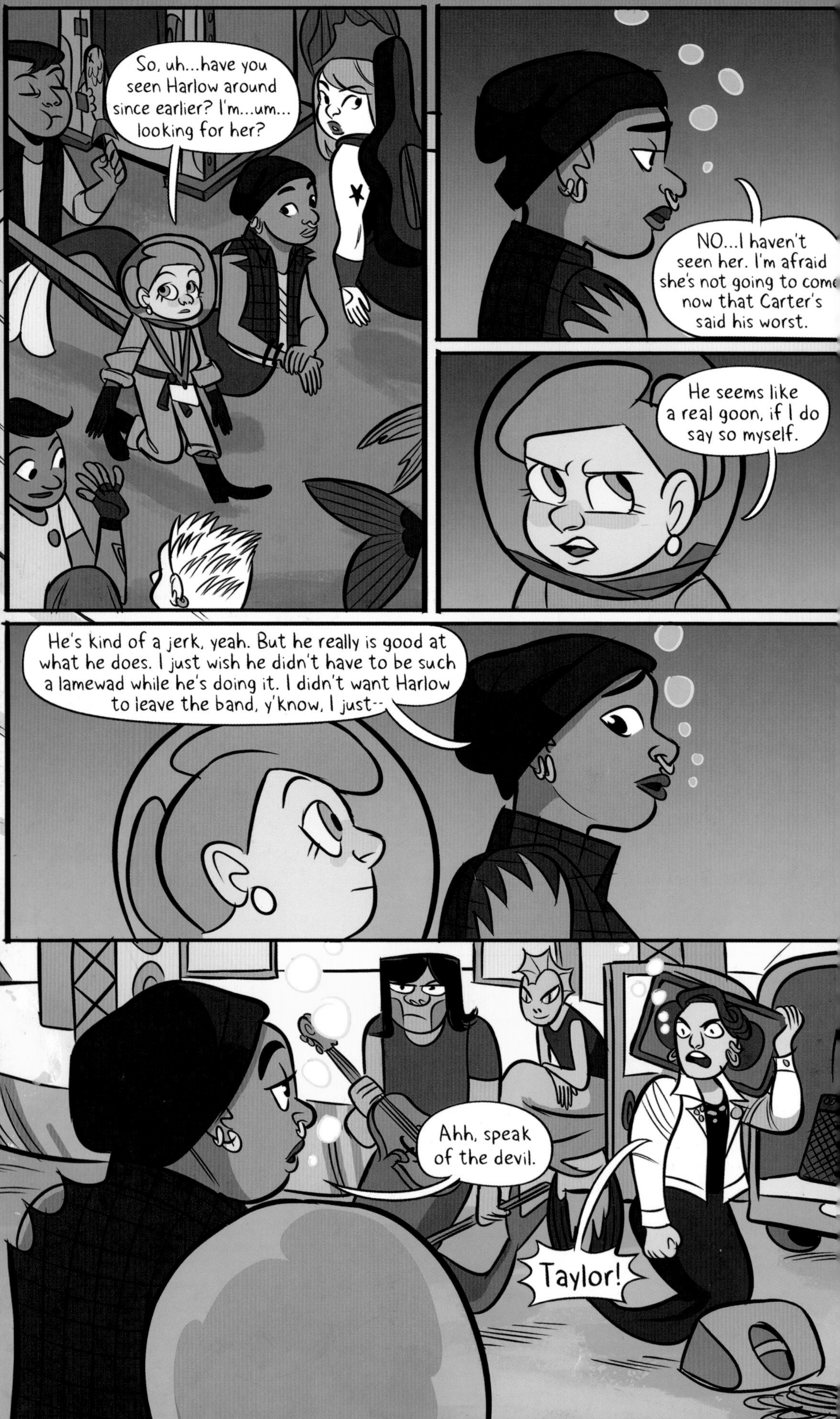
So, uh...have you seen Harlow around since earlier? I'm...um... looking for her?
NO...I haven't seen her. I'm afraid she's not going to come now that Carter's said his worst.
He seems like a real goon, if I do say so myself.
He's kind of a jerk, yeah. But he really is good at what he does. I just wish he didn't have to be such a lamewad while he's doing it. I didn't want Harlow to leave the band, y'know, I just--
Ahh, speak of the devil.
Taylor!

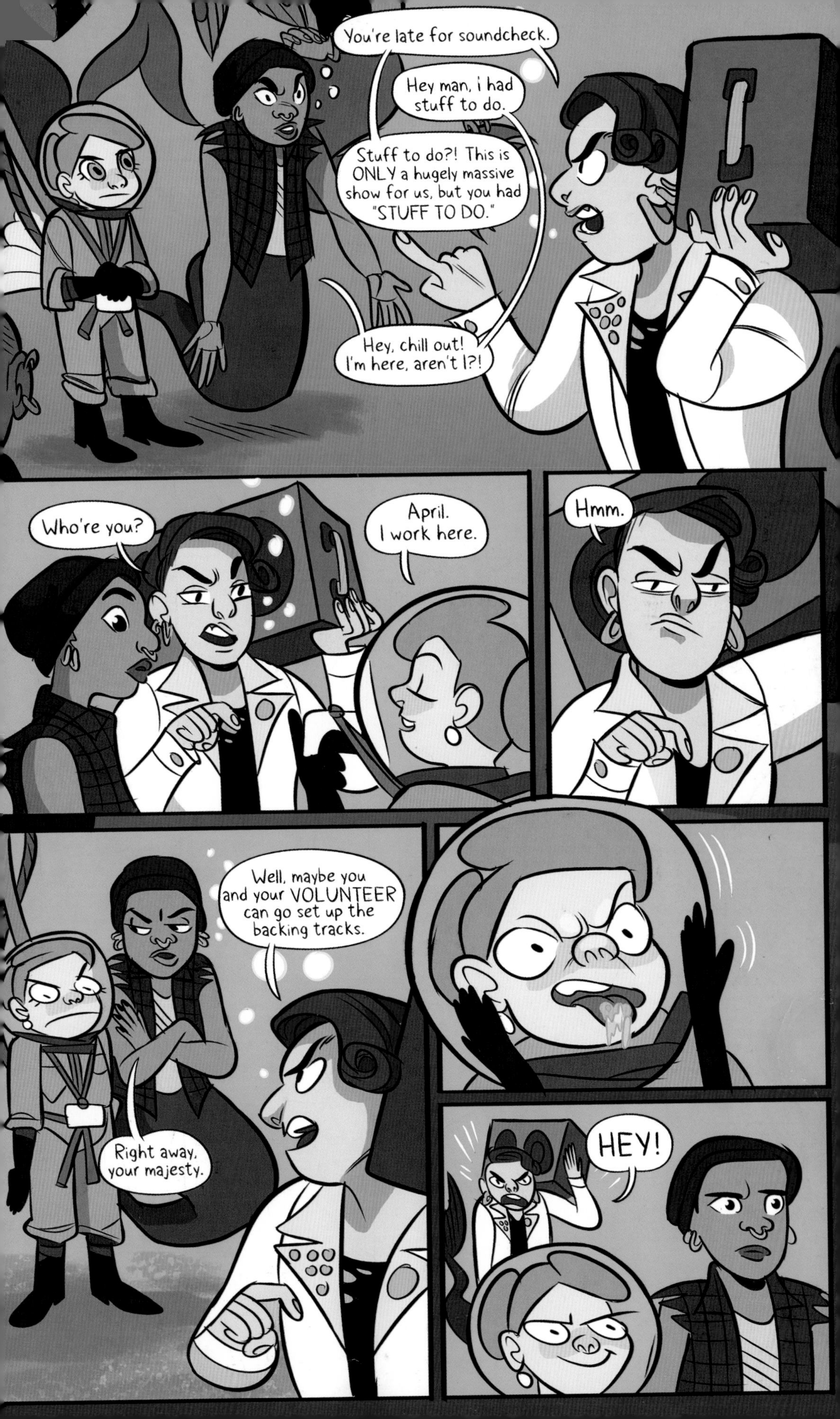
You're late for soundcheck.
Hey man, i had stuff to do.
Stuff to do?! This is ONLY a hugely massive show for us, but you had "STUFF TO DO."
Hey, chill out! I'm here, aren't I?!
Who're you?
April. I work here.
Hmm.
Well, maybe you and your VOLUNTEER can go set up the backing tracks.
Right away, your majesty.
HEY!

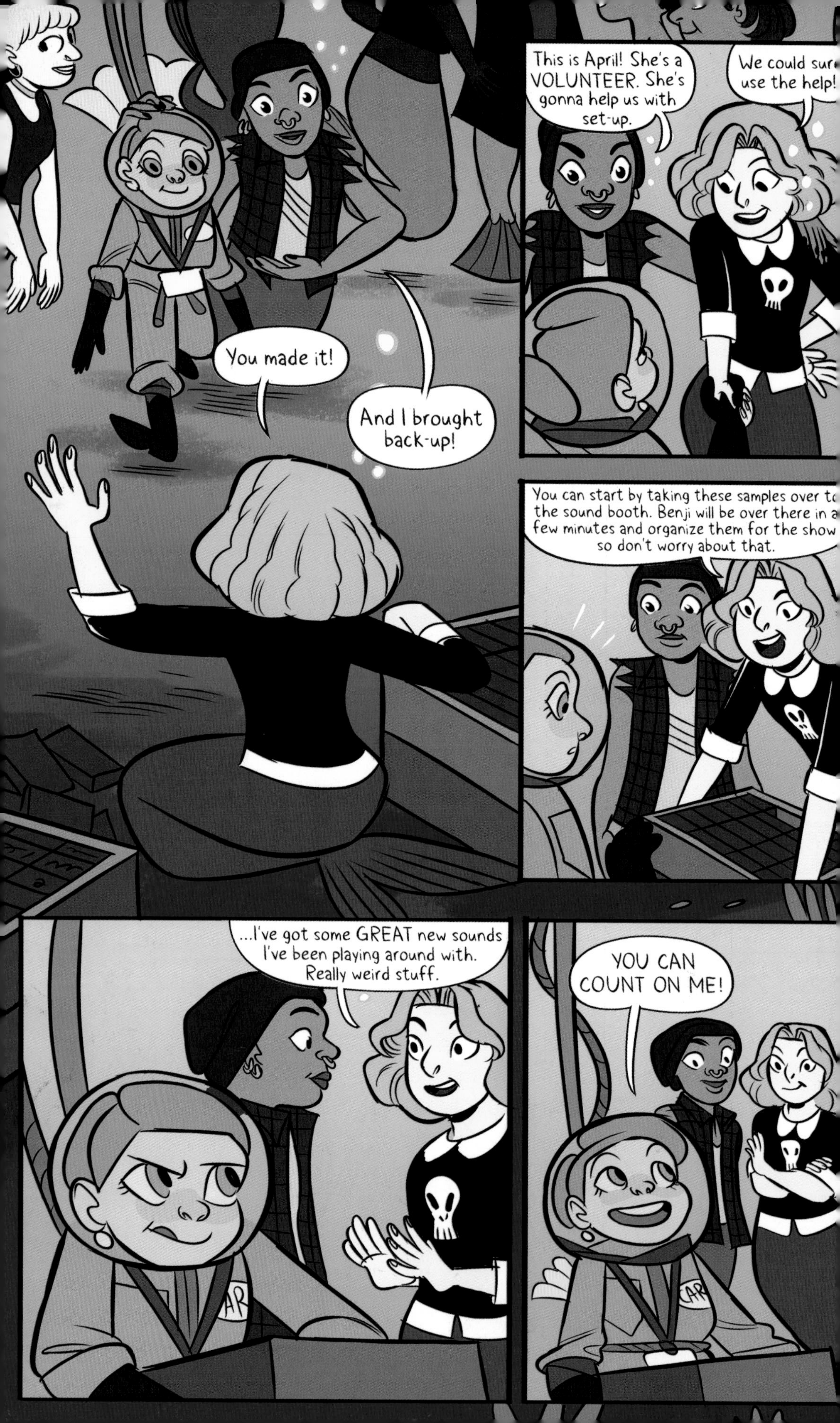
You made it!
And I brought back-up!
This is April! She's a VOLUNTEER. She's gonna help us with set-up.
We could sur
use the help!
You can start by taking these samples over to the sound booth. Benji will be over there in a few minutes and organize them for the show so don't worry about that.
...I've got some GREAT new sounds I've been playing around with. Really weird stuff.
YOU CAN COUNT ON ME!

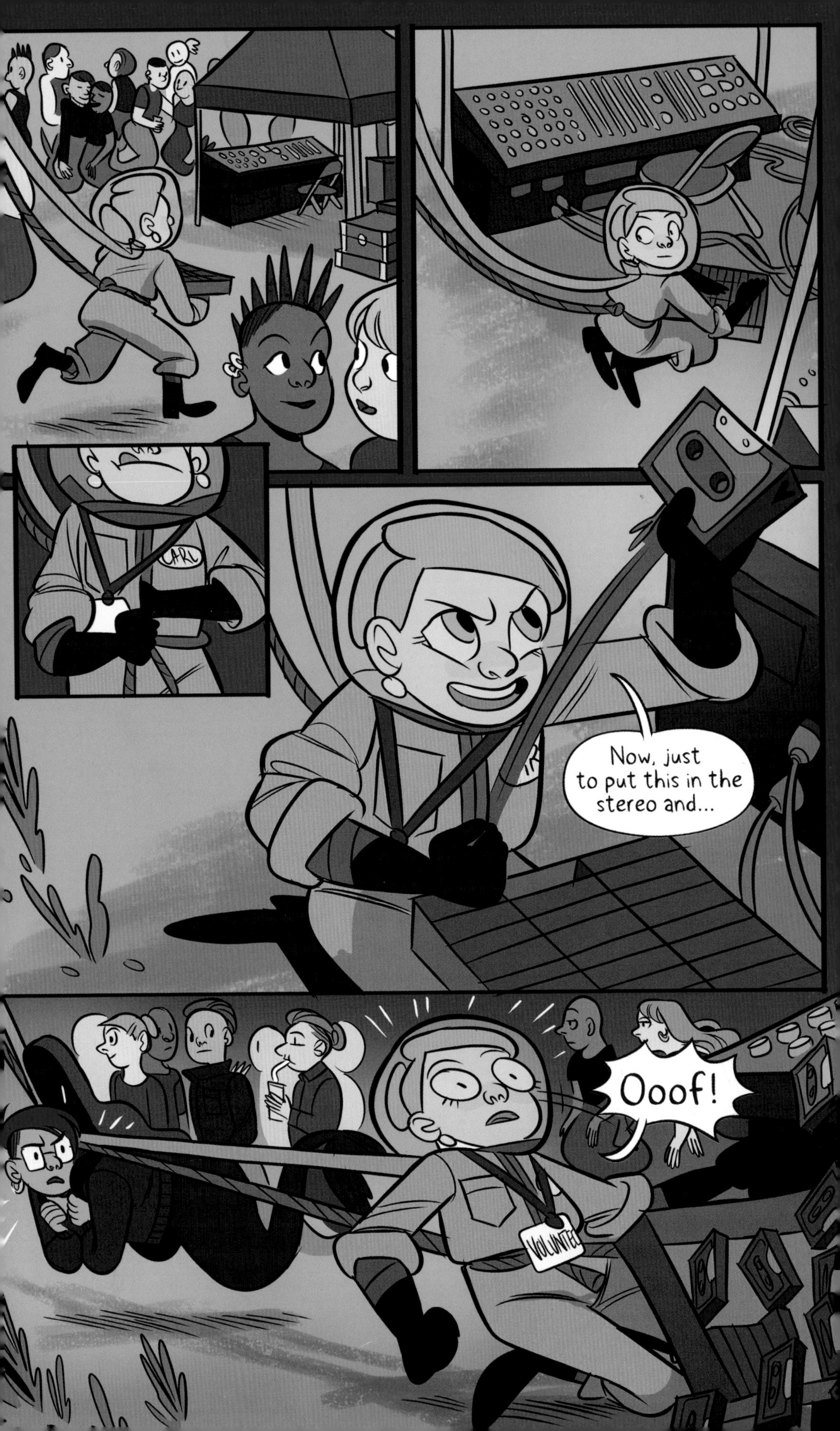
Now, just to put this in the stereo and...
Ooof!

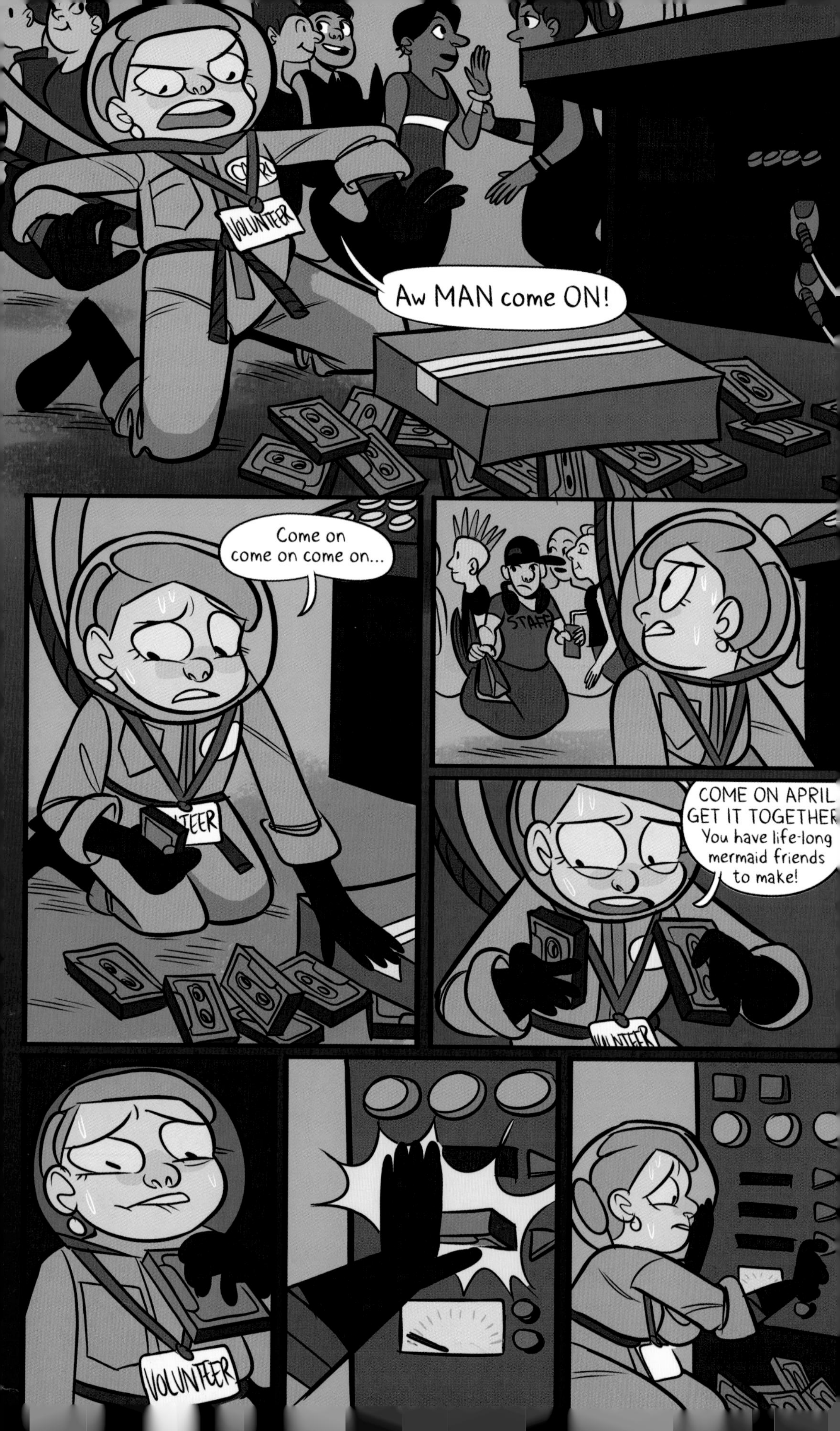
VOLUNTEER
Aw MAN come ON!
Come on come on come on...
STAFF
COME ON APRIL GET IT TOGETHER
You have life-long mermaid friends to make!
VOLUNTEER

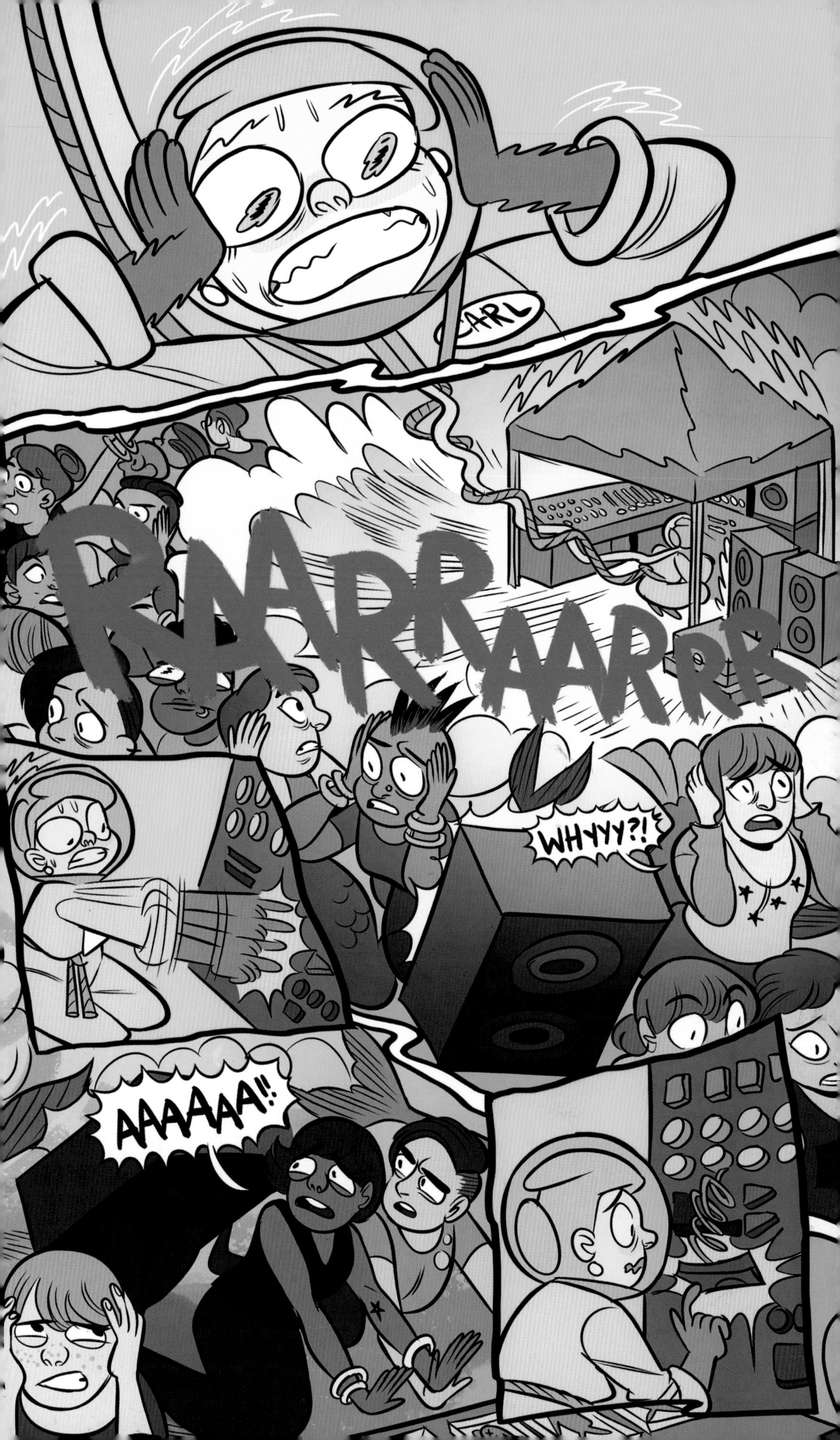
CARL
RAARRAARRR
WHYYY?!
AAAAAA!!

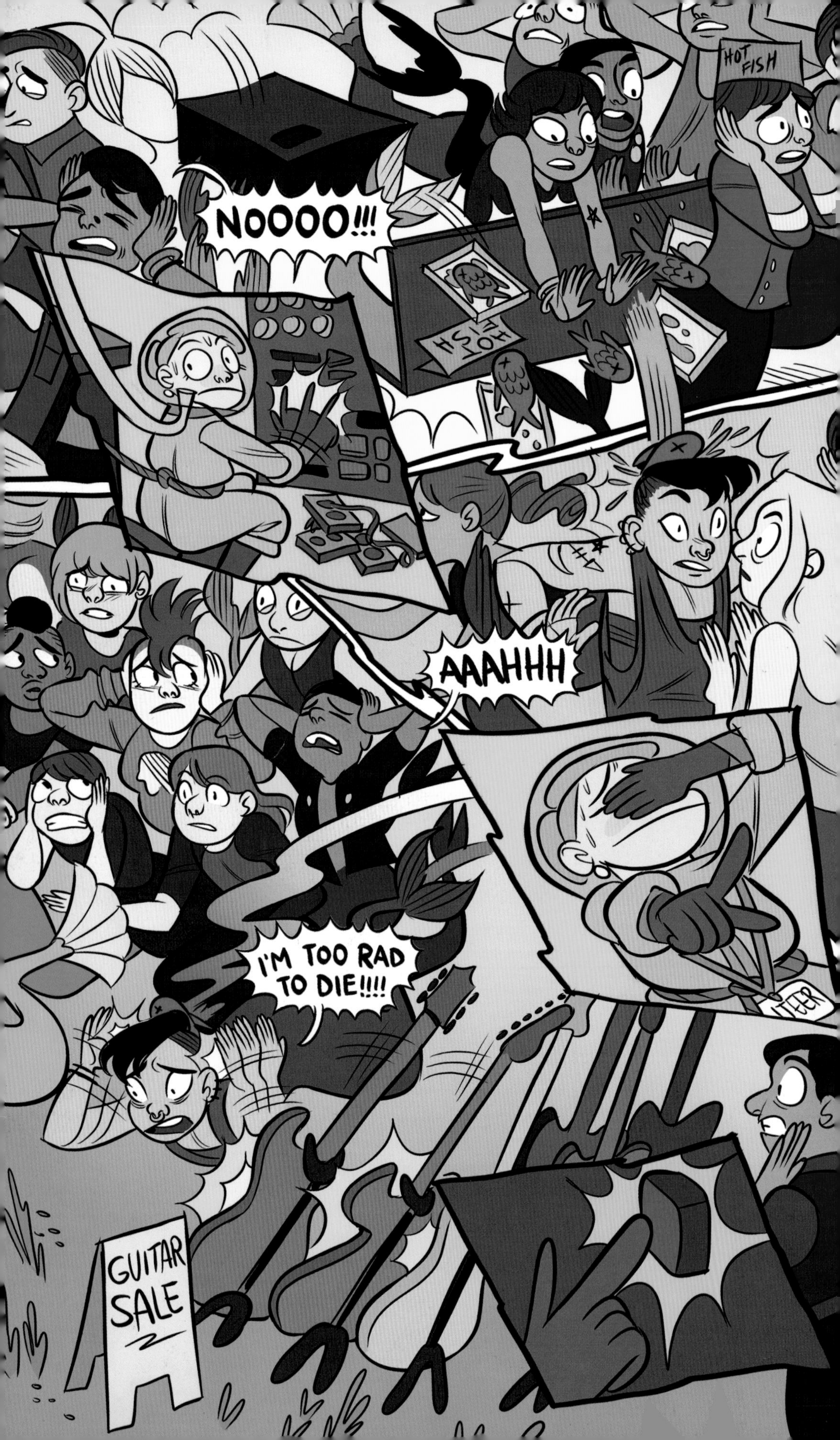
HOT FISH
NOOOO!!!
HOT FISH
AAAHHH
I'M TOO RAD TO DIE!!!!
GUITAR SALE

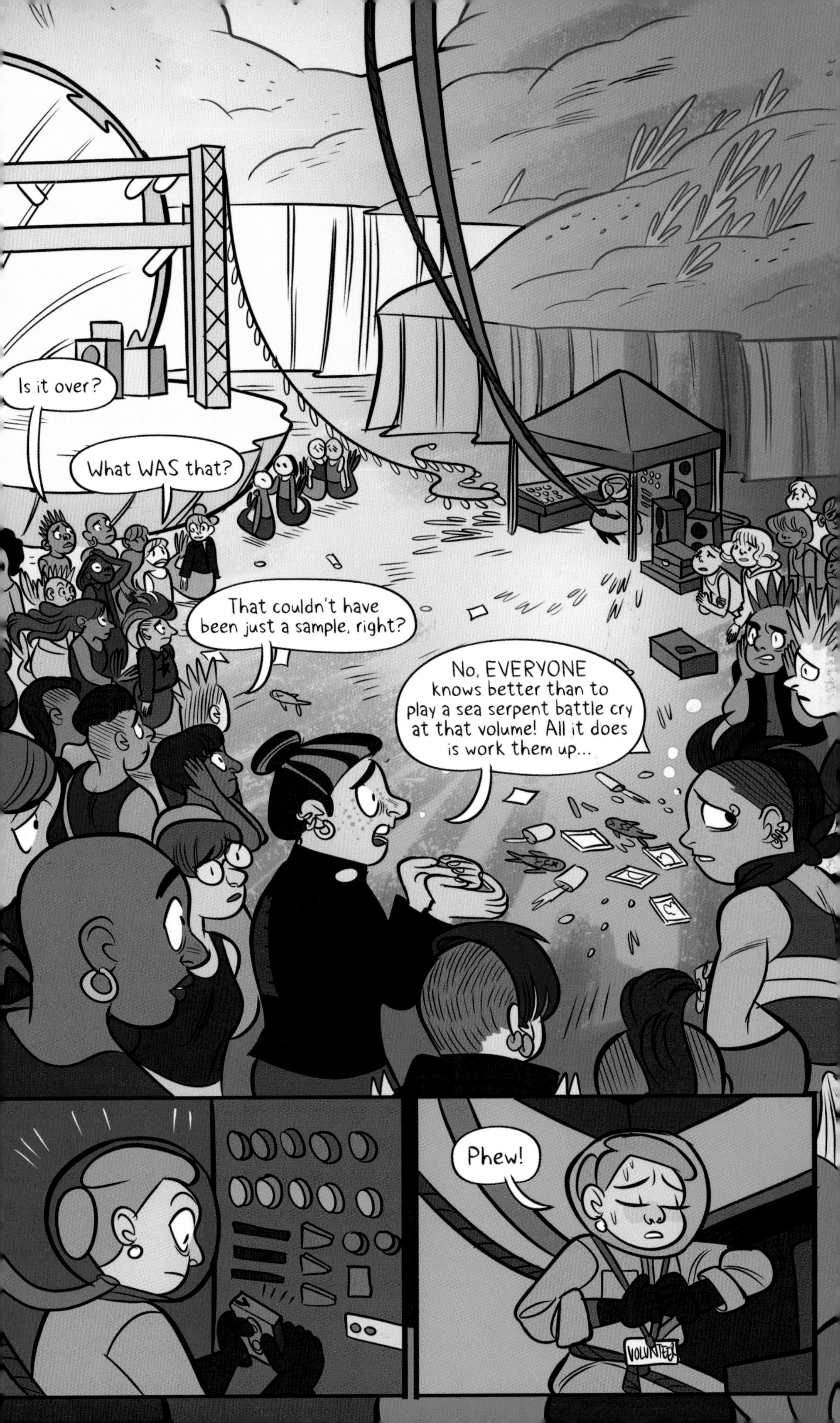
Is it over?
What WAS that?
That couldn't have been just a sample, right?
No, EVERYONE knows better than to play a sea serpent battle cry at that volume! All it does is work them up...
Phew!
VOLUNTEER

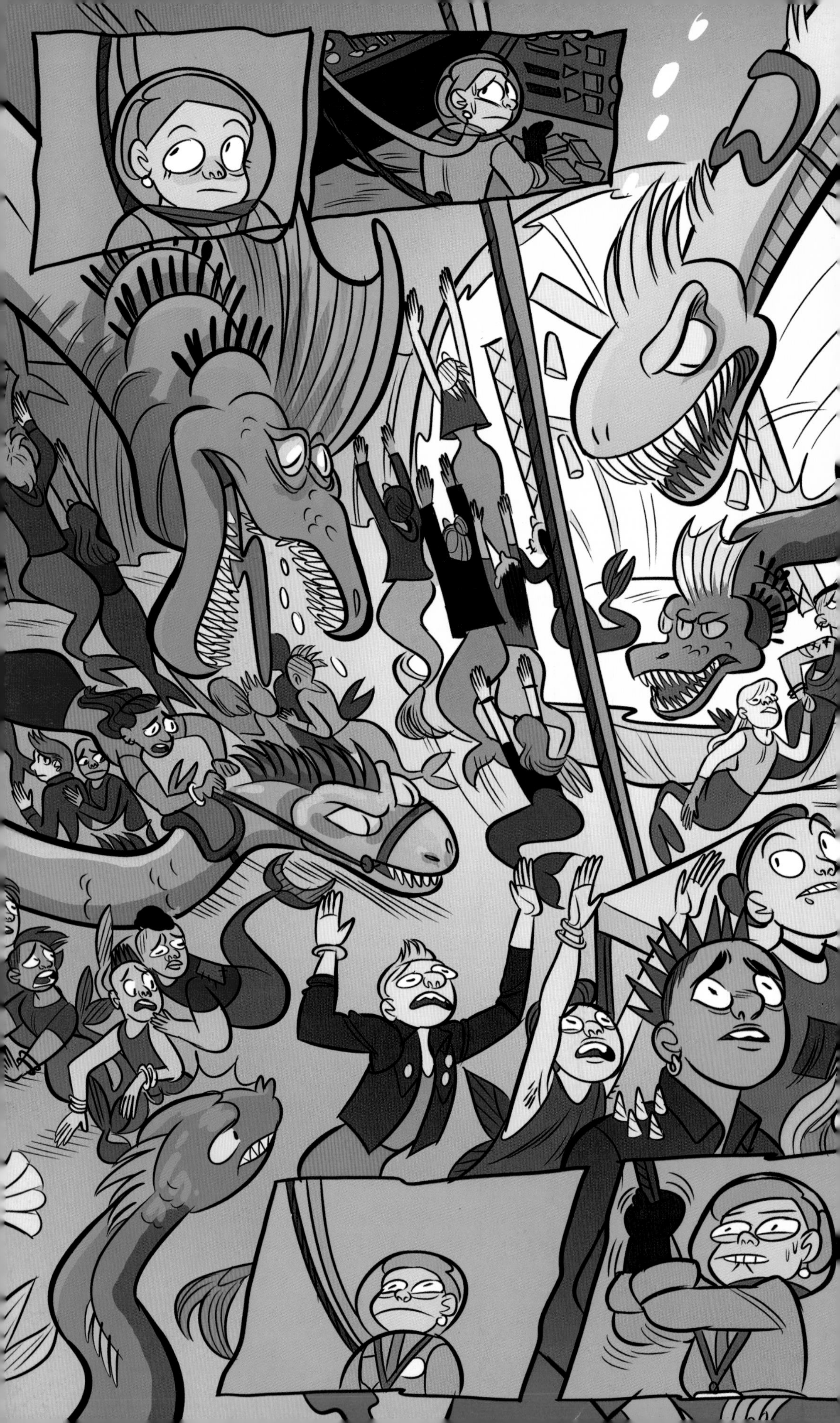

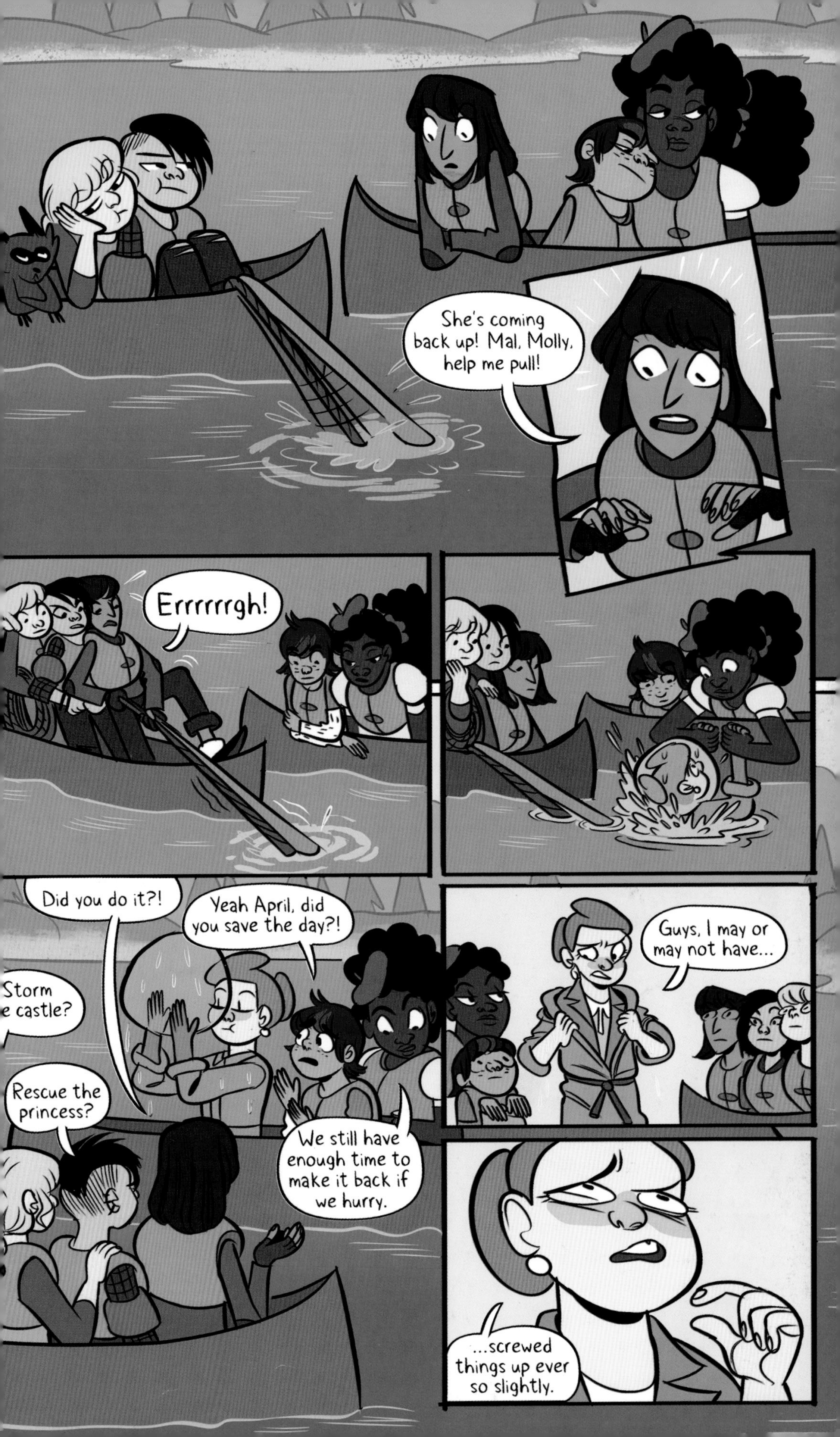

She's coming back up! Mal, Molly, help me pull!
Errrrrrgh!
Did you do it?!
Yeah April, did you save the day?!
Storm
e castle?
Rescue the princess?
We still have enough time to make it back if we hurry.
Guys, I may or may not have...
...screwed things up ever so slightly.

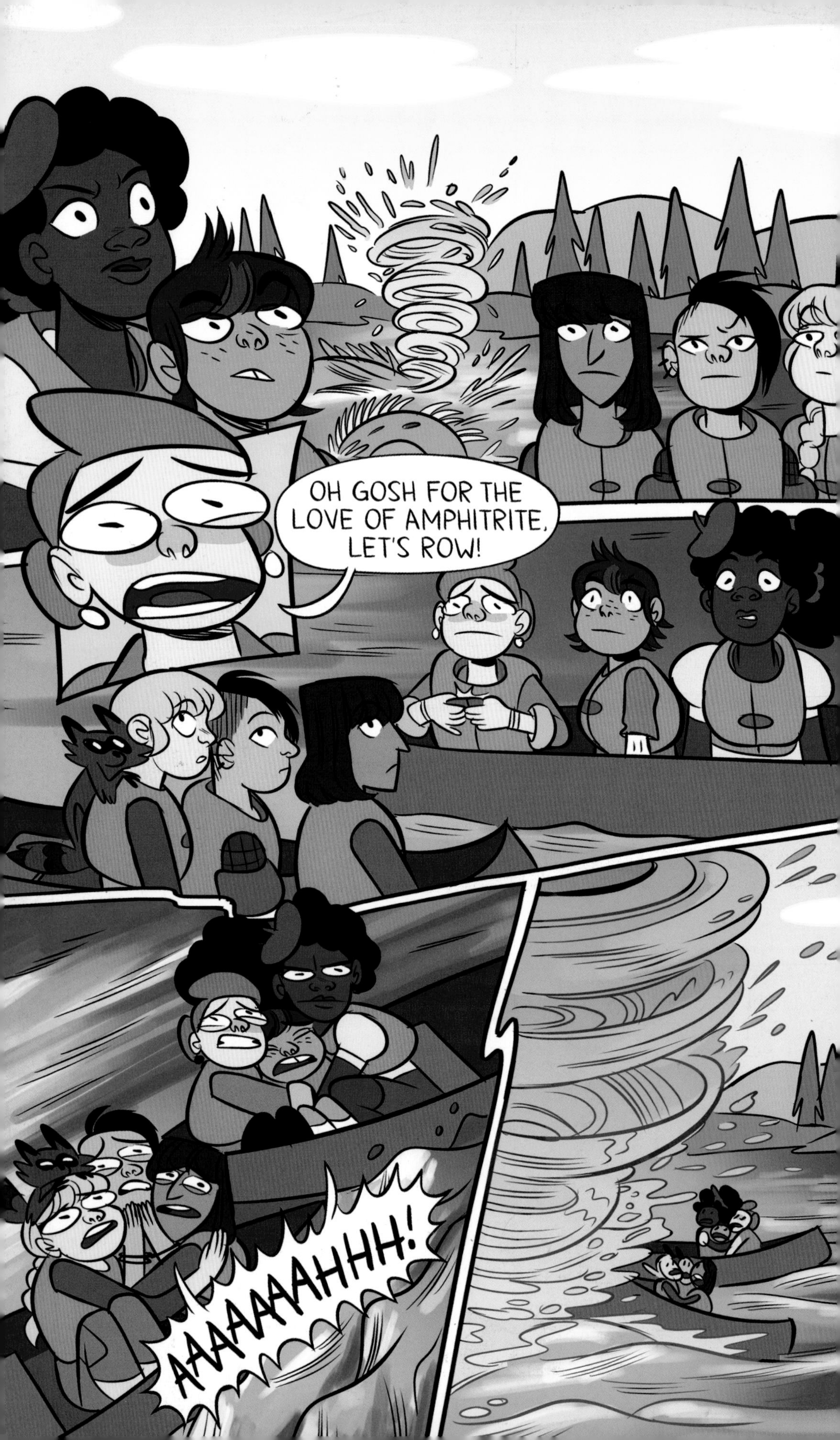
OH GOSH FOR THE LOVE OF AMPHITRITE, LET'S ROW!
AAAAAAAHHH!

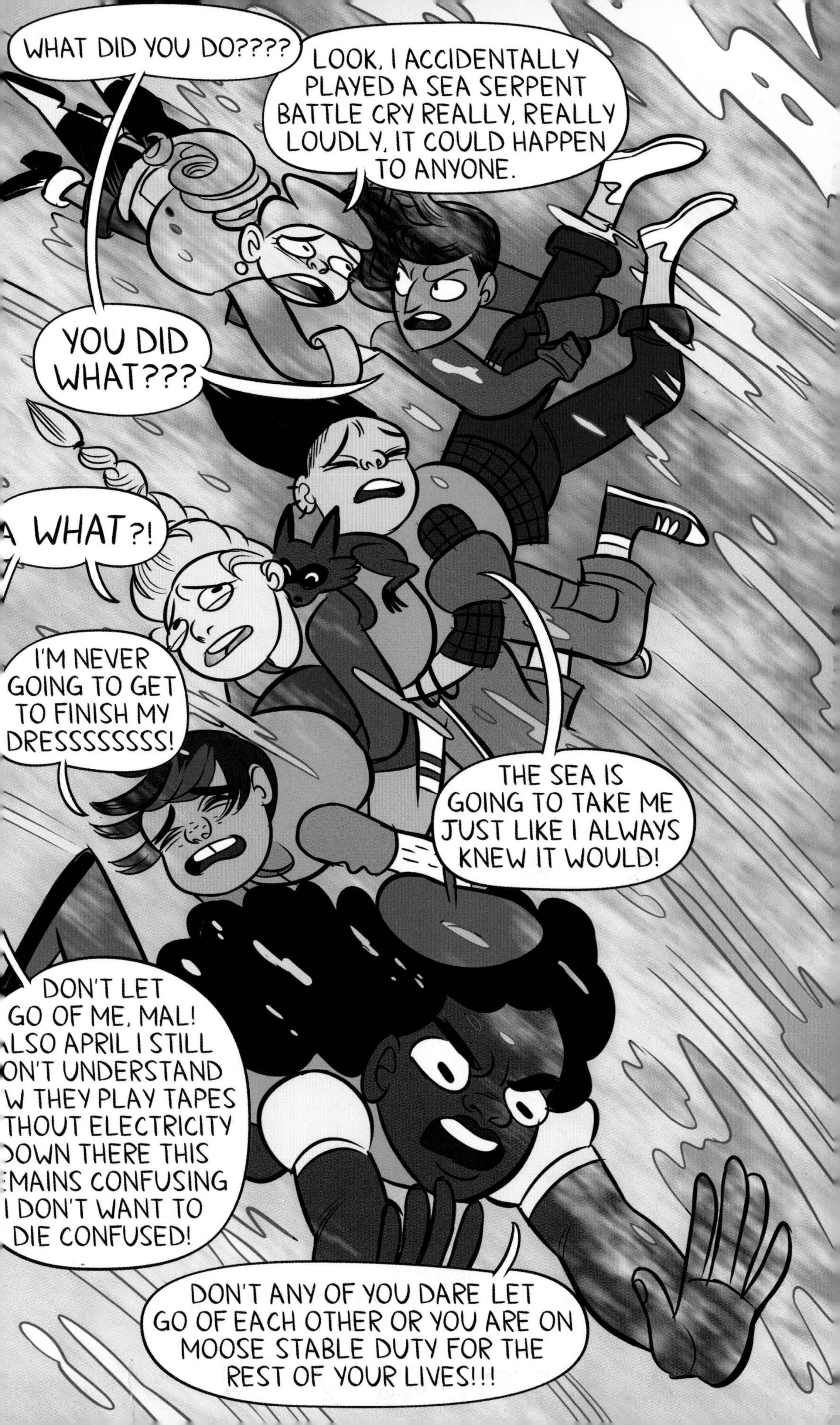
WHAT DID YOU DO????
LOOK, I ACCIDENTALLY PLAYED A SEA SERPENT BATTLE CRY REALLY, REALLY LOUDLY, IT COULD HAPPEN TO ANYONE.
YOU DID WHAT???
A WHAT?!
I'M NEVER GOING TO GET TO FINISH MY DRESSSSSSSS!
THE SEA IS GOING TO TAKE ME JUST LIKE I ALWAYS KNEW IT WOULD!
DON'T LET GO OF ME, MAL! ALSO APRIL I STILL ON'T UNDERSTAND W THEY PLAY TAPES THOUT ELECTRICITY OWN THERE THIS EMAINS CONFUSING I DON'T WANT TO DIE CONFUSED!
DON'T ANY OF YOU DARE LET GO OF EACH OTHER OR YOU ARE ON MOOSE STABLE DUTY FOR THE REST OF YOUR LIVES!!!

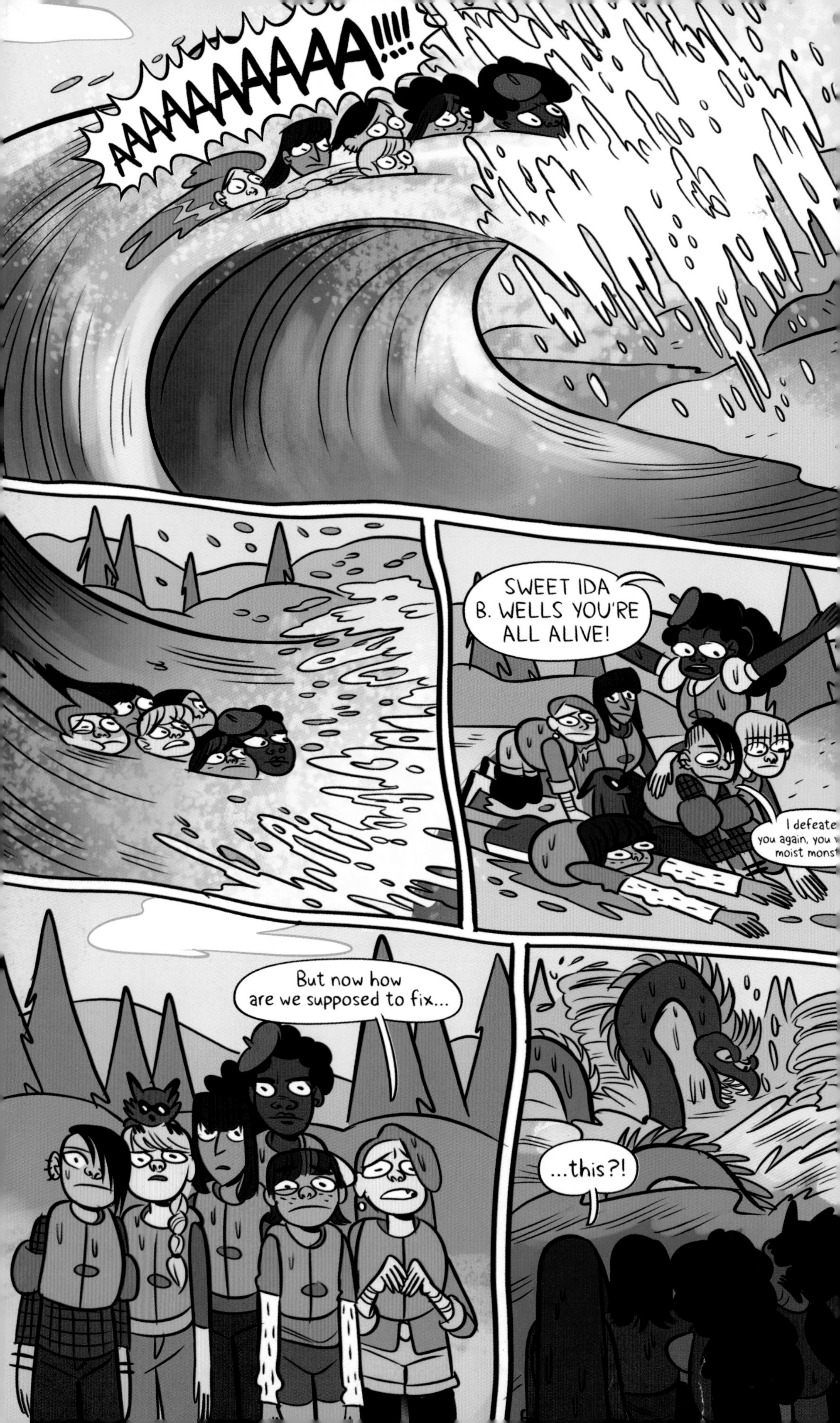
AAAAAAAAA!!!!
SWEET IDA B. WELLS YOU'RE ALL ALIVE!
I defeate
you again, you
moist monst
But now how are we supposed to fix...
...this?!

will co

The i
It help
appearan
dress fo
Further
Lumber
to have
part in
Thiskv
Hardo
have
them

WHEN YOU ACCIDENTALLY PLAY A SEA SERPENT BATTLE CRY.

The
yellow, short sl
emb
the w
choose
slacks,
made o
out-of-do
green bere
the colla
Shoes ma
heels, rou
socks shou
the uniform. Ne
belong with a Lumberjane uniform.

TIME TO FIX THIS!

E UNIFORM

hould be worn at camp
events when Lumberjanes
may also be worn at other
ions. It should be worn as a
the uniform dress with
rrect shoes, and stocking or
out grows her uniform or
ter Lumberjane.
a she has
her
her

GES

HOW TO WEAR THE U

To look well in a uniform deman
uniform be kept in good condi
pressed. See that the skirt is the righ
height and build, that the belt is adj
that your shoes and stockings are in
uniform, that you watch your posture and
with dignity and grace. If the beret is removed
be sure that your hair is neat and kept in place with an
insnspicuous clip or ribbon. When you wear a
Lumberjane uniform you are identified as a member of
this organization and you should be doubly careful to
conduct yourself in a way that will show everyone that
courtesy and thoughtfullness are part of being a
Lumberjane. People are likely to judge a whole nation by
the selfishness of a few individuals, to criticize a whole
family because of the misconduct of one member, and to
feel unkindly toward and organization because of the

nifor
helps to cre
in a group.
active life th
another bond
future, and pr
in order to b
Lumberjane pr
Penniquiqul Thi   re Lady
Types, but m   es will wish to have one. They
can either bu   orm, or make it themselves from
materials available at the trading post.

FRIENDSHIP TO THE MAX?

LUMBERJANES FIELD MANUAL

CHAPTER TWENTY

Lumberjanes "Automotive" Program Field

KEEPIN' IT REEL BADGE

"There is more to life than fish, most of the time."

Fishing, hunting, gathering, all those good things that will be touched on in the basic survival classes are great things to know. At this camp we want to ensure that each and every Lumberjane leaves this camp with a basic understanding of what to do in a blizzard, how to survive in the desert, and what actions are needed with the ring of fire finally activates. We are happy to say that every Lumberjane that comes to this camp will leave with that knowledge and more. But knowledge and skills aren't the only things we want Lumberjanes to leave this camp with, we want Lumberjanes to have a better understand of themselves when they do eventually leave the wooden walls of their lodges.

There are a lot of distractions in the world outside of camp, and some of those distractions will follow every camper here, but to the best of our abilities we want to ensure that this camp is always a safe and welcoming environment

for every camp who walks these dirt trails. At camp it is important to understand teamwork and friendship but more importantly, it is vital that you learn acceptance for who you are as a camper and gain a better understanding of that means to you. With the *Keepin' It Reel* badge, each camper is encouraged to be themselves, to find and realize that individuality they have that makes them who they are.

To obtain the *Keepin' It Reel* badge, a Lumberjane must learn the art of meditation and focus. As this is a precursor to many of the badges that need to be earned at this camp, by the time a Lumberjane is ready for the *Keepin' It Reel* badge, meditation is the least of their worries. The Lumberjane, once ready, will then figure out what they need in order to complete this badge by wandering around the camp. They will know what the object is as soon as they come across, remember this badge is all about gut instincts and not actual methods.

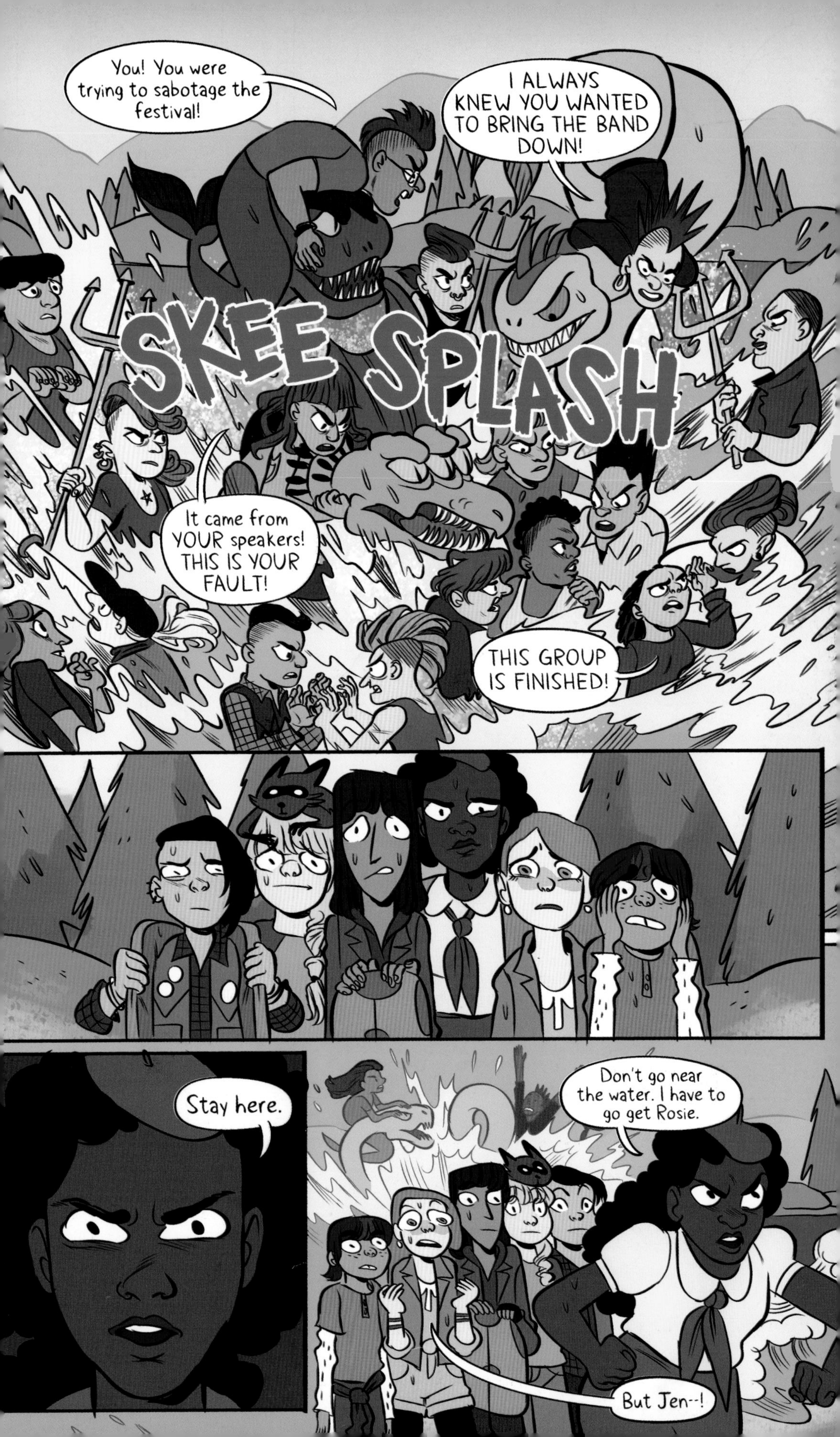
You! You were trying to sabotage the festival!
I ALWAYS KNEW YOU WANTED TO BRING THE BAND DOWN!
SKEE SPLASH
It came from YOUR speakers! THIS IS YOUR FAULT!
THIS GROUP IS FINISHED!
Stay here.
Don't go near the water. I have to go get Rosie.
But Jen--!

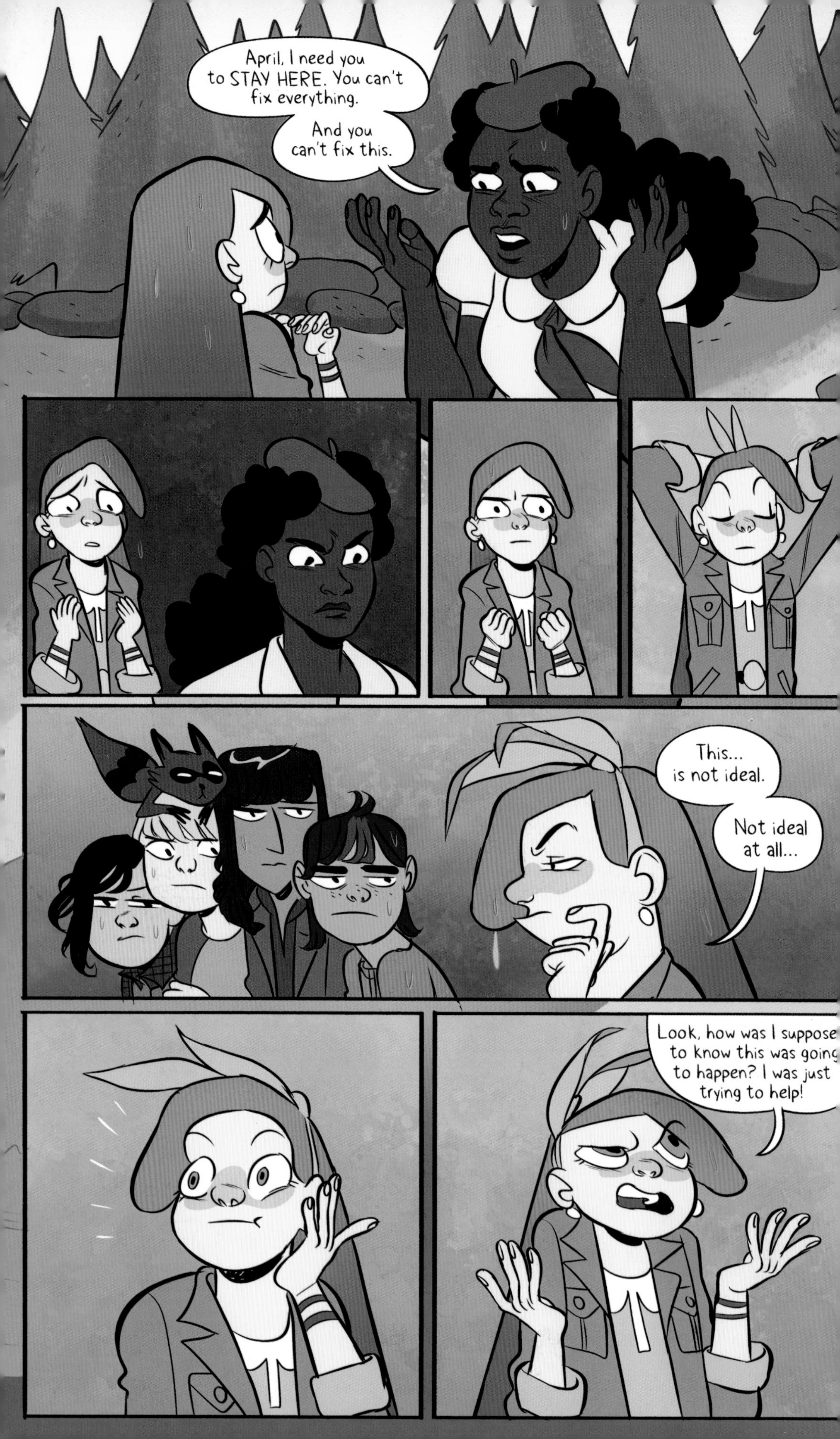
April, I need you to STAY HERE. You can't fix everything.
And you can't fix this.
This... is not ideal.
Not ideal at all...
Look, how was I suppose to know this was going to happen? I was just trying to help!

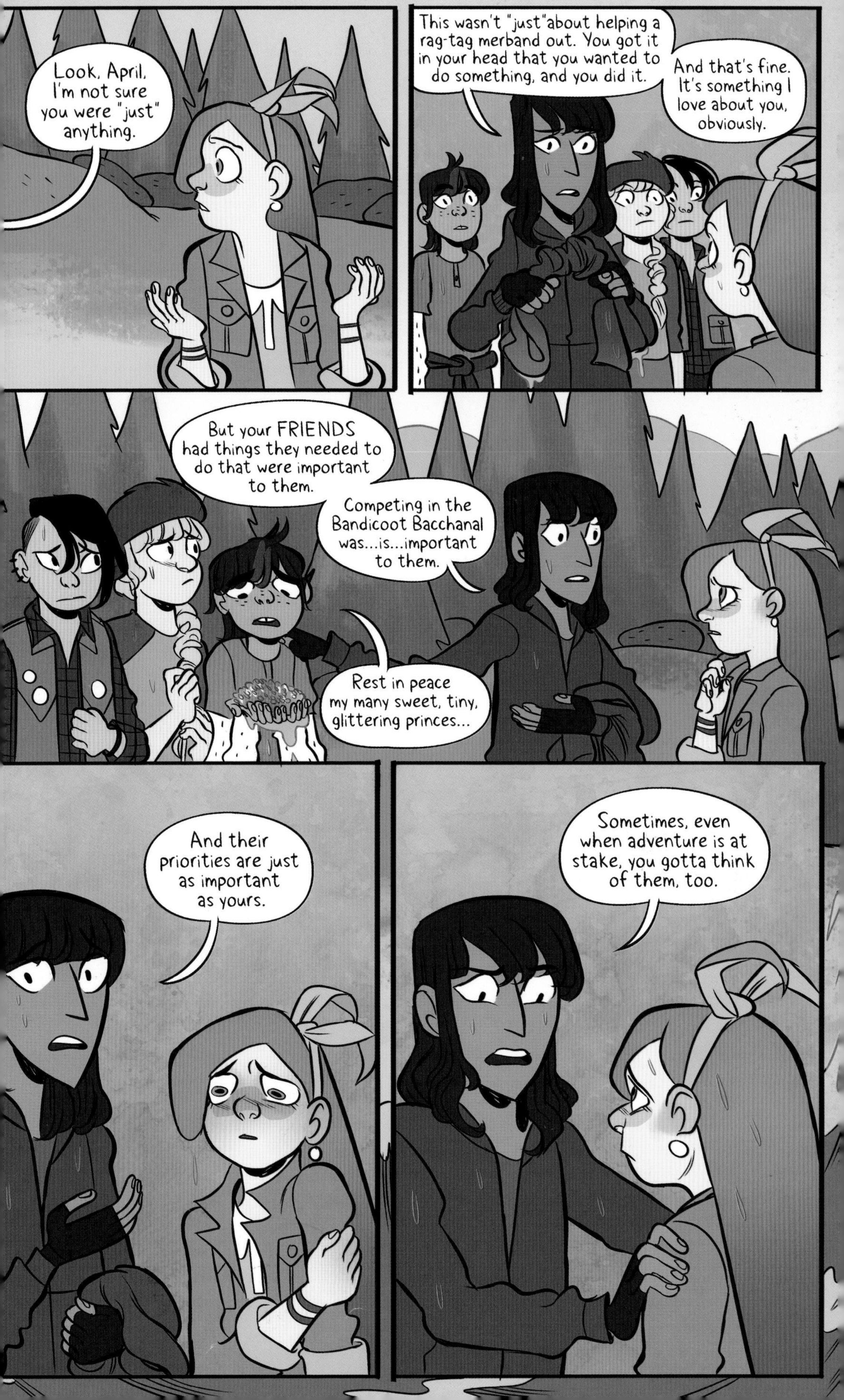
Look, April, I'm not sure you were "just" anything.
This wasn't "just"about helping a rag-tag merband out. You got it in your head that you wanted to do something, and you did it.
And that's fine. It's something I love about you, obviously.
But your FRIENDS had things they needed to do that were important to them.
Competing in the Bandicoot Bacchanal was...is...important to them.
Rest in peace my many sweet, tiny, glittering princes...
And their priorities are just as important as yours.
Sometimes, even when adventure is at stake, you gotta think of them, too.

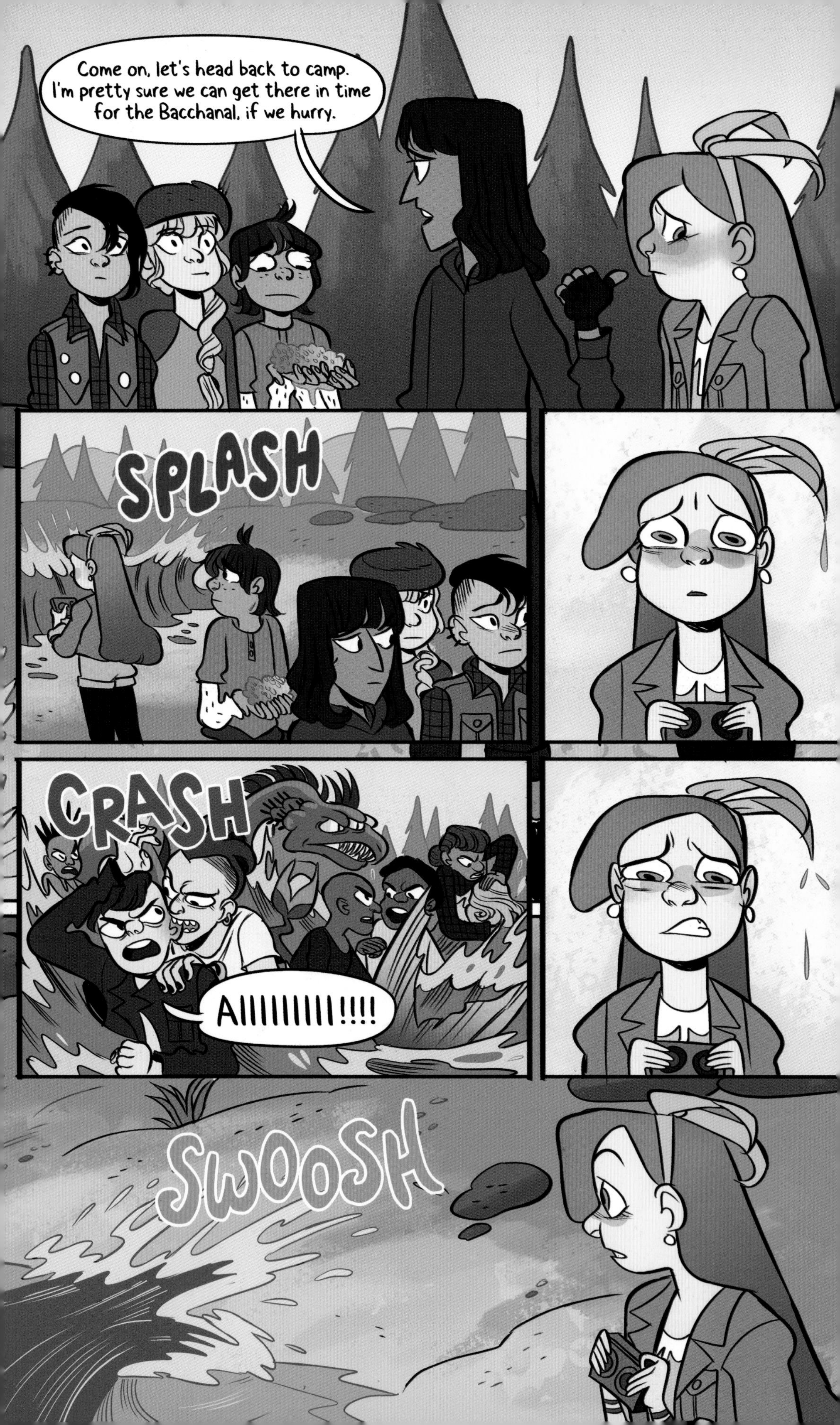

Come on, let's head back to camp. I'm pretty sure we can get there in time for the Bacchanal, if we hurry.
SPLASH
CRASH
AIIIIIIIII!!!!
SWOOSH

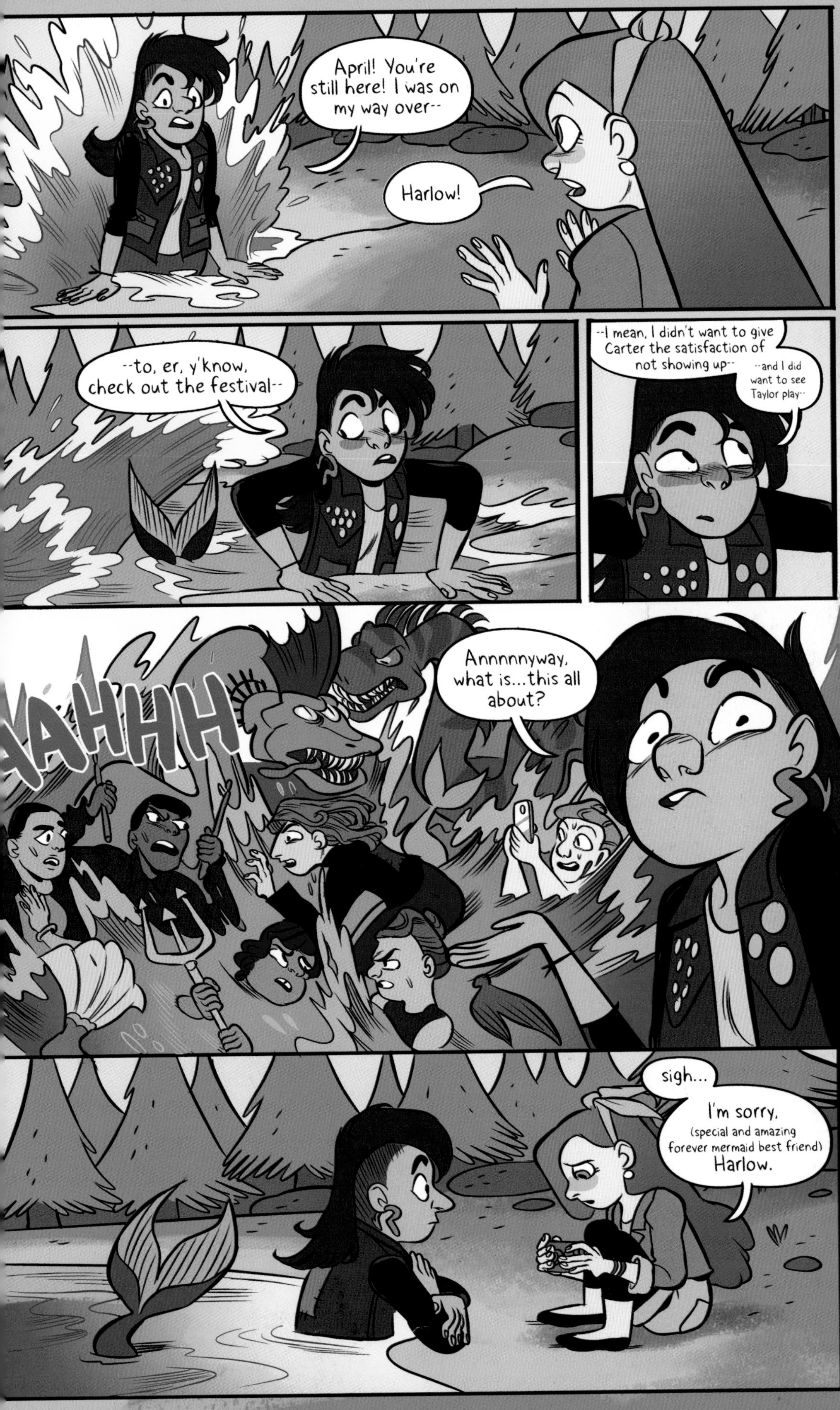
April! You're still here! I was on my way over--
Harlow!
--to, er, y'know, check out the festival--
--I mean, I didn't want to give Carter the satisfaction of not showing up--
--and I did want to see Taylor play--
AHHHH
Annnnnyway, what is...this all about?
sigh...
I'm sorry, (special and amazing forever mermaid best friend) Harlow.

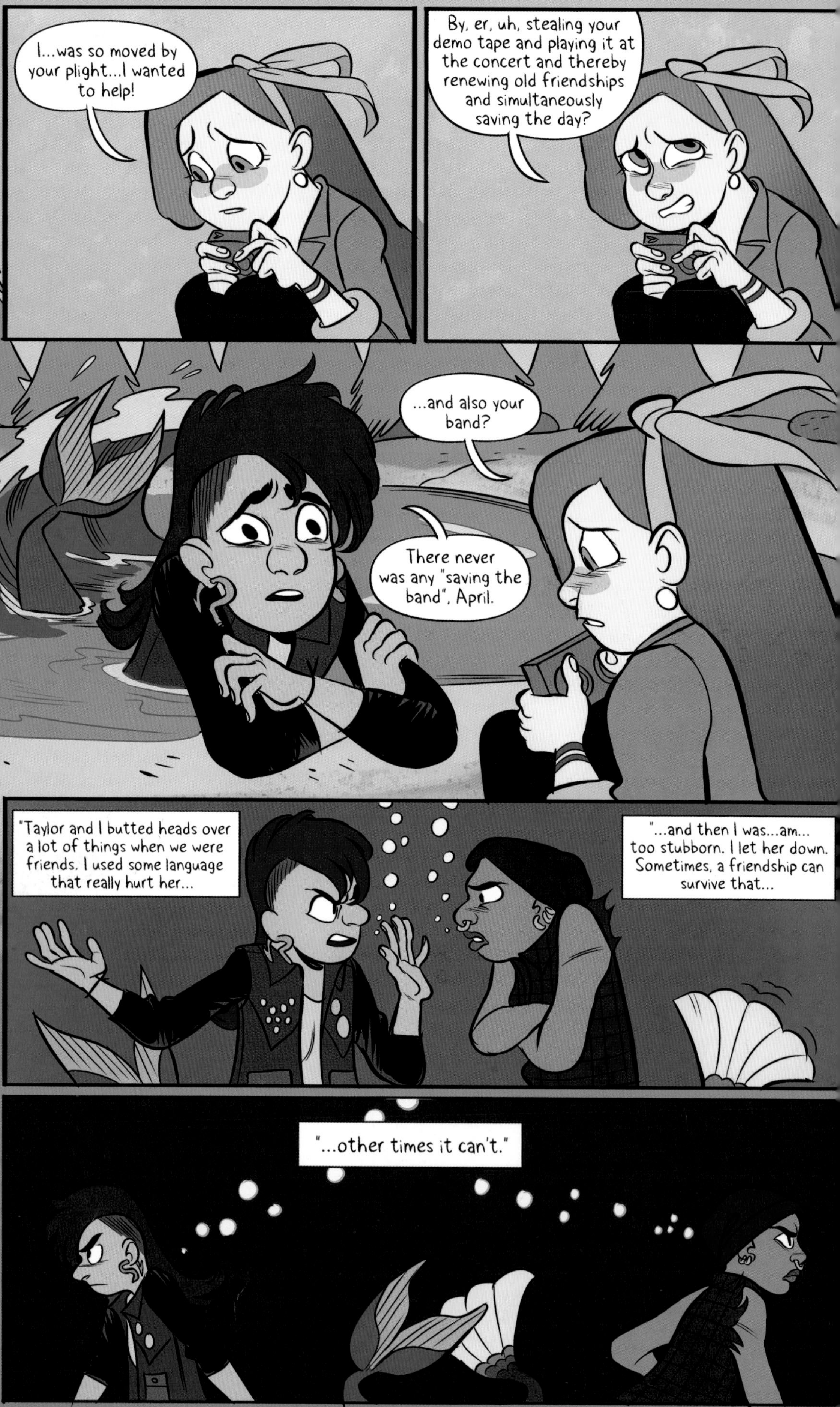
I...was so moved by your plight...I wanted to help!
By, er, uh, stealing your demo tape and playing it at the concert and thereby renewing old friendships and simultaneously saving the day?
...and also your band?
There never was any "saving the band", April.
"Taylor and I butted heads over a lot of things when we were friends. I used some language that really hurt her...
"...and then I was...am... too stubborn. I let her down. Sometimes, a friendship can survive that...
"...other times it can't."

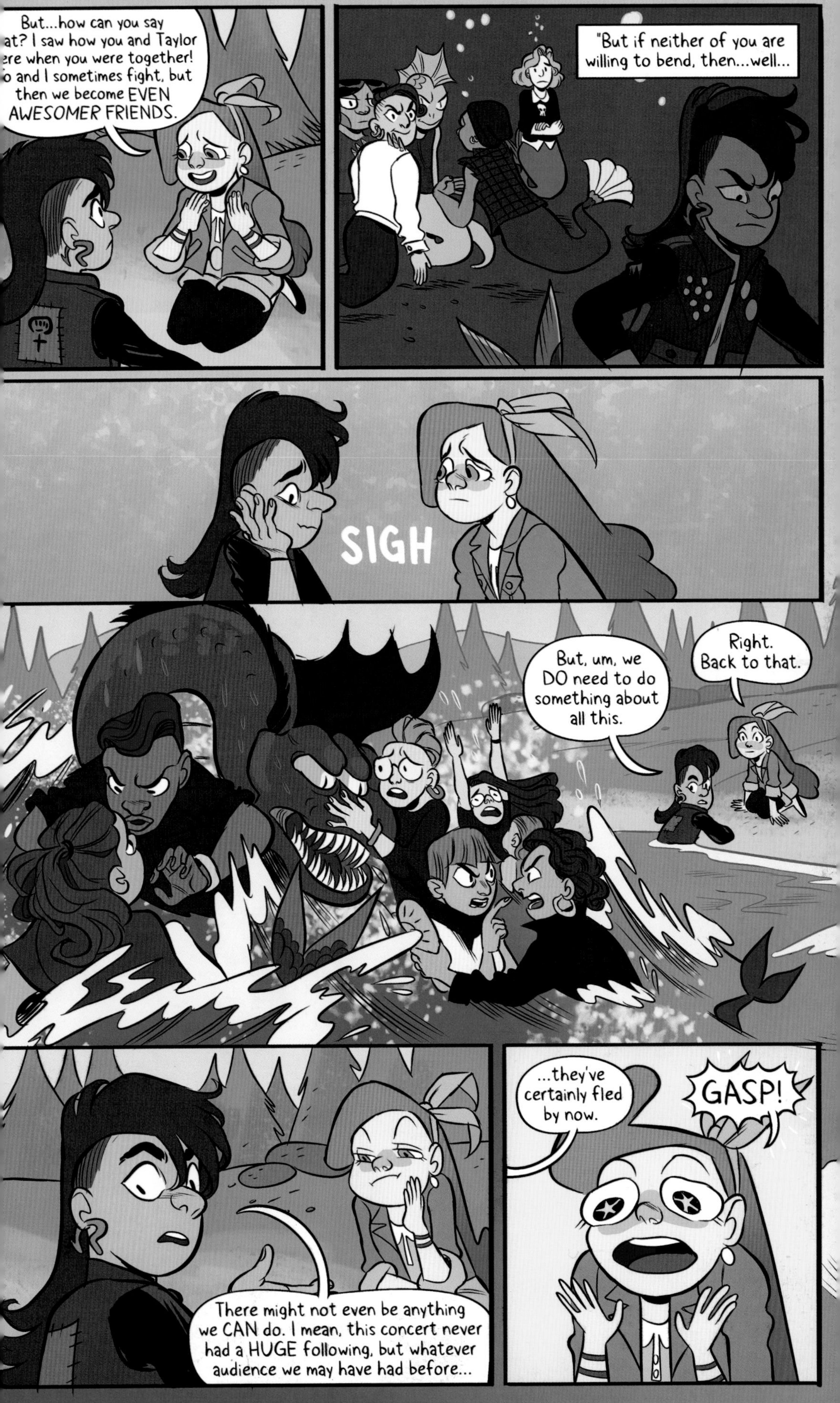
But...how can you say
at? I saw how you and Taylor
ere when you were together!
o and I sometimes fight, but
then we become EVEN
AWESOMER FRIENDS.
"But if neither of you are
willing to bend, then...well...
SIGH
But, um, we
DO need to do
something about
all this.
Right.
Back to that.
There might not even be anything
we CAN do. I mean, this concert never
had a HUGE following, but whatever
audience we may have had before...
...they've
certainly fled
by now.
GASP!

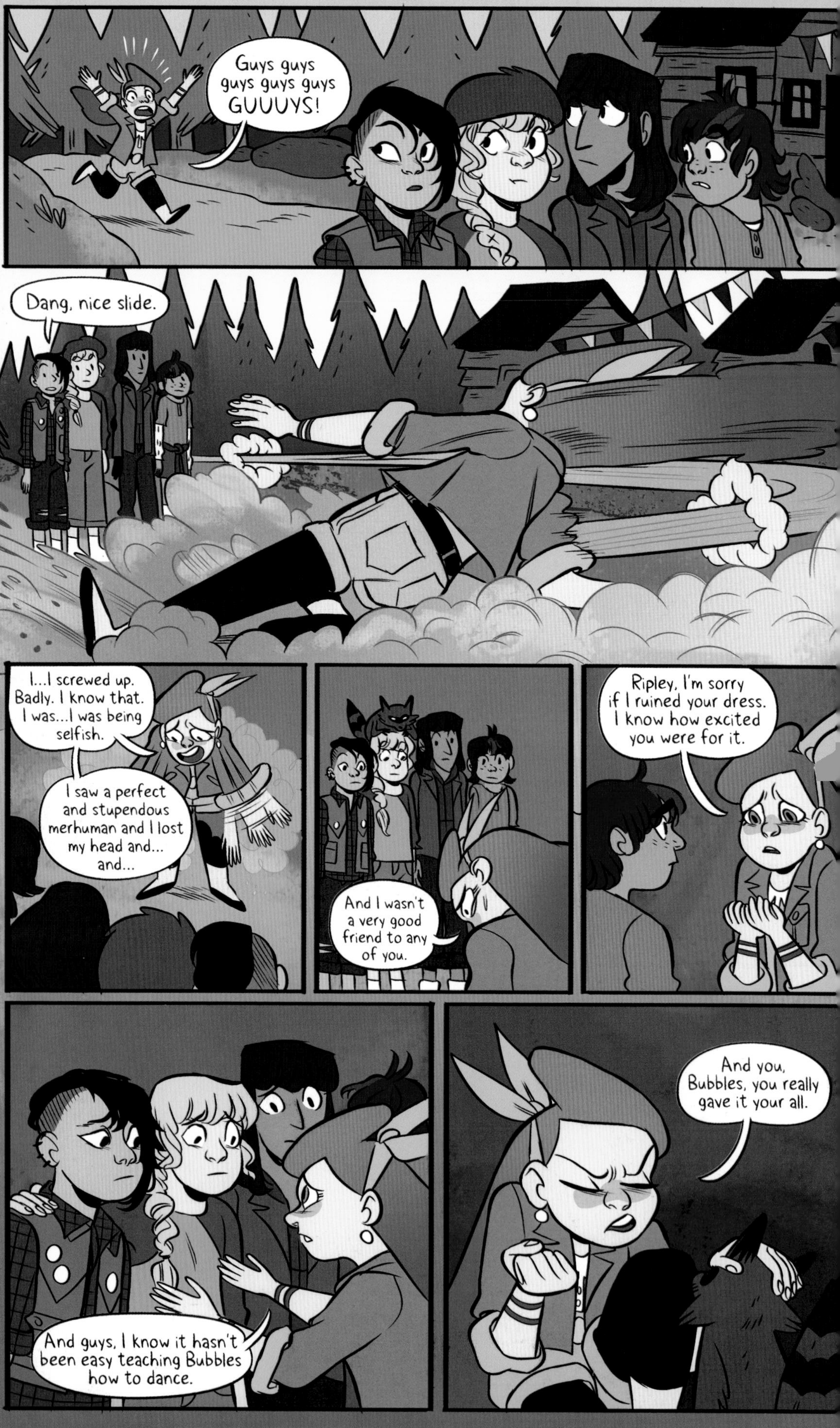
Guys guys guys guys guys GUUUYS!
Dang, nice slide.
I...I screwed up. Badly. I know that. I was...I was being selfish.
I saw a perfect and stupendous merhuman and I lost my head and... and...
And I wasn't a very good friend to any of you.
Ripley, I'm sorry if I ruined your dress. I know how excited you were for it.
And guys, I know it hasn't been easy teaching Bubbles how to dance.
And you, Bubbles, you really gave it your all.

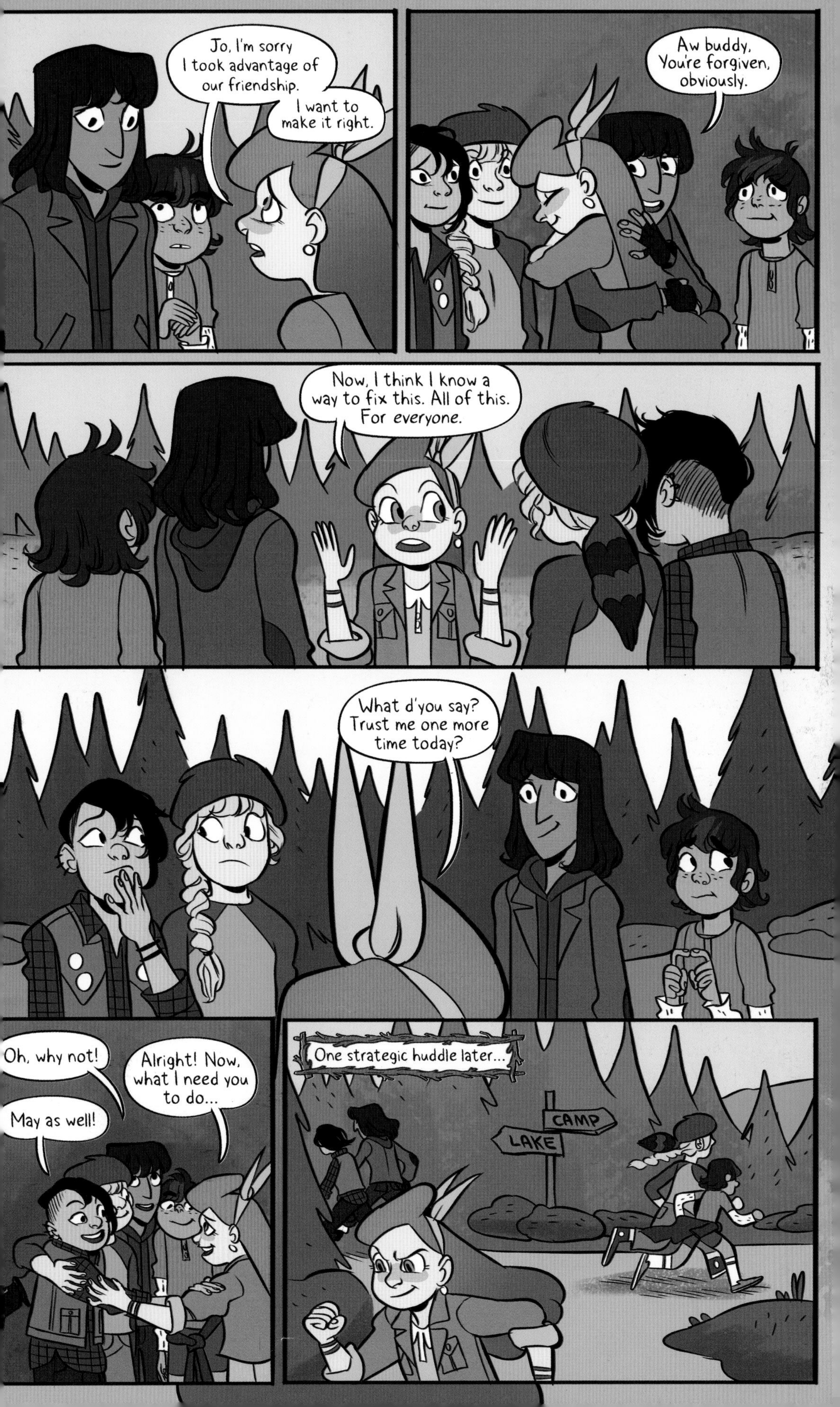
Jo, I'm sorry I took advantage of our friendship.
I want to make it right.
Aw buddy, You're forgiven, obviously.
Now, I think I know a way to fix this. All of this. For *everyone*.
What d'you say? Trust me one more time today?
Oh, why not!
May as well!
Alright! Now, what I need you to do...
One strategic huddle later...
CAMP
LAKE

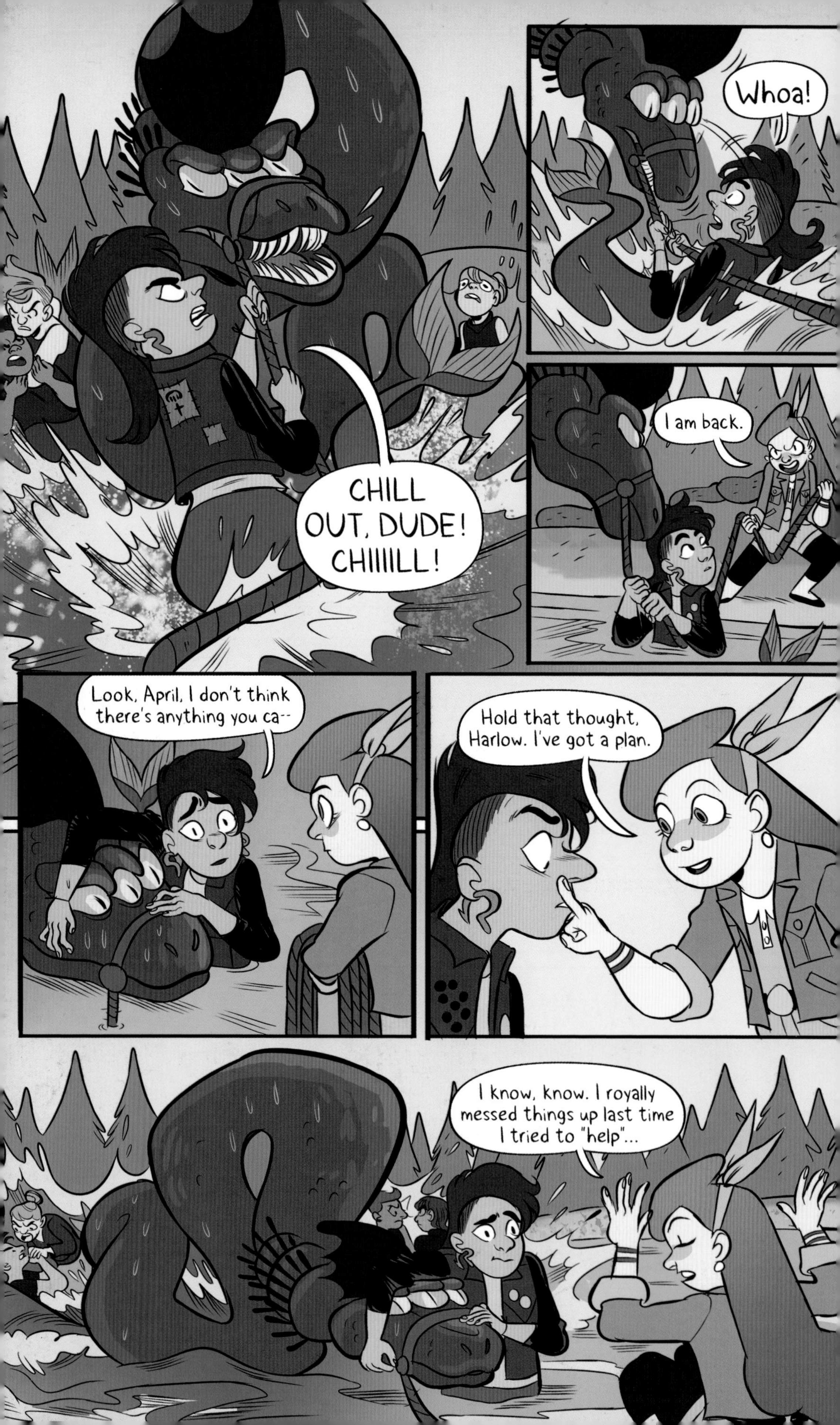
CHILL OUT, DUDE! CHIIIIILL!
Whoa!
I am back.
Look, April, I don't think there's anything you ca--
Hold that thought, Harlow. I've got a plan.
I know, know. I royally messed things up last time I tried to "help"...

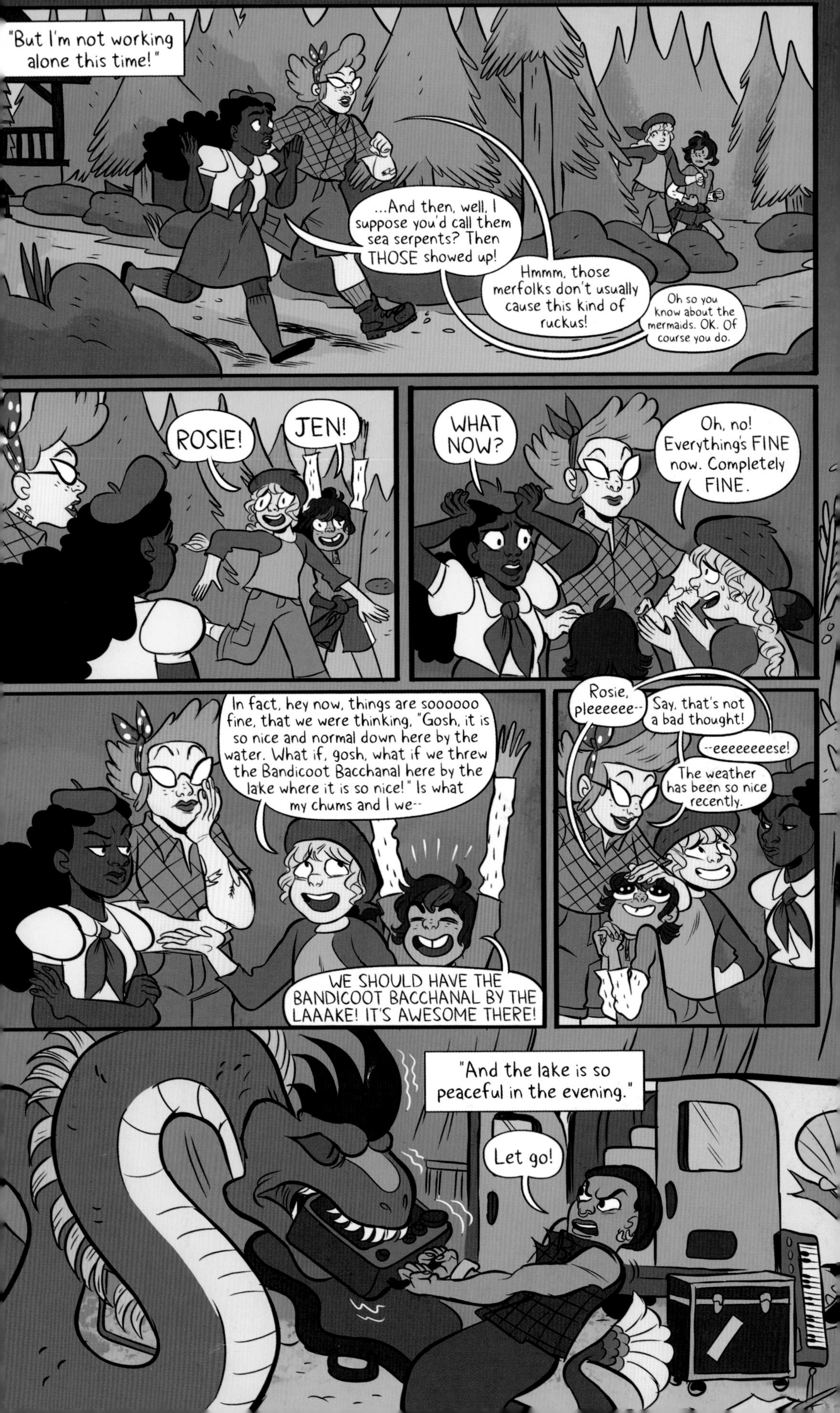
"But I'm not working alone this time!"
...And then, well, I suppose you'd call them sea serpents? Then THOSE showed up!
Hmmm, those merfolks don't usually cause this kind of ruckus!
Oh so you know about the mermaids. OK. Of course you do.
ROSIE!
JEN!
WHAT NOW?
Oh, no! Everything's FINE now. Completely FINE.
In fact, hey now, things are soooooo fine, that we were thinking, "Gosh, it is so nice and normal down here by the water. What if, gosh, what if we threw the Bandicoot Bacchanal here by the lake where it is so nice!" Is what my chums and I we--
WE SHOULD HAVE THE BANDICOOT BACCHANAL BY THE LAAAKE! IT'S AWESOME THERE!
Rosie, pleeeeee--
Say, that's not a bad thought!
--eeeeeeeese!
The weather has been so nice recently.
"And the lake is so peaceful in the evening."
Let go!

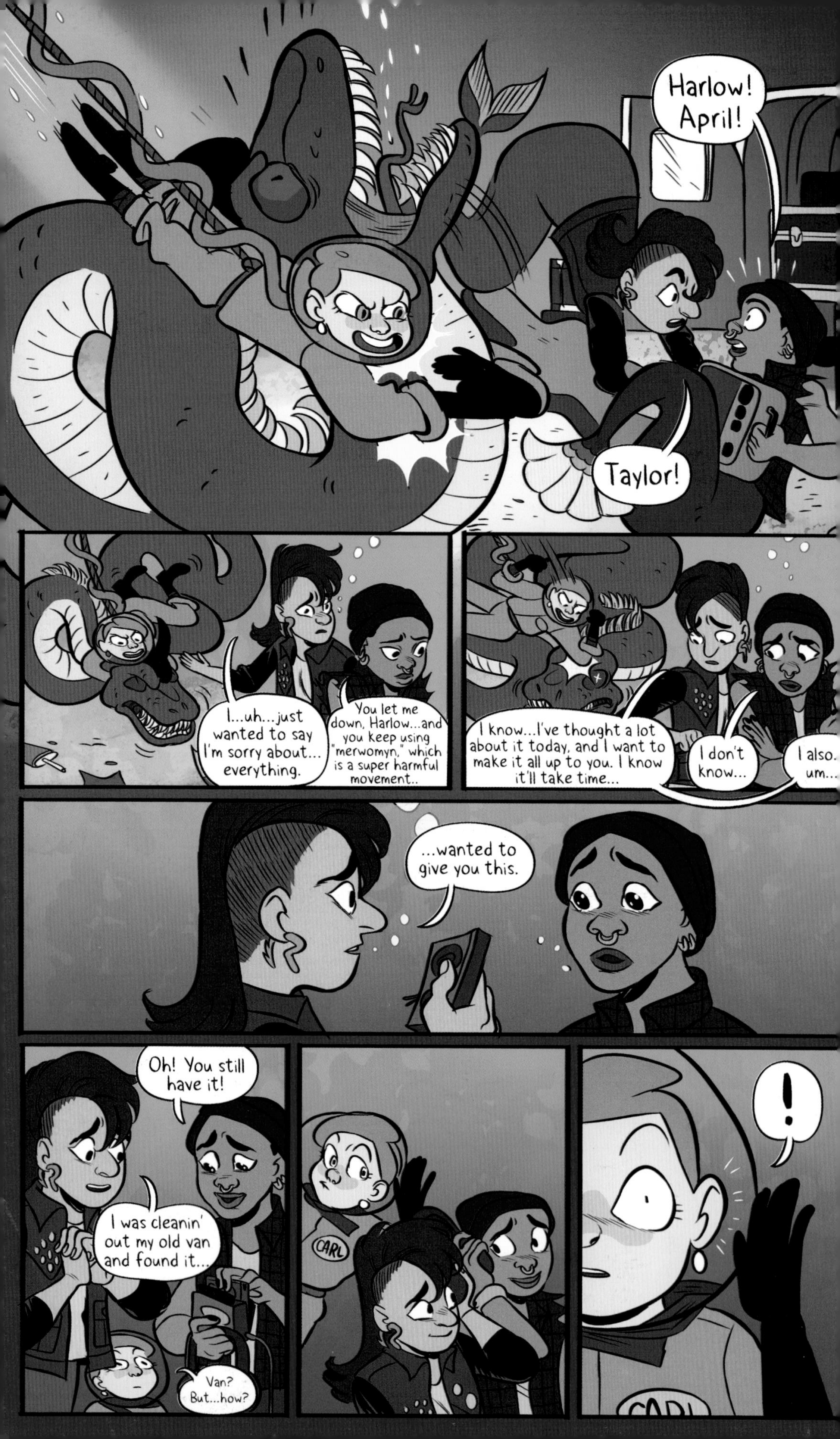
Harlow! April!
Taylor!
I...uh...just wanted to say I'm sorry about... everything.
You let me down, Harlow...and you keep using "merwomyn," which is a super harmful movement..
I know...I've thought a lot about it today, and I want to make it all up to you. I know it'll take time...
I don't know...
I also... um...
...wanted to give you this.
Oh! You still have it!
I was cleanin' out my old van and found it...
Van? But...how?
CARL
!

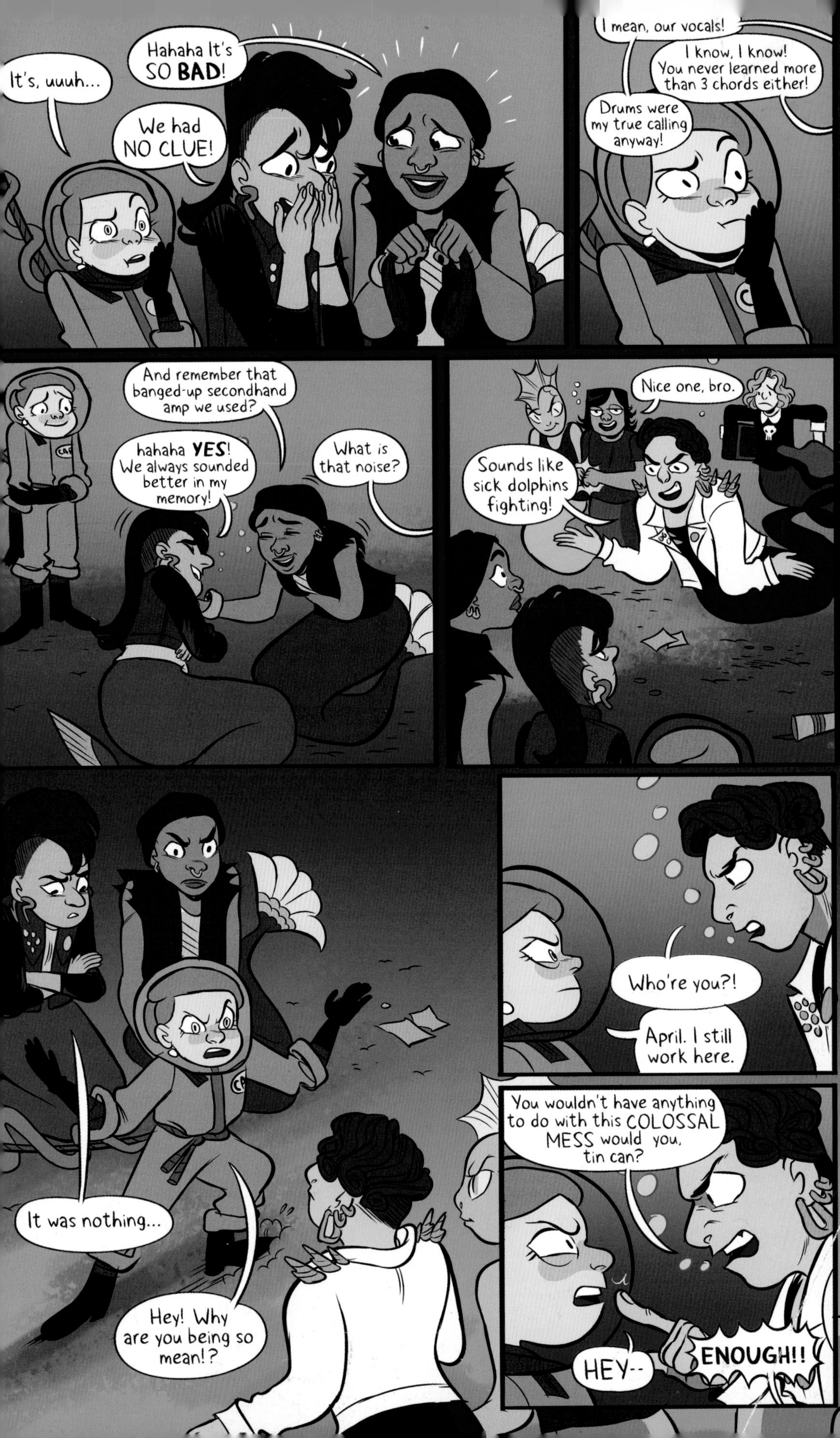
It's, uuuh...
Hahaha It's SO BAD!
We had NO CLUE!
I mean, our vocals!
I know, I know! You never learned more than 3 chords either!
Drums were my true calling anyway!
And remember that banged-up secondhand amp we used?
hahaha YES! We always sounded better in my memory!
What is that noise?
Nice one, bro.
Sounds like sick dolphins fighting!
It was nothing...
Hey! Why are you being so mean!?
Who're you?!
April. I still work here.
You wouldn't have anything to do with this COLOSSAL MESS would you, tin can?
HEY--
ENOUGH!!

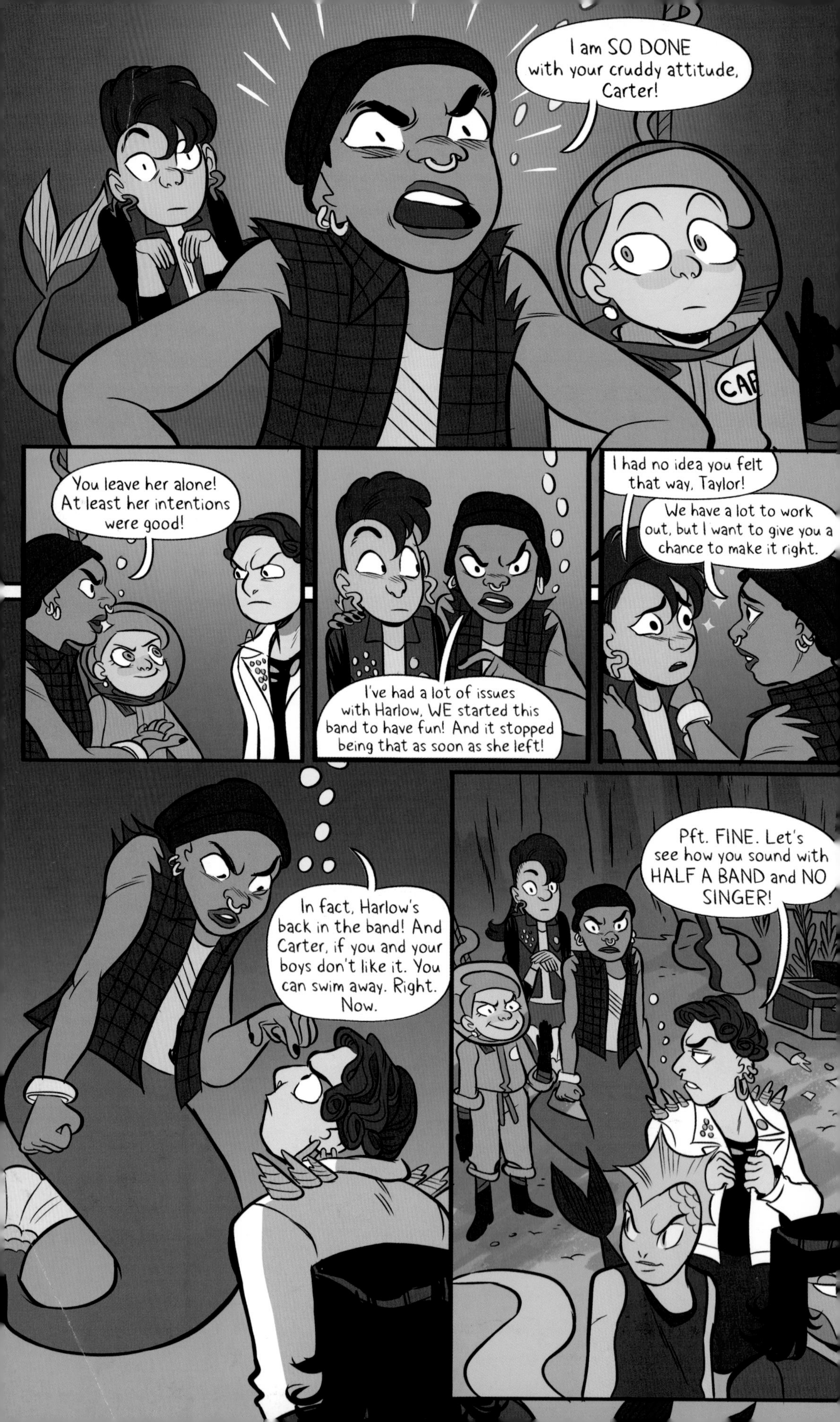
I am SO DONE with your cruddy attitude, Carter!
CAR
You leave her alone! At least her intentions were good!
I've had a lot of issues with Harlow, WE started this band to have fun! And it stopped being that as soon as she left!
I had no idea you felt that way, Taylor!
We have a lot to work out, but I want to give you a chance to make it right.
In fact, Harlow's back in the band! And Carter, if you and your boys don't like it. You can swim away. Right. Now.
Pft. FINE. Let's see how you sound with HALF A BAND and NO SINGER!

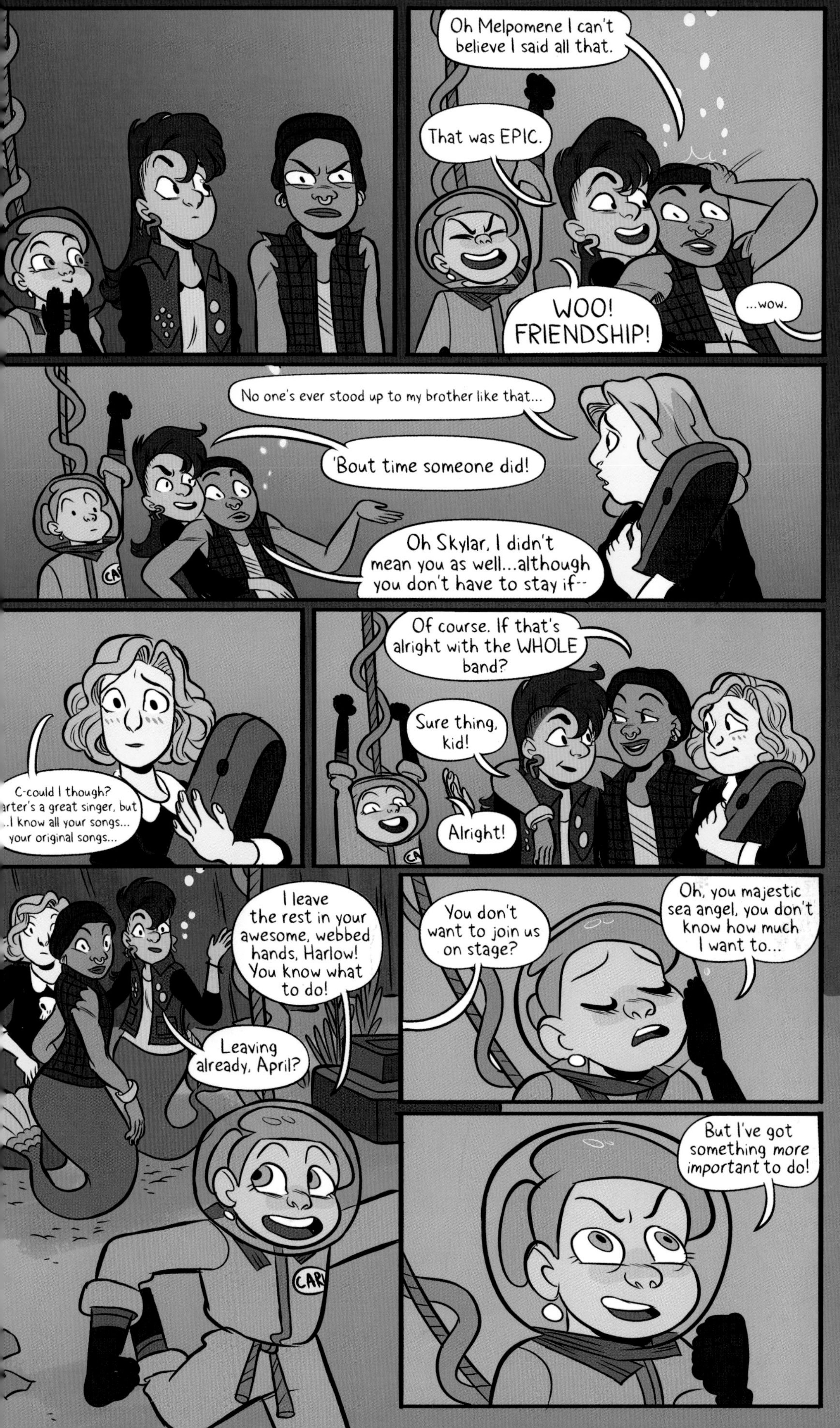
Oh Melpomene I can't believe I said all that.
That was EPIC.
WOO! FRIENDSHIP!
...wow.
No one's ever stood up to my brother like that...
'Bout time someone did!
Oh Skylar, I didn't mean you as well...although you don't have to stay if--
C-could I though?
arter's a great singer, but
..I know all your songs...
your original songs...
Of course. If that's alright with the WHOLE band?
Sure thing, kid!
Alright!
I leave the rest in your awesome, webbed hands, Harlow! You know what to do!
Leaving already, April?
You don't want to join us on stage?
Oh, you majestic sea angel, you don't know how much I want to...
But I've got something more important to do!

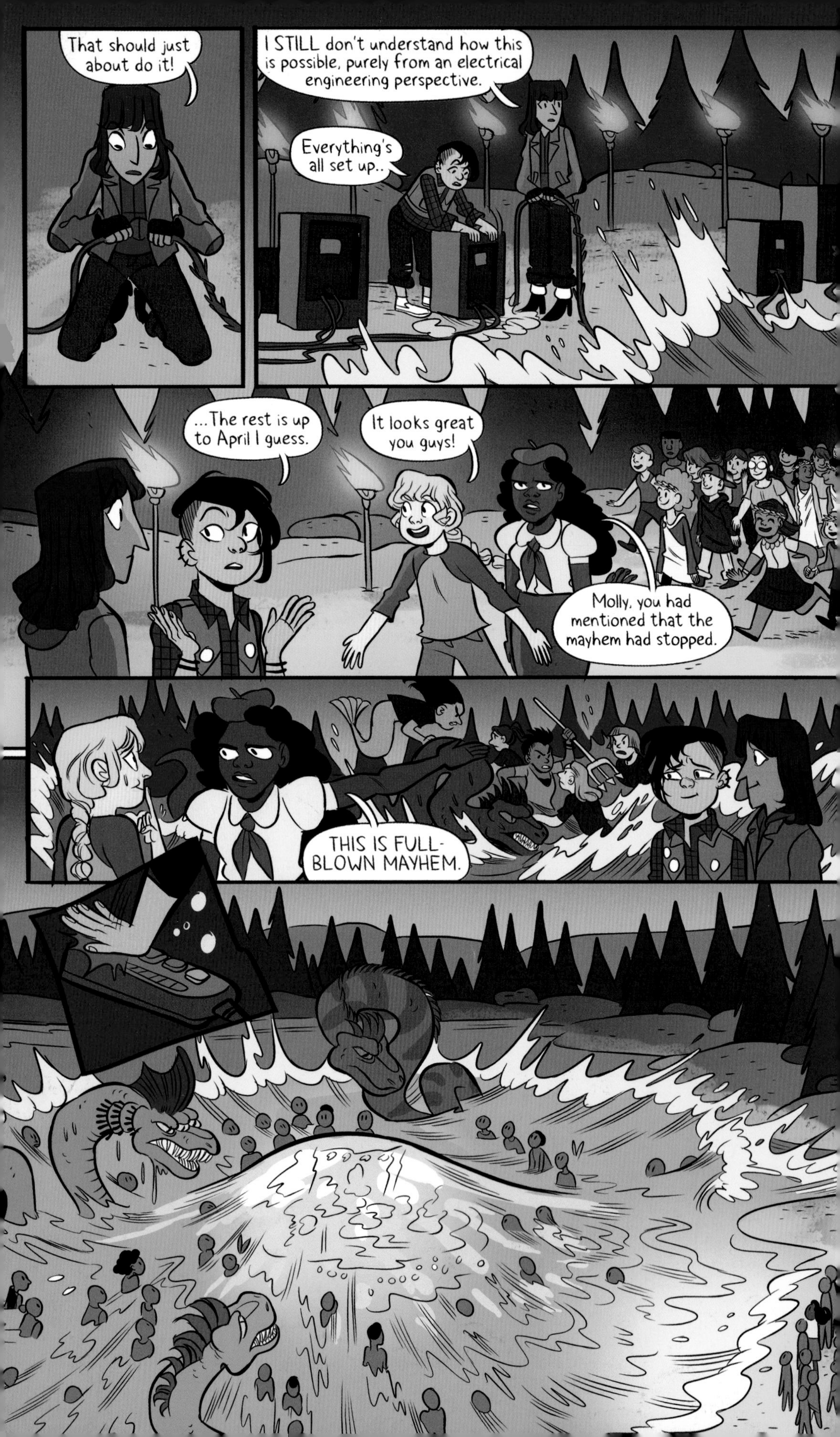
That should just about do it!
I STILL don't understand how this is possible, purely from an electrical engineering perspective.
Everything's all set up..
...The rest is up to April I guess.
It looks great you guys!
Molly, you had mentioned that the mayhem had stopped.
THIS IS FULL-BLOWN MAYHEM.

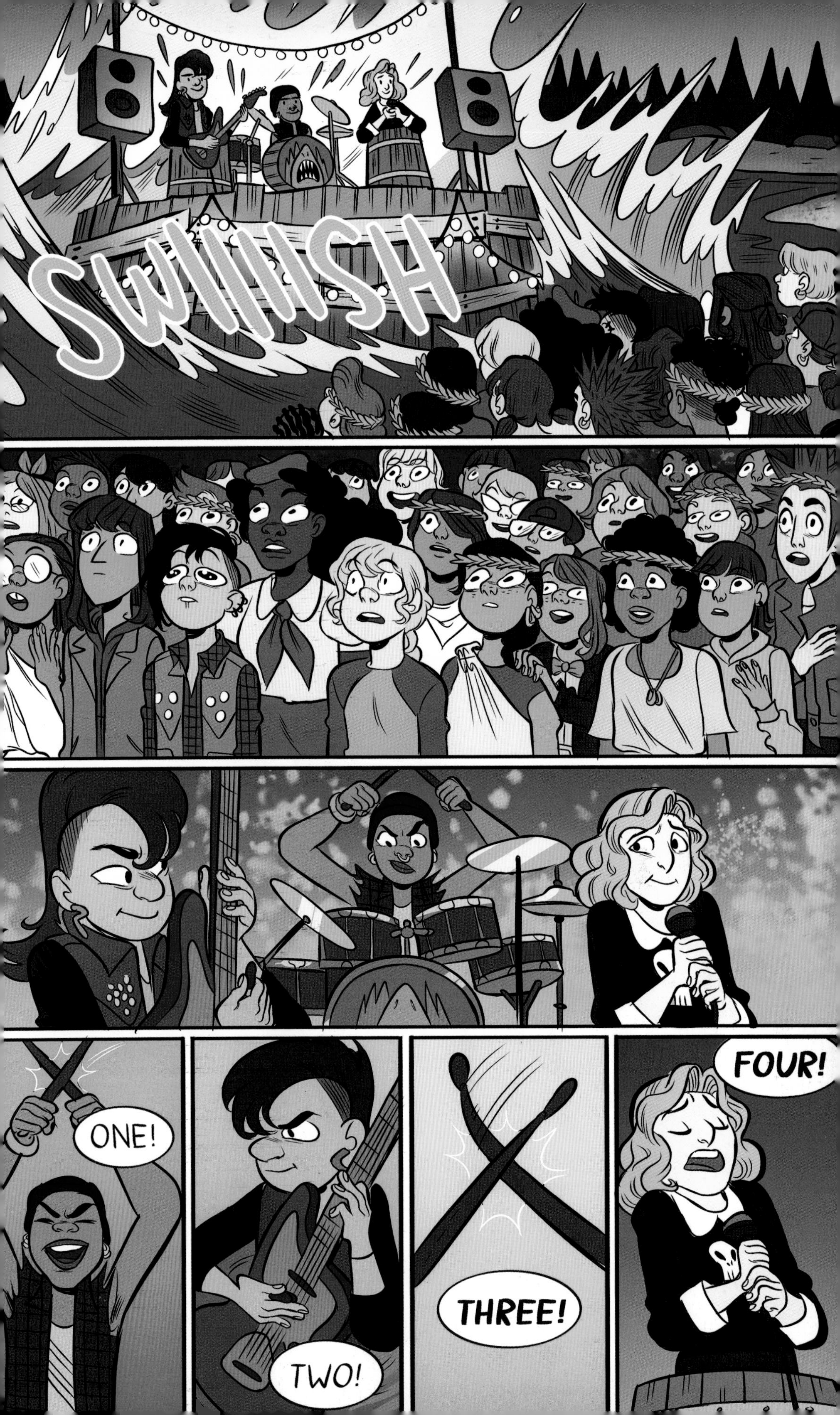
SWIIIISH
ONE!
TWO!
THREE!
FOUR!

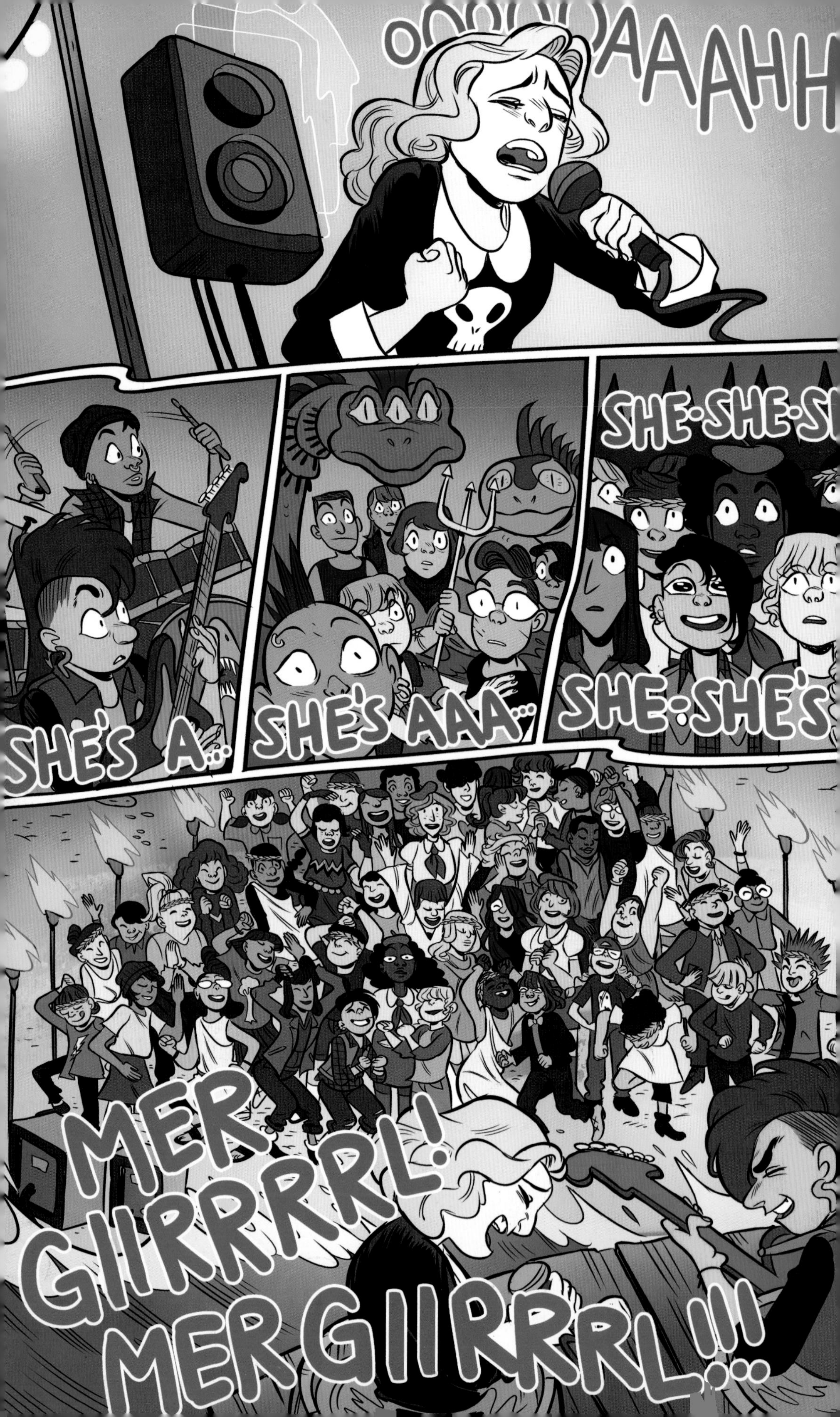
OOOOOOAAAHH
SHE'S A...
SHE'S AAA...
SHE-SHE-SH
SHE-SHE'S
MER GIIRRRRL!
MERGIIRRRL!!!

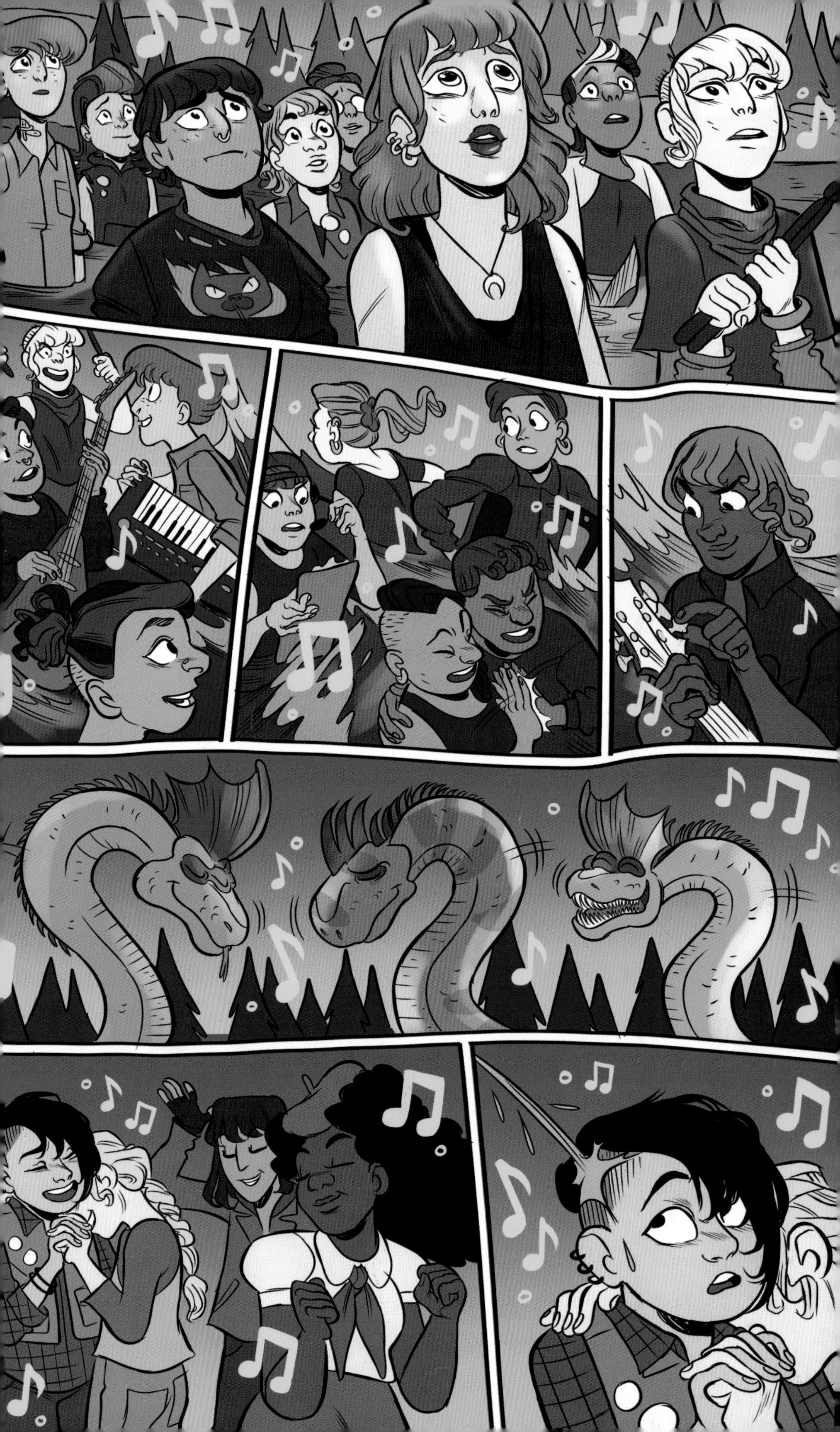

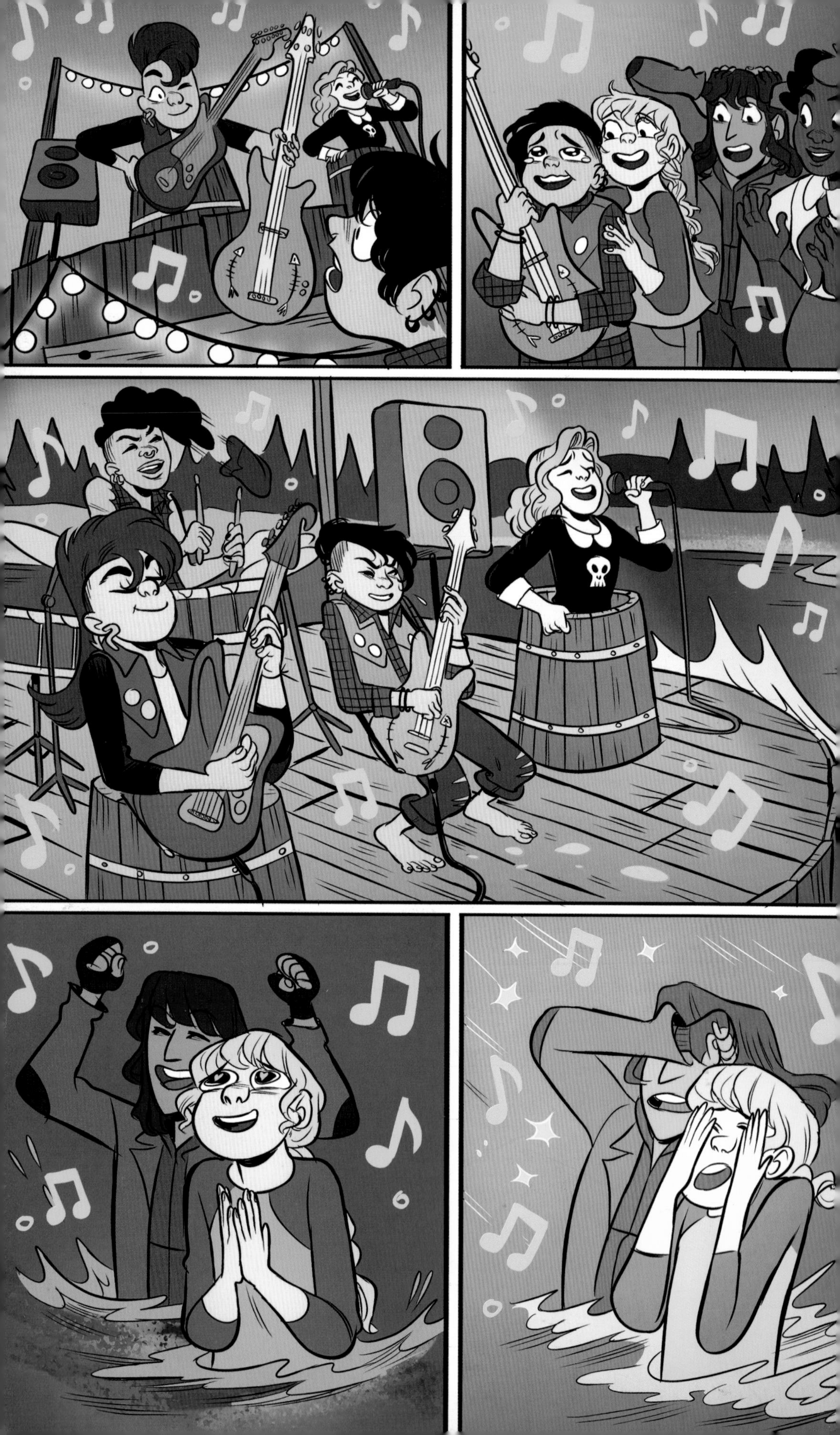

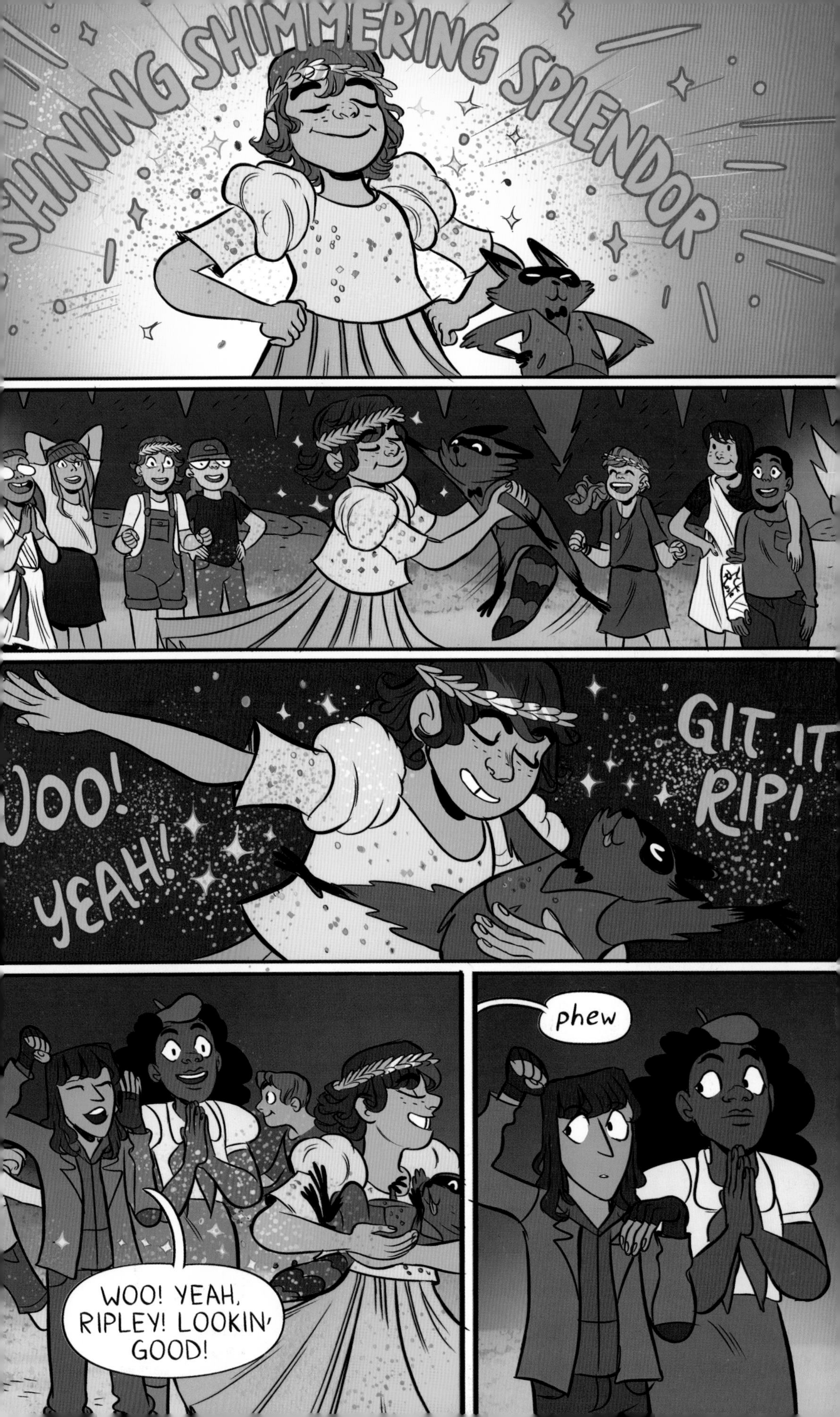
SHINING SHIMMERING SPLENDOR
WOO!
YEAH!
GIT IT RIP!
WOO! YEAH, RIPLEY! LOOKIN' GOOD!
phew

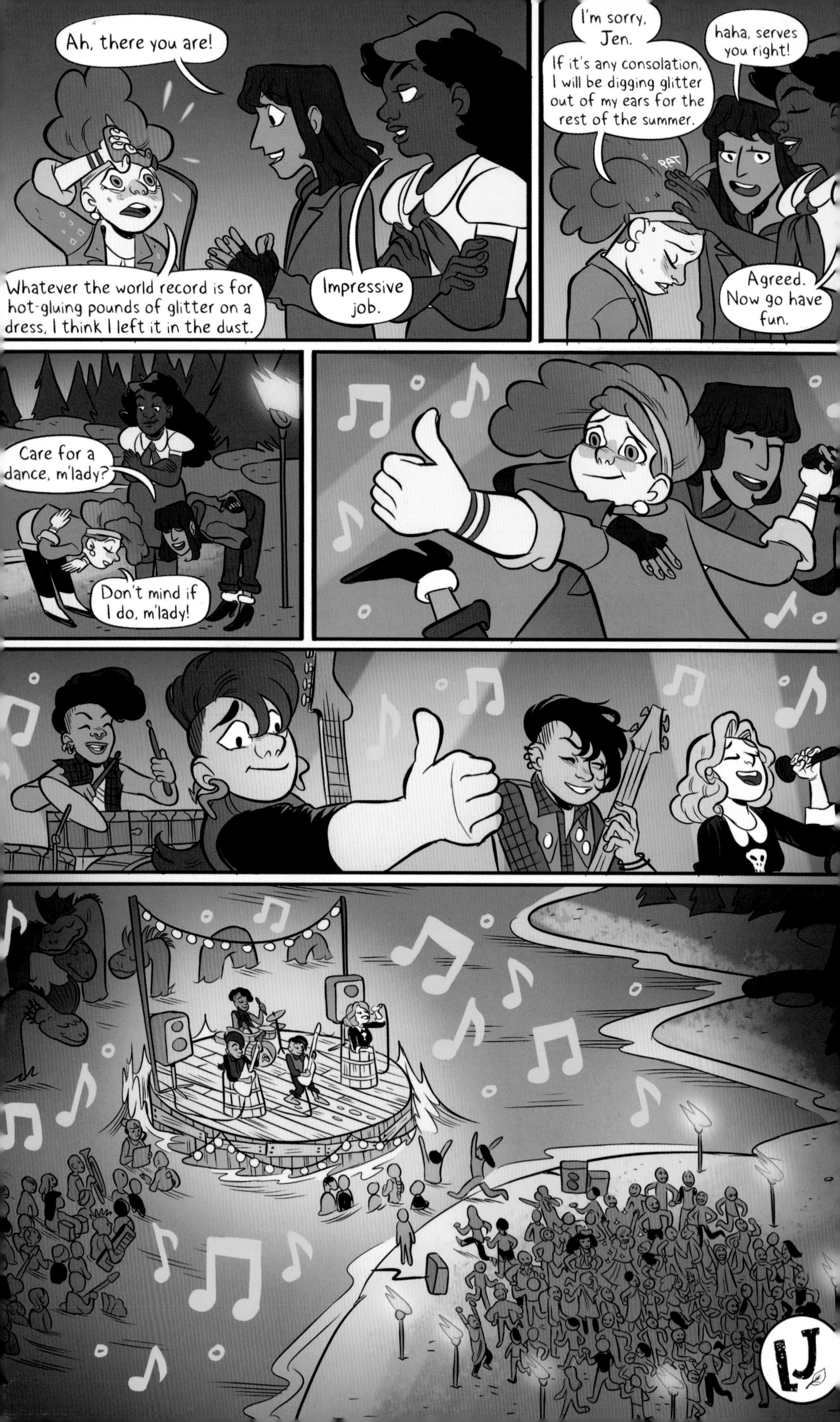
Ah, there you are!
Whatever the world record is for hot-gluing pounds of glitter on a dress, I think I left it in the dust.
Impressive job.
I'm sorry, Jen.
If it's any consolation, I will be digging glitter out of my ears for the rest of the summer.
haha, serves you right!
PAT
Agreed. Now go have fun.
Care for a dance, m'lady?
Don't mind if I do, m'lady!

COVER GALLERY

Lumberjanes. "Wildlife" Program Field

DO THE WRITE THING BADGE

"The is pen might be mightier than the sword, but steel still hurts."

Words are a powerful tool that every Lumberjane scout will have to familiarize herself with. They carry weight, they explain things that actions can barely surmise and they open communication even during the hardest of times. Tone, nuance, and specific wording are all important no matter what language is being used. Lumberjanes will earn their *Do the Write Thing* badge as they fulfill several tasks during their time at camp. These projects will be supervised by the resident wordsmith and it will be up to that counselor to determine if a task is truly finished.

Writing is something that, while it has it's basic rules, everyone will have their own personal style for. Some Lumberjanes embrace the world of fantasy, building detailed worlds that have their own words and understanding of what it means to be have a role in the world. Others stick to the fact, they have the information that they've collected in their years and will put those facts to the page. There will be Lumberjane scouts who will be a little bit of both, and others who will push the envelope and discover that they are something else altogether.

To obtain the *Do the Write Thing* badge a Lumberjane must use her words, her passion for the world around her to create something new. It has to be something that will challenge her fellow scouts as well as push the reader in a positive direction. They need to find the words that inspire. The importance of this badge to recognize the power that words can carry, to know the feelings they can cause and the actions that will occur because of them. Words are not meant to be hidden, they are meant to be read, spoken, and shouted across the camp but every young lady at this camp will be prepare for the consequences if the words are used incorrectly.

Issue Thirteen
BROOKE ALLEN

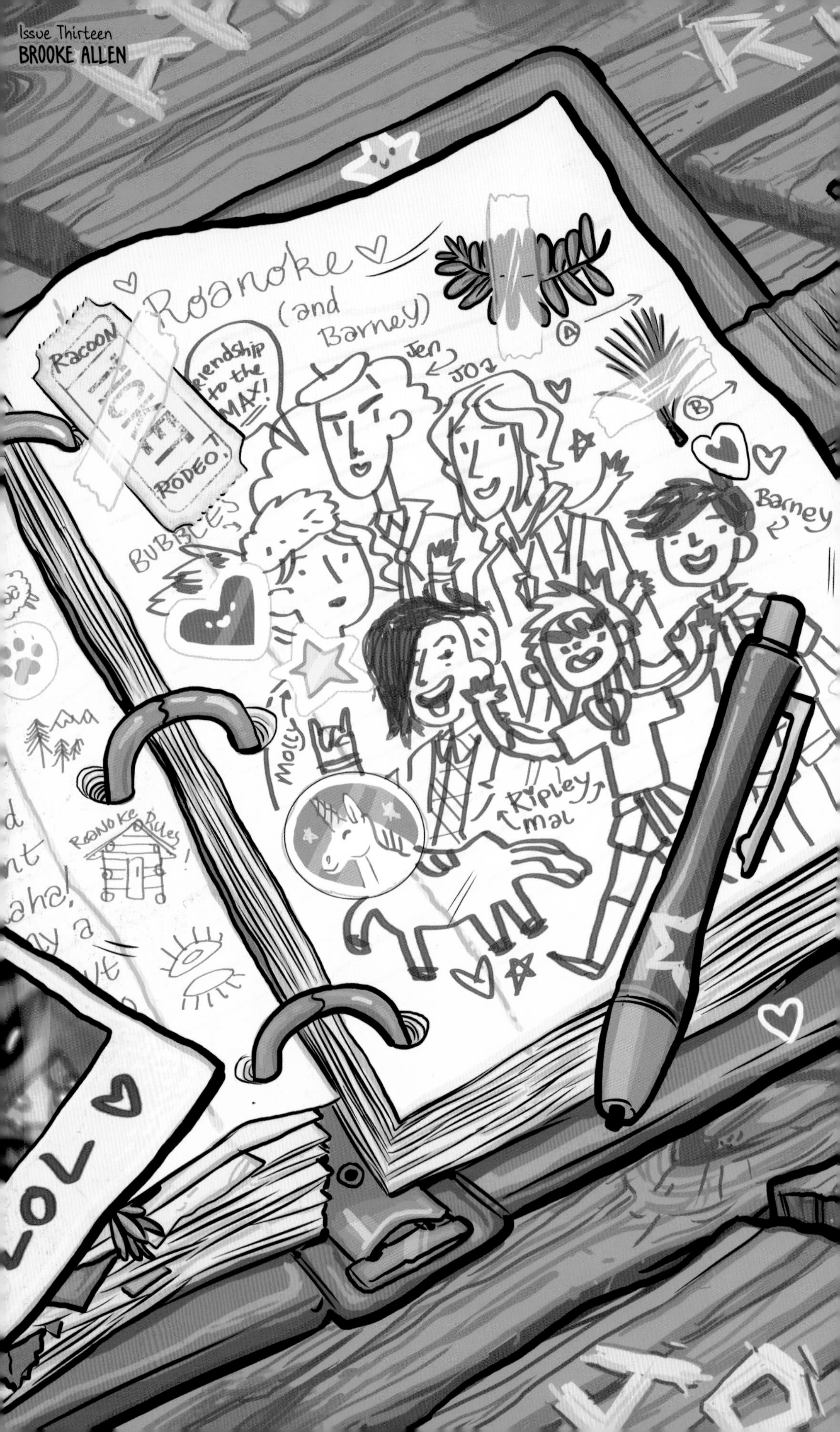

Roanoke
(and Barney)
riendship to the MAX!
RACOON RODEO
Jen
JO
Barney
BUBBLES
Molly
Ripley
Mal
Roanoke Rules!

Issue Thirteen Variant
JOY ANG

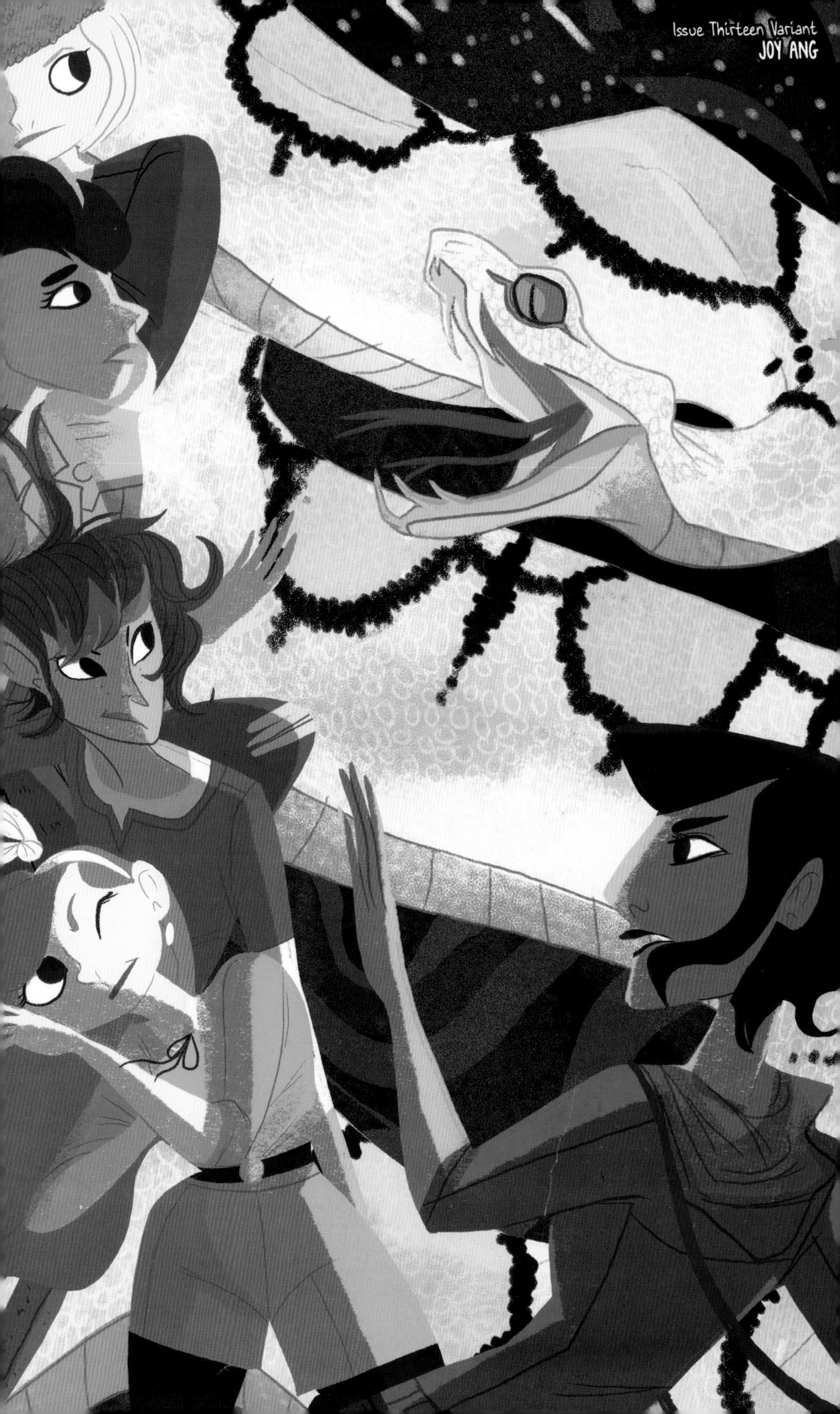

Issue Thirteen Denver Comic Con Exclusive
LIZ PRINCE

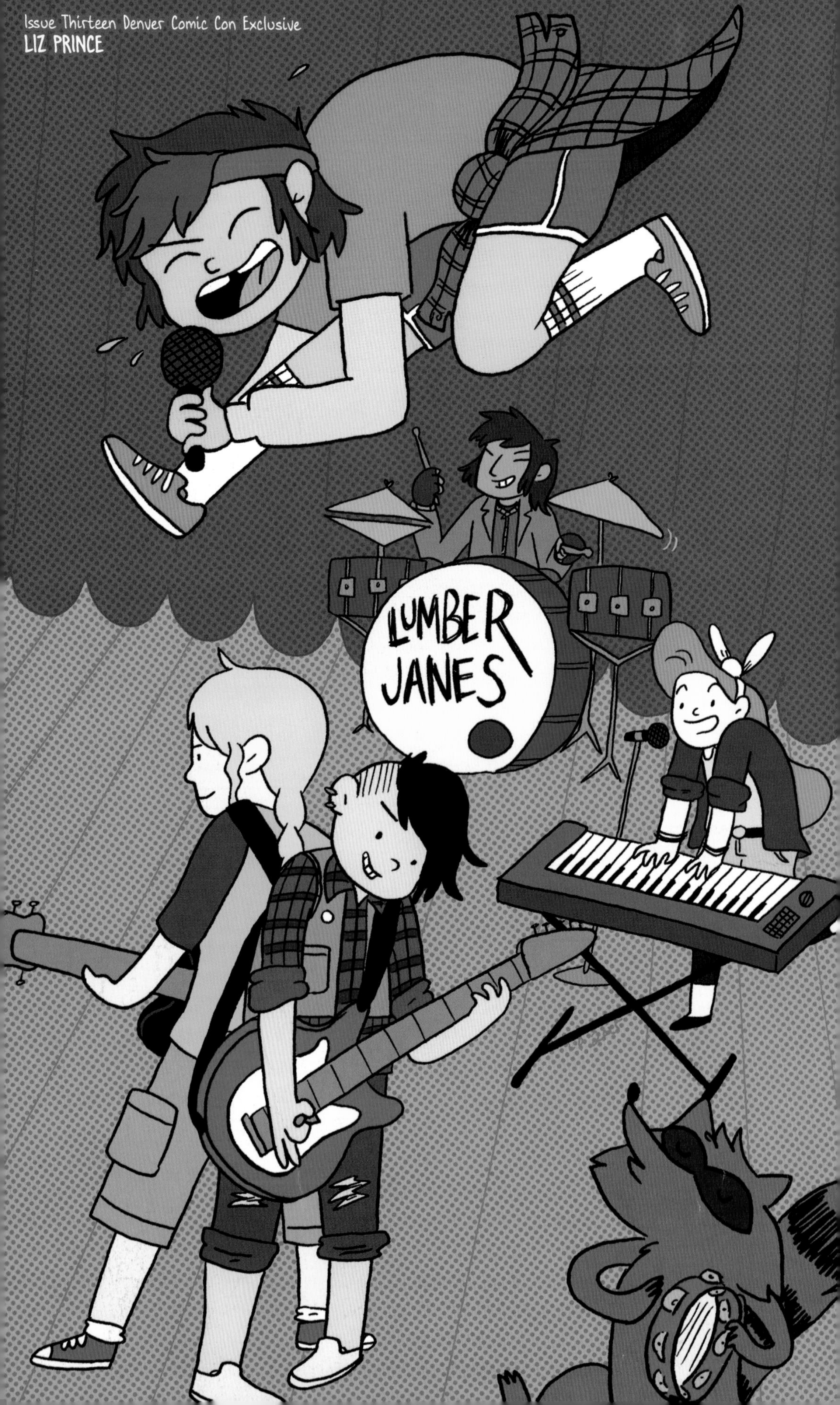

LUMBER JANES

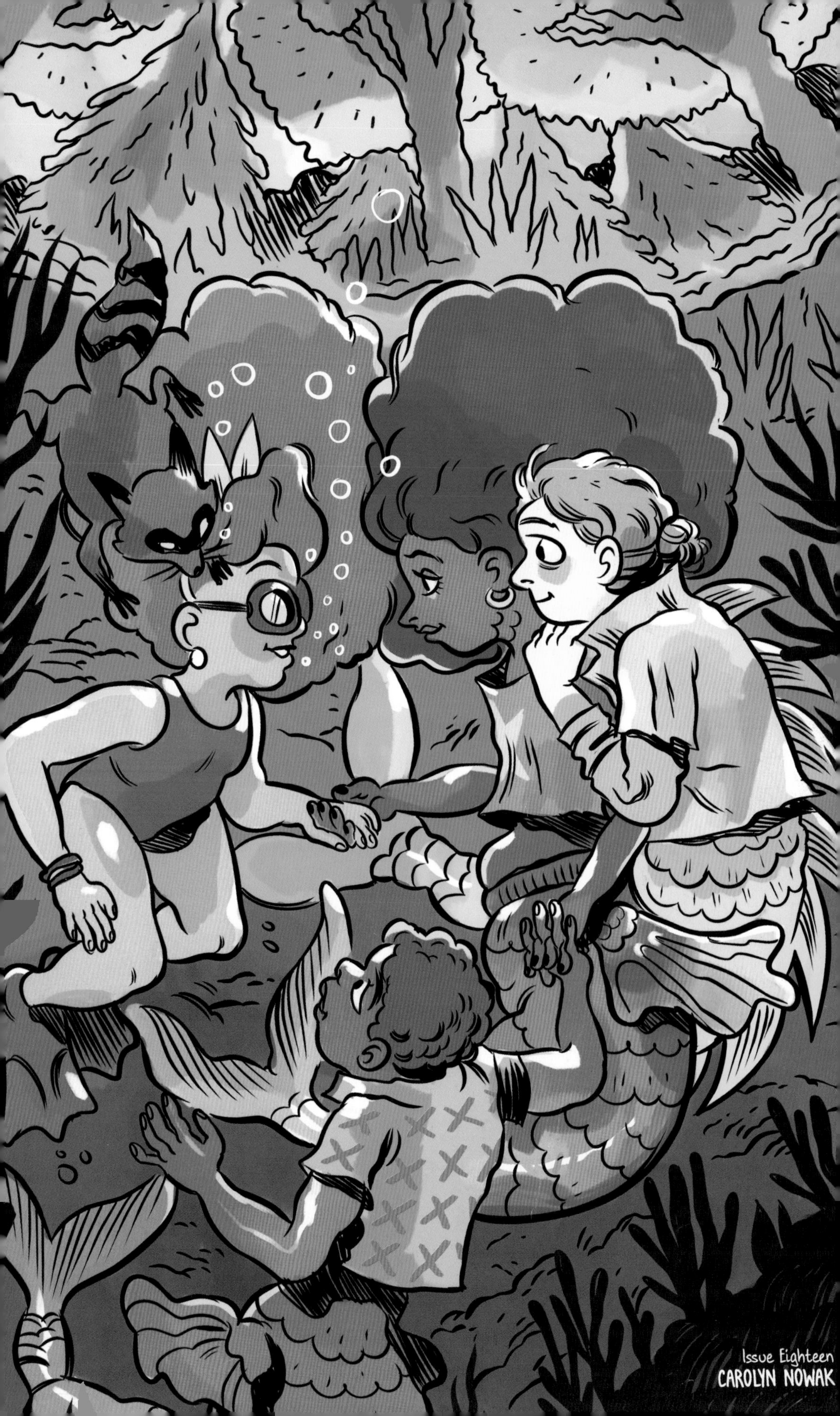
Issue Eighteen
CAROLYN NOWAK

Issue Eighteen Variant
LAUREN DAWSON

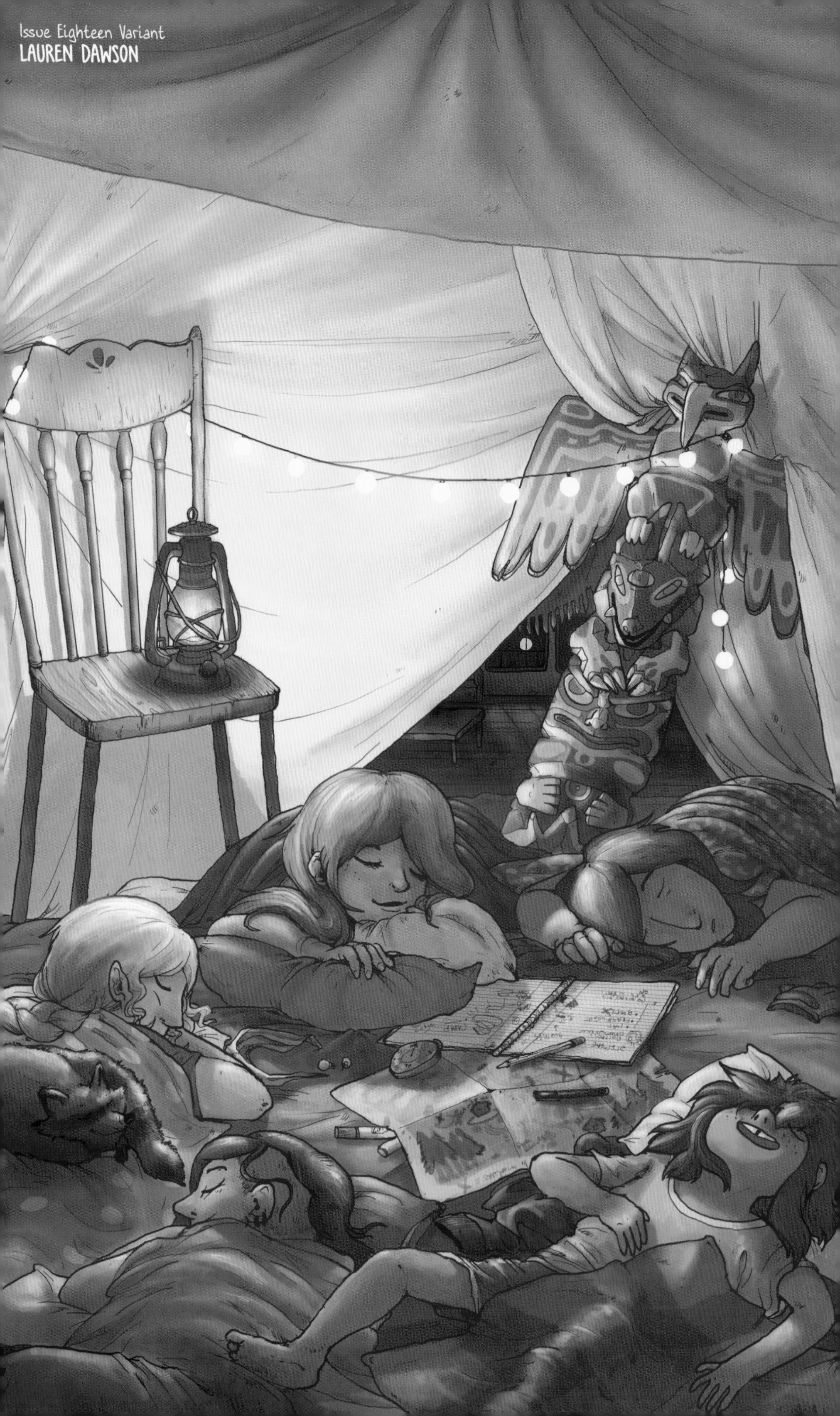

Issue Eighteen CAB Comics Exclusive
RACHEL DUKES

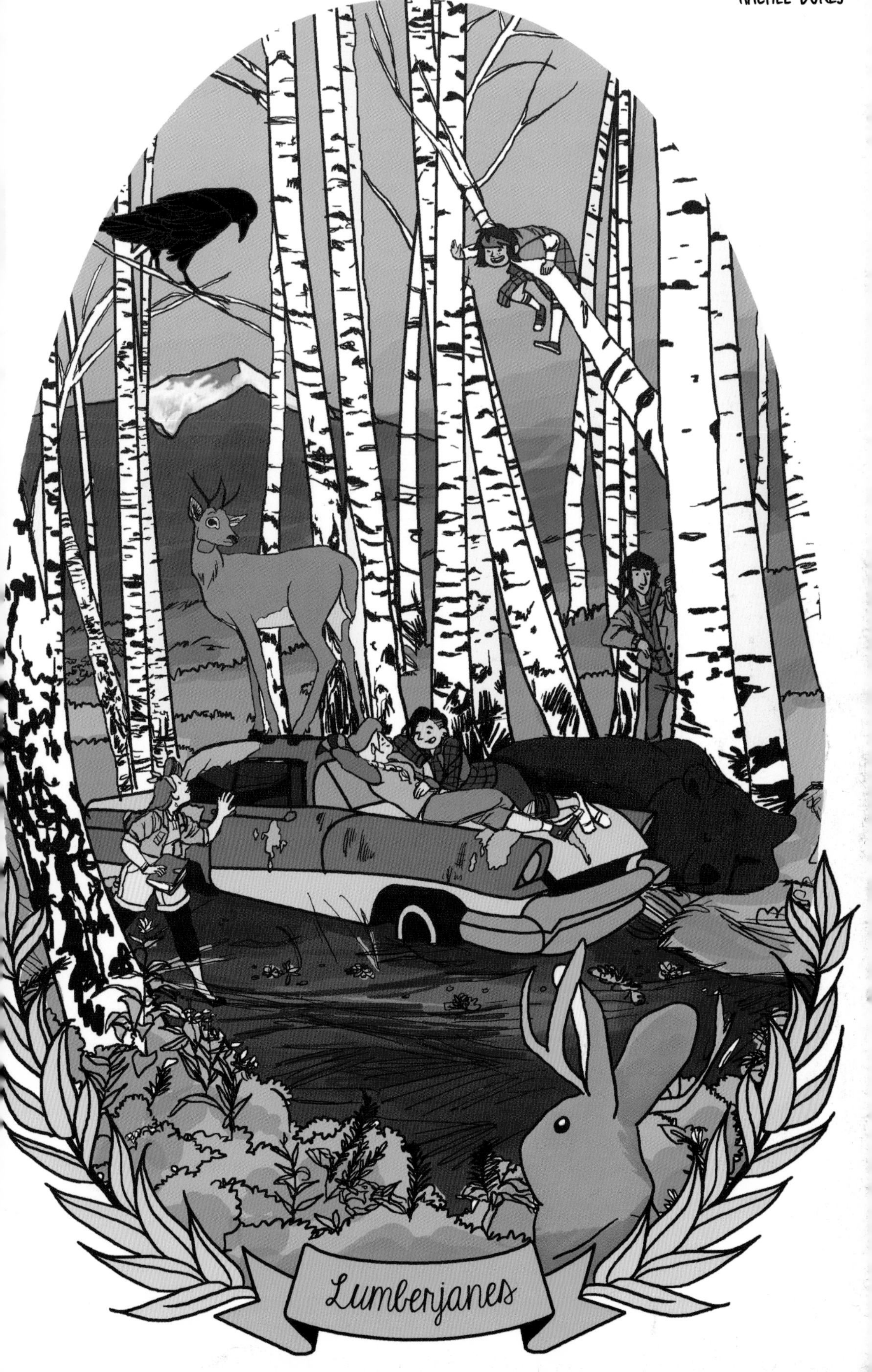
Lumberjanes

Issue Nineteen
CAROLYN NOWAK

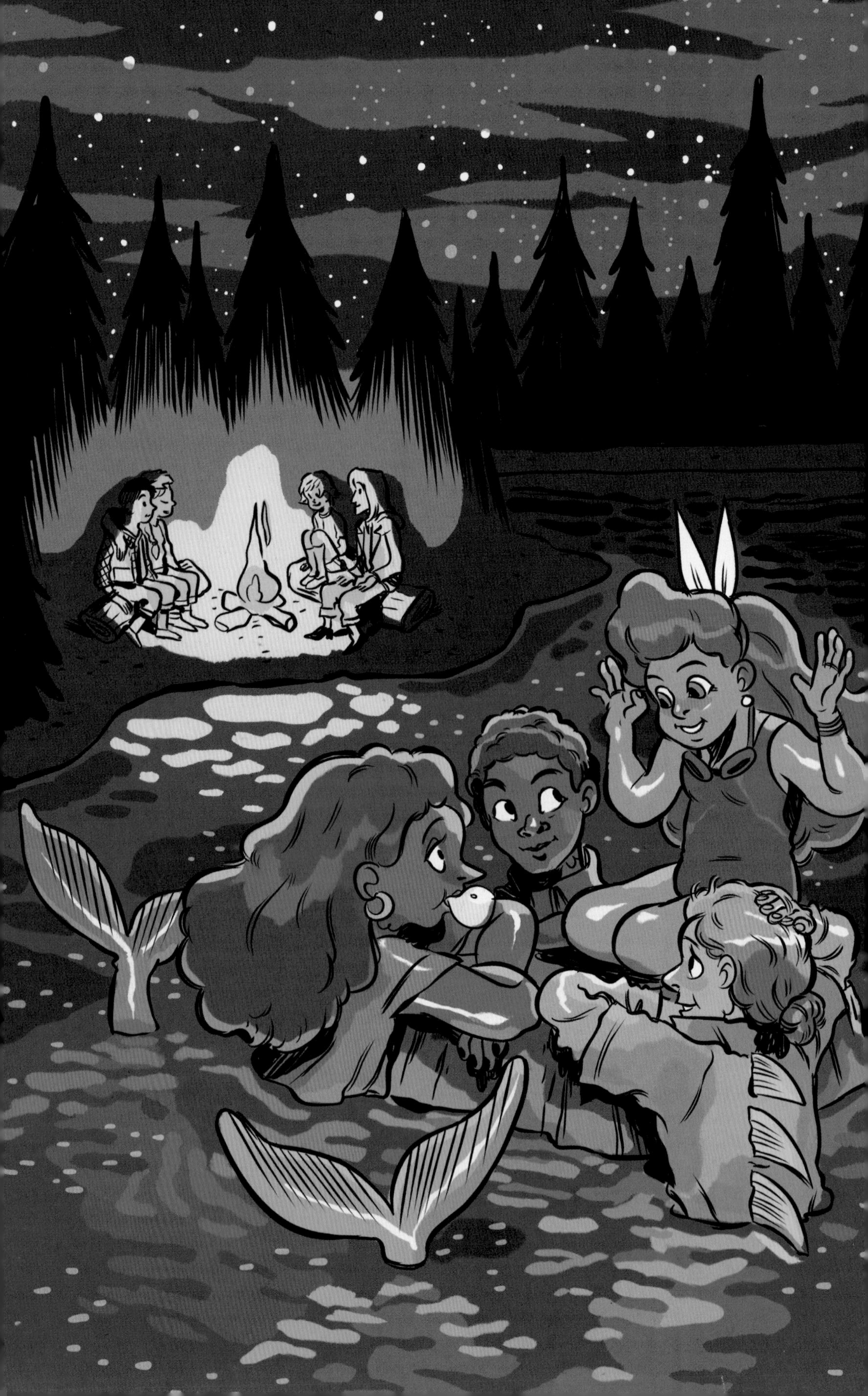

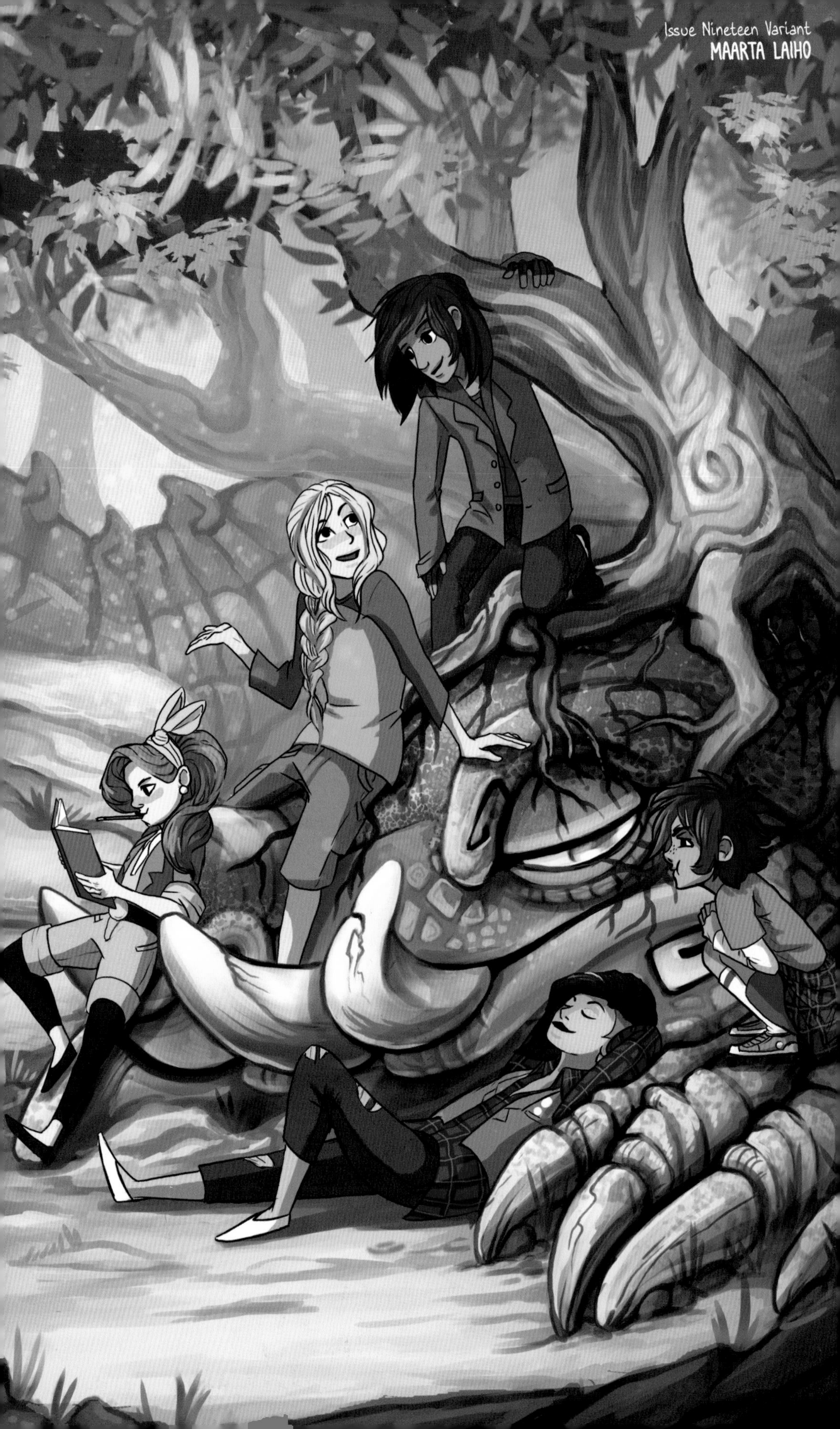

Issue Nineteen Variant
MAARTA LAIHO

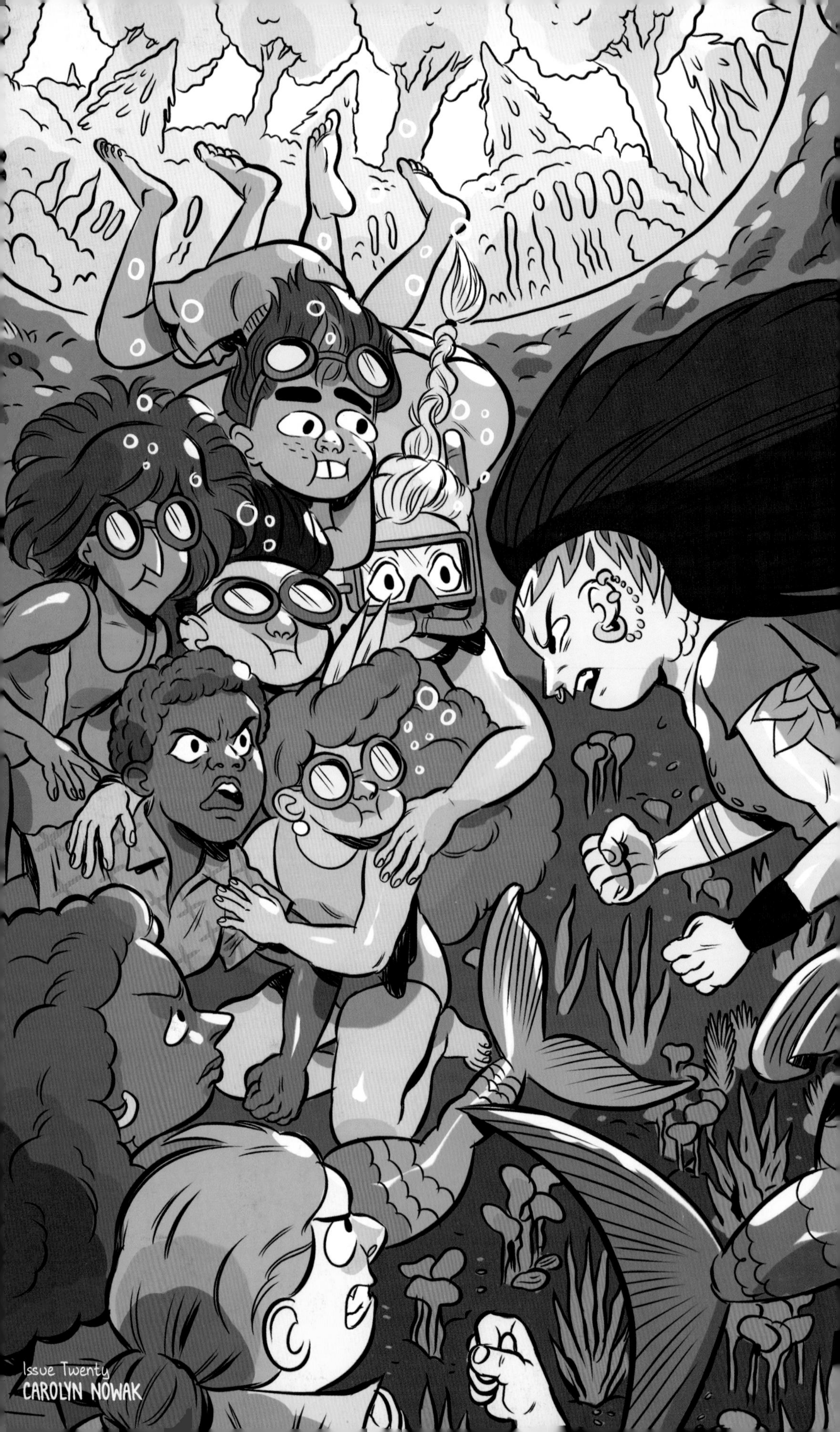
Issue Twenty
CAROLYN NOWAK

Issue Twenty Variant
SHANNON MAY

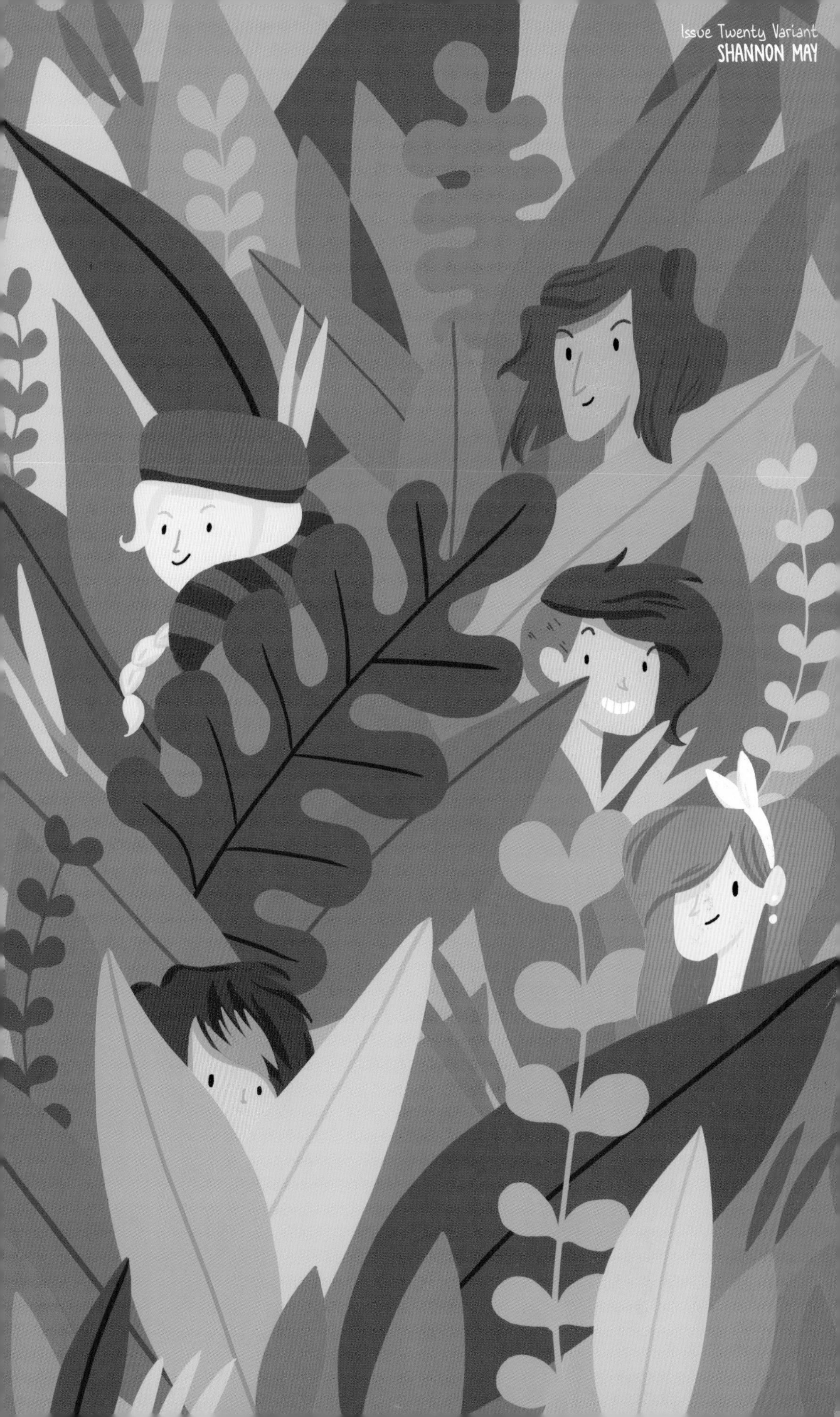

LJ

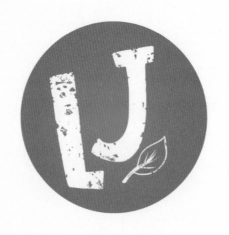